THE CROOKS WHO CONNED MILLIONS

Dedication

This book is dedicated with great affection to the memory of Janet Shepherd Figg (1957–2005), who sadly never saw it completed, but was always a good friend and an inspiration.

THE CROOKS WHO CONNED MILLIONS

TRUE STORIES *of* FRAUDSTERS
& CHARLATANS

Linda Stratmann

SUTTON PUBLISHING

First published in the United Kingdom in 2006 by
Sutton Publishing Limited · Phoenix Mill
Thrupp · Stroud · Gloucestershire · GL5 2BU

British Library Cataloguing in Publication Data
A catalogue record for this book is available from the British Library.

ISBN 0-7509-4243-6

Typeset in 11/14pt Sabon.
Typesetting and origination by
Sutton Publishing Limited.
Printed and bound in England by
J.H. Haynes & Co. Ltd, Sparkford.

Contents

List of Illustrations

Text   *page*

Acknowledgements

I would like to extend my grateful thanks to everyone who has helped me in the considerable research required for this book. The staff at the British Library, Colindale Newspaper Library, the Family Record Centre and the National Archives have, as always, all been enormously helpful. Many thanks also to Sarah Colbourne of the Hallward Library, University of Nottingham, Professor Paul Johnson of the London School of Economics and Sorrel Cittadino. A special thank-you is due to Eamon Dyas for his fascinating tour of *The Times* archives and Mary of the delightful www.missmary.com for unearthing a wonderful article about Mlle Lenormand. The unsung hero of all my work is my husband, Gary, who tolerates with good humour the many hours I spend sitting behind a door marked 'Go Away!'

Introduction

The nineteenth century was a time of optimism, with public confidence in the rewards of trade and exploration, and excitement at new inventions and discoveries. Never before had ordinary members of society had such a variety of opportunities to invest their humble savings in banks and businesses, and never before had rogues and charlatans of all kinds had a larger or richer field in which to perpetrate their frauds. Improvements in communications and travel brought a hunger for knowledge of the world, but this very eagerness sometimes led to uncritical acceptance of any story that seemed fresh and sensational. It is tempting to assume that people then were more gullible than we are today, but society encouraged an admiration of and implicit trust in the nobility, the educated and those with a conspicuous outward show of success. These figureheads were the heroes and superstars of the day, lauded by the popular press, respected by the masses, and their names alone were sufficient to lend credibility to any enterprise.

I have gathered ten stories, arranged chronologically, of some of the most audacious and extensive frauds of the nineteenth century. All had a disastrous impact on large numbers of people, and for some resulted in financial ruin, political disgrace, imprisonment, intellectual humiliation or suicide. All examine the crucial interface between the fraudster and the victim, since inevitably each wanted something from the other. The driving forces were money and celebrity. The methods of perpetrating the fraud may have differed – word of mouth, masquerade, public announcements, pamphlets, official documents and outright forgery – but all did no more than invite the victim into the snare. Entrapment occurred sometimes through trusting innocence and a need for financial security, sometimes from greed, often in the face of dire warnings from observers who were not swept along in the tide of enthusiasm. Those with a desire for fame and respect tried to boost their own standing by attaching themselves to an individual who had gained sudden publicity, and when the story was a good one, people just wanted it to be true. All these scenarios illustrate not only the depths to which people will sink to defraud others, but the scale of human credulity that provided them with so many victims.

In the stories that follow it is sometimes unclear who the hoaxer actually was. There can be no doubts about Whitaker Wright, whose personal control over an empire worth millions enabled him to falsify company accounts when he gambled away investors' funds in shady Stock Exchange deals, but did George Hollamby Druce really mastermind his claim to the £16 million Portland estate or was he himself the tool of a crooked solicitor? Naval hero Thomas Cochrane went to prison for a colourful and complex fraud worthy of one of his great victories; but was he the victim of a miscarriage of justice?

A fraudster can often become his own victim. What starts as a carefully designed plot can develop into a personal obsession, until the boundary between falsehood and reality blurs. Fraudsters can come to believe passionately in the truth of their claims, and feel wronged and cheated of their rights to the end of their days, sometimes even passing the torch to their children. Alexander Humphrys undoubtedly knew exactly what he was doing when he forged documents showing he was the Earl of Stirling, but his later rantings speak of self-delusion and paranoia.

Most fraudsters refuse to admit guilt even in the face of overwhelming evidence of their crimes. Even Ernest Terah Hooley, who cheerfully stated that many of his deals were extremely dubious, still managed to convince himself that on balance he was a benefactor to society. Thousands of small investors would no doubt have disagreed with him.

Not all these fraudsters are unmitigated rogues. It is hard not to admire Mary Baker, the high-spirited shoemaker's daughter who overcame her humble upbringing and conned the intellectuals of her day into believing she was a foreign princess. Others are less attractive, such as John Sadleir, the cold-hearted schemer who brought untold misery to the small farmers he represented in parliament.

We may hope that by studying past frauds we can protect ourselves in future, but there will always be fraudsters and there will always be victims: only the methods change. People still need to believe.

Linda Stratmann

ONE

The Price of Omnium

At 1 a.m. on Monday 21 February 1814, John Marsh, keeper of the Packet Boat public house in Dover, was enjoying a quiet pipe with local hatter Thomas Gourley when he heard a violent and insistent knocking at the door of the Ship Inn opposite and a loud voice demand that a post-chaise and four be brought at once. The night was dark, bitterly cold and misty, yet Marsh left his warm fireside to see what was happening, calling to Gourley to follow him with candles. His curiosity was understandable, since Dover was on constant alert for news from the Continent.

This was a critical period in European history and a time of agonising public suspense. Following his disastrous Russian campaign of 1812, Napoleon was in retreat but far from beaten. Rejecting attempts by Britain and her Allies to negotiate a peace in November 1813, he concentrated his forces in France. In January and February 1814 Napoleon's armies won a series of victories, which were eagerly followed in the British press. While the spectre of invasion had vanished, Napoleon – alive, free and at the head of an army – remained a potent threat. The peace of Europe depended on the fate of one man, and in Britain news of his final defeat was awaited with breathless expectation.

Outside the Ship Inn was a stranger in a grey military greatcoat and fur cap. The Ship's servants opened the door and admitted him: Marsh and Gourley followed, not wanting to miss the excitement. Soon the landlord, Mr Wright, appeared. In the candles' glimmer the stranger looked agitated, his bewhiskered and pock-marked face reddened by the cold. Under the greatcoat, which was very wet, he wore an unfamiliar-looking scarlet uniform trimmed with gold, much dirtied as if from battle, with a silver star on the breast and a medallion around his neck. He announced that he had just arrived from France, was the bearer of the most important dispatches that had been brought to the country in twenty years, and demanded that, in addition to the post-chaise for himself, an express messenger be provided at once, as he wished to send an urgent letter to Port-Admiral Foley in Deal. Everyone scattered to attend to his demands without question. A closer look

1

might have revealed that the dirt of battle had been simulated with boot-blacking, while the observers would have been surprised to know that a few minutes earlier their visitor had been standing by the nearby millstream throwing hatfuls of water over his coat to give the impression of a dousing with sea-spray.

William St John, an agent for a London newspaper who was staying at the Ship, found the stranger pacing impatiently about the coffee room. St John approached and asked about a messenger he had been expecting, but the officer said he knew nothing about that, and dismissed him brusquely, saying that he wanted to be left alone as he was extremely ill. The agent did as requested, just as pen, ink and paper were brought.

The letter, addressed 'To the Honorable J. Foley, Port Admiral, Deal', revealed the officer to be Lieutenant-Colonel du Bourg, aide-de-camp to the distinguished military commander Lord Cathcart. Saying that he had just landed in Dover from Calais, the news he brought was explosive. The Allies, he wrote, had obtained a final victory over Napoleon, and, most import-antly: 'Bonaparte was overtaken by a party of Sachen's Cossacks, who immediately slaid [*sic*] him, and divided his body between them. – General Plastoff saved Paris from being reduced to ashes. The Allied Sovereigns are there and the white cockade is universal; an immediate peace is certain.'[1]

It was what everyone had been hoping for. Wright's servant William Ions drew up to the front door on a pony, was handed the letter and set off at once for Deal. But this was not the only express sent from Dover that night. Even at that late hour the news spread rapidly, and hastily prepared messages were dispatched to London. Du Bourg offered to pay Mr Wright in gold napoleons, but the landlord was unsure how much these coins were worth and was unwilling to accept them. Reluctantly, the supposed messenger from France pulled some English pound notes from his pocket, explaining that they had been there for some months. His task done, du Bourg took his seat in a post-chaise bound for Canterbury, and sped away into the frosty night.

It was 3 a.m. before William Ions arrived in Deal and delivered the letter to Admiral Foley's servant. The Admiral read the letter in bed, then rose to question Ions about its origins. His suspicions may have been aroused by the letter being addressed to 'J. Foley', since his name was Thomas. The sender must have anticipated that Foley would at once transmit the news by telegraph (a system of moving wooden shutters mounted on towers) to the Admiralty offices in London, but here the plan foundered, thanks to that great unpredictable, the English weather. Even as it grew light, the fog remained so thick that it was impossible to use the telegraph. Neither was Foley as gullible as had been hoped, since he dispatched his own messenger to Dover to check the credentials of du Bourg.

It was several hours before the galloping expresses brought the news to London, and when they did few people could have been more interested in its ramifications than the members of the Stock Exchange.

By 1814 the London Stock Exchange had acquired most of the features we would recognise in it today. The present-day building had been opened in 1802; there was an official code of rules, first printed in 1812, and an authorised price list. Dealing was a specialised profession, though not a popular one with the public. Samuel Johnson's dictionary famously described the stock-jobber as 'a low wretch who gets money by buying and selling shares in the funds'.[2] One type of deal, time-bargains, was especially frowned upon – indeed they had been made illegal in 1734, but despite this remained common. Speculators would agree to buy stocks at a fixed price at some future date, but without actually paying for or taking possession of their purchases, gambling on a rise in price before payment was due, which would enable them to sell at a profit. Anyone who held, even briefly, important news unknown to other speculators could make a fortune in just a few hours. To control these bargains, the Stock Exchange Committee had established eight regular settlement days in each year, when the promised payments and deliveries had to be made.

The main stocks dealt in were government securities, a popular investment since the establishment of the national debt in the reign of William III. These funds were subject to great fluctuations in price, and their value was dependent not only on the economy but on whether the country was at peace or war. One important fund for speculators – Omnium – was an especially sensitive barometer of news. In 1802 the commentator Simeon Pope, addressing investors in Omnium, stated:

> It seems . . . somewhat paradoxical that while the immense funded property of the country rests on a foundation which is cemented with its greatest and dearest interests, that it should be subject to be operated on by almost every tide of vague opinion, and agitated by fluctuations of *rise* and *fall*, by the mere fleeting rumour of the day – the too common offspring of scheming manoeuvres and venal fabrication.[3]

Since communication from abroad could be slow and uncertain, news reports causing sudden changes in the market were impossible to correct quickly, and great efforts were made by the Stock Exchange to establish a reliable system of messengers.

The business of the Stock Exchange opened each weekday morning at 10 a.m., but on Monday 21 February 1814 messengers from Dover and Northfleet had started to pour into London before that hour, each one confirming Napoleon's defeat, and dealers were seized with excitement at the prospect of substantial gains. Some may have been wary at first, but soon most were caught up in the tide of greedy expectation, and the floor of the Exchange opened in a scene of noise and confusion. There was a particular sense of urgency, since the next settlement day was the following Wednesday.

Omnium opened at 27½ (all prices were quoted in pounds sterling) but quickly rose since everyone in the know clamoured to buy; it soon soared to 29. In the midst of the flurry the Stock Exchange dispatched messengers to government offices to obtain confirmation of the rumour. Had Foley been able to send his telegraph, it would have set an official seal on the news, rapidly forcing prices still higher, but this was not to be. The poor weather did mean, however, that no further information of any kind was available.

The news flew around London and soon the City was in a state of great agitation. People ran to shops and offices, looking in and shouting out what they had heard, one man claiming to have seen a letter from the Lord Chancellor confirming the report. As the tidings passed so they received embellishments, which added to the believability of the tale:

> it was boldly stated that two Messengers had, in the course of the morning, arrived at the Foreign Office, decorated with the white cockade, the favourite colour of the BOURBONS, and worn by all the military under the former government.[4]

In one story, Napoleon had been murdered by his own troops; in another, the Cossacks had marched into Paris with the tyrant's head on a pike. Citizens who could leave their businesses and homes poured out onto the streets determined to celebrate in a spirit of universal joy. Public offices were besieged with eager enquirers, and all businesses in London seemed to come to a standstill, save one – the Stock Exchange, where the price of Omnium was still climbing, and appetite for the stock seemed insatiable. Still more profits were anticipated by the springing-up of a thriving business in side bets on Napoleon's fate.

While London remained in a state of feverish excitement, other remarkable scenes were being enacted in Dartford, where Phillip Foxall, landlord of the Rose Inn, had received a note at 7 a.m. from an acquaintance, Ralph Sandom, asking him to send over a chaise and pair to him in Northfleet and have ready four good horses to go on to London. The chaise was duly sent and it returned quickly, driving at a furious pace. The occupants were Sandom and two strangers dressed in blue coats and cocked hats with white cockades. Sandom revealed that the men were French officers and were very tired as they had been in an open boat all night and had news of the very greatest consequence. Foxall gave them a fresh chaise and they dashed away at speed. He failed to notice that the officers' coats, which were not even identical, were not of a military cut, that their hats were such as could be bought anywhere and the white cockades had been home-made by sewing ribbon on to paper.

Before Sandom and his companions entered London, which they reached in the late morning, the horses and carriage were decorated with boughs of laurel. The three men entered the heart of the city, driving over London Bridge, down Lombard Street, along Cheapside, over Blackfriars Bridge, and down the New Cut. As they went they cried out slogans such as *Vive le Roi!* and *Vivent les Bourbons!* and distributed slips of paper with similar messages. The occupants of the chaise, believing that they were the first to bring the glad tidings to the city, were surprised to be greeted by crowds in the streets who already seemed to know the news and who mobbed their vehicle so that they were frequently obliged to stop. The post-boys naturally anticipated that their important passengers would alight at some government office, but to their surprise the journey finally came to an end at the Marsh Gate hackney coach stand, where the men got out, took off their military hats, put on round ones, and calmly walked away.

During the morning, lack of confirmation of the news from Dover had caused the price of stocks to slide, but at the new sensation brought by Sandom's French officers, prices soared even higher than before, eventually reaching 33, bringing a fresh frenzy of buying. As late as 2 p.m. the *London Chronicle* reported that it was still believed that Napoleon was dead and the Allies in possession of Paris, although it denied the rumour that the guns of the Tower of London had been fired. Meanwhile, large crowds had gathered outside Mansion House waiting impatiently for the Lord Mayor to appear with an official announcement.

The announcement never came. There was no news. Napoleon, as messengers were able to confirm by the afternoon, was very much alive.

Admiral Foley's enquiries had revealed that the pound notes supposed to have been in du Bourg's pockets for months had been endorsed in London only six days previously. Du Bourg was an impostor, and so, it appeared, were the two French officers who had ridden so triumphantly through London and carefully avoided any contact with government offices.

> To this scene of joy and of greedy expectation of gain, succeeded in a few hours, that of disappointment, shame at having been gulled, the clenching of fists, the grinding of teeth, the tearing of hair, all the outward and visible signs of the inward commotions of disappointed avarice in some, consciousness of ruin in others, and in all, boiling revenge, so strongly and beautifully, or rather so horribly depicted by the matchless pencil of Hogarth.[5]

It was not only wealthy speculators who suffered, but many humbler investors who could ill-afford a loss. Purchases had also been made that day on behalf of the official trustee who managed the assets of charities devoted to the relief of the poor.

As the crowds dispersed and the turbulent day ended, the Stock Exchange Committee quickly concluded that this was not simply a rumour that had got out of control but a conspiracy to defraud investors. The profits made that day were placed in the hands of trustees, and a subcommittee of ten men was assembled to investigate the affair. One of its first actions was to follow the trail of the mysterious Lt-Col du Bourg. This was easy enough, as he had travelled by post-chaise all the way to London, scattering the glad news and gold napoleons as he went. From the Ship Inn at Dover he had driven via the Fountain in Canterbury, the Rose, Sittingbourne, the Crown, Rochester, and the Granby at Dartford. Once in London du Bourg became suddenly less willing to draw attention to himself, and transferred to a hackney coach, in which he drove to 13 Green Street. After making some enquiries of the servant there, he was admitted, taking with him only his sword and a small leather case. His greatcoat was now buttoned firmly up to his chin, so only the dark collar and not the scarlet breast of his uniform was visible. Later enquiries revealed that 13 Green Street was the home of one of the greatest naval heroes in British history, Lord Thomas Cochrane.

Thomas Cochrane was the eldest son of the 9th Earl of Dundonald. Born in 1776, Cochrane had established a naval career of outstanding brilliance in combat and command. A distinctive, rather than handsome, man, he was well over six feet in height, with red hair and a prominent nose. Popular both with the general public and the men who served with him, he had, however, made some dangerous enemies in high places by his bluntly outspoken efforts to expose corruption in the Admiralty. On the morning of 21 February 1814 he had been engaged in two important projects, the fitting-out of his new command, the *Tonnant*, and work on the invention of a new naval signalling lamp, for which he intended to register a patent.

He had breakfasted at the Cumberland Street residence of his uncle, Andrew Cochrane Johnstone, a tall elegantly dressed man in his late forties with long powdered hair. Also at the table was 38-year-old Richard Gaythorne (sometimes spelt Gathorne) Butt, their stockbroker, a tall thin man in his late thirties with light hair and a florid complexion. At 10 a.m. the three men took a hackney carriage, but Thomas Cochrane alighted at Snows Hill to visit the workshop of Mr King, a lamp-maker, while the other two, as was their habit on weekdays, proceeded to the Stock Exchange. Shortly before 11 a.m., Cochrane's servant Thomas Dewman arrived at Mr King's with a barely legible note, saying that a military-looking gentleman had called on a matter of great urgency. Cochrane's brother, William, who had been serving in Spain, was dangerously ill, so bracing himself for bad news and abandoning all thought of his lamp, Cochrane hurried home. To his surprise, he was met not by a messenger from abroad but a man he was already acquainted with, Charles Random de Berenger. (In Cochrane's affidavit made three weeks later he stated that he had not expected the visit. De Berenger, on the other hand, claimed in 1816 that it was a pre-arranged visit and that Cochrane was a part of the conspiracy, but this was after he had unsuccessfully tried to extort money from Cochrane. De Berenger's account of the meeting should therefore be regarded as suspect.)

De Berenger was born in Prussia in 1772. His father, Baron de Beaufain, had owned lands in America worth over £30,000 (about £1.5 million today), but being a Loyalist opponent to the revolutionary war, his assets were confiscated by the State. In 1788 father and son came to England to try to obtain indemnity from the British Government. The Baron's efforts failed and he died six years later, leaving his son with a worthless title and a strong sense of having been cheated of his inheritance. De Berenger was a man of many talents – a clever self-taught artist, amateur scientist and excellent rifle shot. In 1814 he had for some years been serving as an officer with the Duke of Cumberland's sharpshooters, whose uniform included a dark green jacket. Always anxious to make money, he bombarded anyone he could think of with plans for improved methods of conducting warfare and inventions he was convinced would make his fortune. An attempt to start a charity for distressed artists had resulted in large personal losses and some bitterness, as an existing charity took the view that his intentions were untrustworthy. He had recently been making architectural drawings for Andrew Cochrane Johnstone, and as a result had dined at the latter's house, where he had been introduced to Lord Cochrane.

De Berenger's new acquaintances had given him the prospect of better fortunes. Admiral Alexander Cochrane, another of Thomas Cochrane's uncles, had offered to take him to America and had recommended him for the rank of lieutenant-colonel; but de Berenger had recently learned that, because of his status as an alien, the plan had not been approved. He was currently in debt to the tune of some £350 and had been committed to the King's Bench debtors' prison, although he was able to live within the 'Rules', that is, instead of being incarcerated he was permitted to lodge within a 3-mile radius of the prison itself. Despite these setbacks, he was still hopeful of being able to settle his debts and go to America. On 25 January Admiral Alexander had sailed without him, but he had recently approached Lord Cochrane suggesting that he might go out with him on the *Tonnant* instead.

De Berenger, despite having waited indoors for some time, was still wearing his grey military greatcoat buttoned to his chin. His face was red with cold when he arrived, making his pock-marked skin appear blotchy, but both this and the redness had faded by the time Cochrane saw him. The only visible part of his uniform was the dark collar and drab breeches encased in dark-green overtrousers. He began with great uneasiness to apologise profusely to Cochrane for taking the liberty of summoning him, saying that only his personal difficulties and distressed state of mind had induced him to do so. To Cochrane's astonishment he then launched into a tale of woe, saying that his last hope of obtaining an appointment in America had gone, that he had no prospects but only debts he was unable to pay. He hoped that with Cochrane's approval he could at once board the *Tonnant*, where he could find honourable employment exercising the sharpshooters. Cochrane, still reeling with relief that his brother was not dead, was more inclined to be sympathetic than he might otherwise have been. He said that he would do everything in his power to help, but it was not possible for his visitor to go immediately to the *Tonnant*, where the cabin had no furniture, nor even a servant. De Berenger tried to brush this difficulty aside, but Cochrane added that he could not take a foreigner without permission from the Admiralty. If de Berenger could get that permission he would be pleased to take him. De Berenger was deeply disconcerted at this response. He said he had not anticipated any objections, and indeed had come away fully prepared to board the *Tonnant* that day. Dressed as he was, he could neither return to his lodgings nor approach anyone he knew in official positions who might help him. He asked for a civilian hat to wear instead of his military cap. Cochrane lent him one, and when trying it on de Berenger commented that his uniform was visible under his greatcoat. Cochrane, who was some eight inches taller than de Berenger, was obliged to lend him a long black coat of his own. According to Cochrane, de Berenger removed the grey coat and put the black one on in a back room while he was not present. With the greatcoat and green overtrousers tied up in a bundle, de Berenger at last departed, clearly in some emotional distress.

Cochrane gave no more thought to this strange visit, and during the next week completed his preparations, joining the *Tonnant* on 1 March. Meanwhile, the Stock Exchange Committee had been compiling a list of those it wished to interview. The trading records for 21 February were examined to see which substantial investors had made money by disposing of Omnium and other government stocks early that day. It was soon apparent that, while most investors had been eagerly buying up Omnium, only three had made large disposals. One of these was Thomas Cochrane; the others were his uncle, Andrew, and Richard Gaythorne Butt.

Andrew Cochrane Johnstone, son of the 8th Earl of Dundonald, was born in 1767. He must have had considerable personal charm, enabling him to combine his military career with a series of successful schemes aimed at lining his pockets at the expense of others. In 1793 he married an heiress, Lady Georgiana Hope-Johnstone, and added her surname to his own. Four years later he became Governor of the Island of Dominica. His rule, according to the *Dictionary of National Biography*, 'was marked by tyranny extortion and vice'.[6] He was recalled and court-martialled, but because of the complexities of the case he was given the benefit of the doubt and acquitted. His next move was to bribe his way into parliament as MP for the rotten borough of Grampound, a position he knew would exempt him from criminal prosecution. Georgiana had died in 1797, leaving him with a daughter, Elizabeth, and in 1803 he married a widow who was a cousin of Josephine Bonaparte. Two months later the resumption of hostilities with France necessitated a separation. His letters to his wife were returned unopened, and he never saw her again. Returning to the West Indies he was appointed auctioneer and agent to the Navy for its conquests there, which gave him ample opportunity to carry out some major financial swindles. Placed under house arrest, he escaped, returned to England and in 1812 was again elected to parliament. There he made a substantial sum of money offering to sell rifles to the Spanish allies. The rifles were never shipped, and his creditors found themselves barred from suing him: it must have stung somewhat when they found that the frigate they had placed at his disposal had been used for a lucrative sideline in smuggling. During his infamous career Cochrane Johnstone acted with supreme self-interest and a callous indifference to the fate of those unfortunate enough to cross his path, although he seems to have had both affection and admiration for his nephew Thomas.

It was natural that Cochrane Johnstone should have been attracted to the Stock Exchange as a means of making money. With no expertise of his own, he engaged Richard Gaythorne Butt, a former naval clerk turned successful speculator, to manage his affairs. Thomas Cochrane, on the other hand, took little interest in the Stock Exchange, and it was not until October 1813 that he became a speculator. Butt had tried to induce him to invest in government securities, saying he could make gains without advancing any principal. Cochrane declined to enter into speculations he did not understand, but a few days later Butt brought him the sum of £430, saying it was the gain on investments he had made on Cochrane's behalf. Cochrane still refused to take the offer seriously and told Butt to sport with the money until he lost it. Over the next few months Butt placed £4,200 to Cochrane's account, and ultimately Thomas Cochrane, seeing that Butt could be as good as his word, and believing him to be an honourable man, agreed to let him handle his investments.

On the day of the Stock Exchange fraud, Thomas Cochrane, Andrew Cochrane Johnstone and Richard Gaythorne Butt held between them stocks valued in excess of one million pounds, an amount which at today's prices would be equivalent to £45.5 million. Selling virtually all their holdings on that day, they had netted profits of £10,500 (equivalent today to about half a million) in the course of one hour. Had the weather been fine and Admiral Foley more trusting, they might have gained up to ten times that amount.

Of the three, Thomas Cochrane had been the smallest investor. The whole of his Omnium holdings at 21 February was valued at £139,000. He had bought it on 12 February and left a standing order for it to be sold if the price rose by 1 per cent. On the day of the fraud he had not attended the Stock Exchange, given any orders to sell, or indeed shown any interest in the markets. By contrast, Cochrane Johnstone and Richard Butt were enthusiastic players, their accounts showing numerous transactions through three different brokers.

On 8 March, Cochrane discovered that his name was on the list of those men the Stock Exchange Committee wished to interview. Also on the list were his uncle Andrew, Richard Butt and three men who were unknown to him, John Peter Holloway, Ralph Sandom and Alexander McRae. Cochrane obtained leave to attend to his affairs in London and hurried home, where he made an affidavit describing to the best of his recollection all that had passed on 21 February.

John Peter Holloway was a small investor, a wine and spirit merchant with stocks valued at £40,000. He had given instructions to his broker to sell on 21 February, but not until the afternoon. Questioned by the Stock Exchange Committee, he assured them he knew nothing of the fraud. He was allowed to depart. Ralph Sandom, who had accompanied the supposed French officers in the post-chaise, had no investments, and explained that he was an agent for a newspaper and had been duped like everyone else. He too, was not questioned further. Alexander McRae, a poor man with no interest in the Stock Exchange, had been accused by an informant of involvement in the post-chaise masquerade. He declined to come forward.

The Stock Exchange list of suspects was supposed to be seen only by the Committee, but somehow it found its way into the popular press. Butt and Cochrane Johnstone immediately announced that they were innocent and were preparing to take action for libel, presumably against the newspapers, although neither of them did so. Lord Cochrane, believing that his affidavit would settle the matter, remained convinced that de Berenger and du Bourg could not be the same man, as du Bourg had been described by witnesses as having a red blotchy face. De Berenger was already a wanted man: a warrant had been out for his arrest for some days since he had been reported missing from the Rules of the King's Bench.

To an unprincipled rogue such as Andrew Cochrane Johnstone, Charles Random de Berenger was an ideal tool for one of his money-making schemes. A man of action, down on his luck and with a monstrous chip on his shoulder about his lost fortunes, de Berenger was flattered by the favour of the Cochrane family and hopeful that the connection would lead to advancement. Early in February 1814, an unfounded rumour of Napoleon's death had set the Stock Exchange in a flurry and the Cochranes and Butt had all bought heavily in government stocks. With settlement day approaching, there was an urgent need for good news. According to de Berenger's account of the plot,[7] Cochrane Johnstone began sounding out de Berenger, taking care to introduce the fraudulent scheme in the guise of a joke. He said how easy it would be to bring a pretend messenger to London, laughingly suggesting a bearded Cossack warrior with a pike. De Berenger, failing to see the humour in this, only commented that such a figure would not be believed. Cochrane Johnstone persisted, asking de Berenger what he might propose, and after further conversation the idea emerged of an officer arriving at Dover. The subject was dropped, but the next time they met Cochrane Johnstone, all pretence of humour abandoned, asked de Berenger to draw up a plan of how the deception might be accomplished, representing it as a 'stratagem . . . daily practised, never punished, never looked into and above all, one that could save Lord Cochrane and himself from ruin'.[8]

De Berenger objected that it would ruin his prospects in America if he was found out, whereupon Cochrane Johnstone bit his lip, looked displeased and pointedly accused him of refusing to help those who had helped him, reminding him that it was to the Cochranes he owed the opportunity in America. Over the next few days, Cochrane Johnstone, who was adept at changing his tactics from oily persuasion to emotional blackmail without missing a beat, openly displayed great anxiety over his investments, claiming that he and his nephew stood to lose £150,000 (about £7 million today). De Berenger, still not convinced that his benefactor was serious, reluctantly agreed to draw up a plan. He was quite unaware that Cochrane Johnstone had already assigned him the role of the impostor.

Invited to a meeting at the stockbroker's office in Sweetings Alley on 19 February – at which de Berenger claimed that Cochrane Johnstone, Thomas Cochrane and Butt were all present (Cochrane and Butt were to deny they had been there) – there was much despondency and talk of serious losses. De Berenger, according to his own account, succumbed to an emotional appeal from Butt. 'Baron, cannot YOU help us in some way or other: if you do not, WE ARE ALL RUINED.'[9] Believing that he alone could save the Cochranes, to whose fates his own advancement was so closely connected, de Berenger consented. Provided with funds, he purchased the gold napoleons, a leather dispatch case and the military clothing he required, including an aide-de-camp's uniform in scarlet with dark-blue collar and cuffs, and for decoration a Russian medal and a Masonic emblem. He travelled to Dover on 20 February with his costume in a trunk, and took a room at an inn, where, after careful preparation, he set out to play his part.

When de Berenger left Cochrane's home in Green Street after the uncomfortable interview of 21 February, he hurried back to his lodgings, where he washed and shaved. Later he went out to dine. All the talk at the table was of the hoax that morning. The diners 'rejoiced that for once the tables had been turned on a nest of wasps, that had grown grey in practices of deceit and iniquitous gain'.[10] The efforts of the three men in the post-chaise, about whom de Berenger knew nothing, came in for some ridicule. On the following day, however, Cochrane Johnstone was in sombre mood and revealed that great pains were being taken to discover and punish those connected with the plot. The greatest vengeance, he added gloomily, was to fall on the sham du Bourg. De Berenger failed to take the hint, saying he thought it would all blow over and that he was very unlikely to meet the people who had seen him on his journey. Nevertheless, he did take Cochrane Johnstone's advice that it would be wise to dispose of the scarlet uniform, which he cut up, tied in a bundle with some lead, screws and coal, and dropped in the Thames.

On 26 February Cochrane Johnstone brought a note to de Berenger's lodgings to arrange a meeting, which took place the following morning. Cochrane Johnstone said that he had been told by the Lords of the Admiralty that they knew who the messenger was. As he depicted his own terrible fate, his eyes filled with tears. If discovered, the bargain would be cancelled and he would lose his seat in the House – the only thing that prevented his being put in prison. He spoke movingly of his nephew's gallant deeds and the great and brilliant prospects that awaited him. Lord Cochrane was a brilliant gem lost to his family, a hero whose name would be blotted from the proud lists of his country. Seeing that his listener's sympathy was now thoroughly engaged, he drew a picture of his nephew as wretched, despairing and contemplating suicide. His own daughter, he said, was in delicate health, and dangerously ill. He was by now sobbing so hard he was almost unable to speak, gulping that his only uncertainty was whether he would first hear of his daughter's death or his nephew's self-destruction. He then dramatically revealed that it lay in de Berenger's power alone to avert this misery – he must fly and fly at once. De Berenger hesitated. He said that he would flee the next day but that he needed to settle with his creditors first.

Alarmed, Cochrane Johnstone insisted de Berenger depart that very night, even offering to arrange for the settlement of his debts. There was no time for him to put his affairs in order; they would all be ruined if de Berenger did not leave immediately. Cochrane Johnstone tried to increase the pressure by adding that when he had called to leave the note he had seen Bow Street officers lurking about de Berenger's lodgings looking for him. (Even the gullible de Berenger did not swallow this one.) Reassuringly, he said that he and Lord Cochrane and Butt had all decided they would provide for him for life. He must travel to Amsterdam, where he, Cochrane Johnstone, would join him and hand him funds which would enable him to go to Paris or America.

De Berenger, still anxious about the remaining fragments of his reputation, hesitated, then said he would still prefer to leave on the following day. Cochrane Johnstone, almost frantic, exclaimed: 'Then you are BENT on our ruin?'[11] He assured his dupe that his very first business the next day would be to call on de Berenger's creditors and settle the outstanding amount, only he must go, to save the lives of Lord Cochrane and his daughter, and himself from an agony of imprisonment. At last de Berenger agreed. He left London that night. On 17 March a warrant was issued for his arrest.

On 24 March, George Odell, a waterman, was dredging for coals in the Thames and brought up the bundle containing the scarlet uniform and medals worn by du Bourg, which he handed to the Stock Exchange.

The investigative committee had still failed to trace the elusive Alexander McRae. McRae was later described as 'a person in most desperate circumstances',[12] to which he took great exception, although he never revealed how he made a living. His name had come to the notice of the Stock Exchange because he had been unwise enough to believe that an accountant called Thomas Vinn, a friend who could speak French, would be happy to be involved in a 'very particular interesting business'.[13] The two men had met by appointment in the Carolina Coffee House on 15 February, where McRae enthusiastically offered Vinn the opportunity to make his fortune. Vinn was suspicious, and asked if there was anything illegal in the proposal, but McRae assured him there was not – it was something practised daily by men of consequence and affluence. Failing to read Vinn's mood, McRae revealed that the plan was for men to dress as French officers and drive into London from Dartford. He was happy to take credit for the idea, but McRae was in fact no more than the hired minion of the real brains behind the enterprise, whose identity he did not reveal. Vinn soon stopped him, indignant that anyone who knew him would even imagine he might have anything to do with such a scheme. The meeting broke up with some awkwardness, and Vinn hurried off to tell others what he had heard, but, reflecting that he had no proof of his allegations, decided to obtain some and returned to McRae, asking him to meet him later in the Jamaica Coffee House, where he would introduce him to a young man who might help him. They met as planned, but McRae, perhaps sensing that this was a trap, declined at the last moment to be introduced. He did, however, obtain from Vinn the French phrases that were later used by the two sham officers. Soon afterwards Vinn told contacts in the Stock Exchange and some companies he visited about the proposed fraud, but it seems that in the exuberance of the following Monday his warnings were forgotten. After the fraud had been made public, ties of friendship did not prevent Vinn telling all he knew to the Stock Exchange investigators.

McRae had been keeping out of the way of the authorities, but once the fraud was exposed in the newspapers he saw the opportunity to make a large sum of money. He and his confederates were not involved in the du Bourg plot, but recognised that this was a much bigger game played for far higher stakes than the scheme in which he had played a part. On 12 April he sent a letter to Cochrane Johnstone offering to reveal who was behind the Dartford fraud, exonerating the Cochranes and Butt, calculating that they might well be willing to pay handsomely to rescue their good names. No sum of money was mentioned in the letter, but the bearer, who was probably McRae, discussed the arrangements with Cochrane Johnstone. The sum payable was, according to McRae, £3,000 on demand and another £2,000 in instalments (he was no doubt gambling on being able to disappear with the funds before he could be arrested). McRae was, without realising it, becoming enmeshed in the schemes of a man who had been swindling money for far longer and better than he. Cochrane Johnstone had no intention of paying McRae anything. He wrote to the Stock Exchange, enclosing McRae's letter asking for the sum of £10,000. To McRae's dismay copies of the letter were printed with his name on and affixed in every conspicuous place around the Stock Exchange; some were even sent to the Continent. Quite who arranged this is unknown, but it seems probable it was Cochrane Johnstone in an attempt to demonstrate his own innocence.

When Cochrane Johnstone realised the Stock Exchange had declined to reply to his letter, he wrote to them again asking what they intended to do about it. He added that he, Lord Cochrane and Butt were all willing to subscribe £1,000 each towards the reward (which would, if he had been able to extract £2,000 from the others, have left a nice profit of £4,000 for himself). Somehow the Stock Exchange was not inclined to pay, and soon afterwards the scheme crumbled. Mr Holloway, the vintner, went to see the Committee together with a Mr Henry Lyte. Incensed at McRae's attempt to make money by betraying them, they confessed everything. The Dartford escapade had been dreamed up by Holloway, and the two men in the post-chaise with Sandom had been Lyte and McRae. They denied all knowledge of the Dover plan. Holloway and Lyte may have thought that their confession would earn them immunity from prosecution, but they were wrong.

On 4 April a government agent, with a warrant to arrest de Berenger under the Aliens Act, headed north to Sunderland, where a stranger calling himself Major Burne had been trying to get passage to Amsterdam. Burne had moved on, leaving behind him banknotes which were later traced to the hands of Mr Butt and Cochrane Johnstone, but he was finally run to ground in Leith and taken back to London. There the post-boys who had driven du Bourg from Dover to London were brought in to identify him. De Berenger spent much of his time complaining about his treatment and whining that he was so ill as to be on the point of expiry, but he was not taken seriously.

Lord Cochrane questioned his uncle carefully about the plot and received assurances that it was all a great misunderstanding. Not only were his uncle and Butt innocent of any conspiracy, but, said Cochrane Johnstone, de Berenger was not du Bourg, a fact that could be proved by the production of an alibi. On 27 April Lord Cochrane sent a letter to de Berenger asking him to explain publicly his reasons for coming to see him on 21 February. The reply received that same day stated 'nothing could exceed the pain I felt, when I perceived how cruelly, how unfairly my unfortunate visit of the 21st February was interpreted (which with its object, is so correctly detailed in your affidavit)'.[14]

On the same day the London Grand Jury assembled and found a true bill against Lord Cochrane, Cochrane Johnstone, Butt, de Berenger, Sandom, McRae, Holloway and Lyte. They were all committed for trial.

Lord Cochrane, who was probably one of the few people in the country who still did not believe that de Berenger was du Bourg, continued to be confident of acquittal. Believing that his innocence would be his protection, he did not trouble to read his own brief but left the whole affair in the hands of his solicitor and retired to his house in the country, not returning to London until two days before the trial. The only instruction he gave was that his case was to be tried separately from the others. While in the country he received a letter from his solicitor saying that he was to be tried jointly with Mr Butt, and since he believed in Butt's innocence, he consented, adding that he wished no further union with the other defendants. He cannot have been ignorant of his uncle's past and must have been suspicious that if there was a villain in the affair it was he, yet Cochrane remained loyal throughout, and if there was anything he knew to the detriment of his uncle, he said nothing. One possible reason was his fondness for his cousin Elizabeth, who to the end of her life remained convinced that it was for her sake Cochrane chivalrously refrained from placing the blame on her father. It must have been to his great astonishment and dismay when Thomas Cochrane discovered that he was to be tried jointly not only with Butt, de Berenger and his uncle but also with the men of the Dartford conspiracy.

The trial opened on 8 June, and from the start it was assumed by the prosecution that there had been a single conspiracy with two branches, although no connection could be proven. Sandom had once lived within the 'Rules', but there was no evidence that he and de Berenger had ever met. Given the immediately preceding events, and the approach of the crucial settlement date, it is not as unlikely as it may seem at first glance that two people could have had a similar inspiration at the same time.

The crucial question was whether de Berenger was indeed du Bourg. De Berenger's alibi soon crumbled under the strong suspicion that his servants had been bribed to say he had been at his lodgings when du Bourg was in Dover. This sealed the fate of both Cochrane Johnstone and Butt, as the currency paid to de Berenger to finance his escapade could be traced directly back to them. The case against Lord Cochrane was flimsy in the extreme, and mainly rested on his sale of Omnium and the colour of the coat de Berenger was wearing when he arrived at Green Street. Neither Cochrane nor his servants had seen the body of de Berenger's scarlet uniform, and were left only with the impression of a dark collar, which they were all convinced was green. Cochrane had sworn the uniform was green when making his affidavit and never swerved from that opinion. The court chose to believe the testimony of the cab driver Crane, who had deposited de Berenger at Cochrane's door, and swore that the uniform was red, implying therefore that Cochrane had lied. The defence could only suggest that since the uniform of the sharpshooters was green, Cochrane, trying to recall the colour weeks after the event, had simply assumed that de Berenger had worn green. This was weak indeed, for no one could believe that had de Berenger appeared before Lord Cochrane in a foreign scarlet uniform with a medallion and star, it would not have made a very profound impression. The question of whether the scarlet body of the coat was hidden by the greatcoat was not addressed. The trial judge, Lord Ellenborough, was convinced of Cochrane's guilt and summed up for a conviction, stating that when de Berenger visited Cochrane he 'must have appeared to any rational person, fully blazoned in the costume of that or of some other crime, which was to be effected under an assumed dress, and by means of fraud and imposition'.[15]

All eight defendants were found guilty. As they awaited sentencing, de Berenger wrote a letter to Lord Cochrane. He expressed surprise that he had received no message or letter from His Lordship. He complained that he had experienced hardships and ruin on account of his anxiety for the Cochranes' welfare, yet no one had shown any feeling for him: 'fate is not so cruel towards you as it is to me,' he continued, 'for with your means you can live any where, but my want of means forces me to seek a living, which every where will be opposed by my debts, and by the disgrace I suffer under, CERTAINLY *on your account*. . . . What is your intention to me, – how do you mean to heal my wounds.'[16]

By now Lord Cochrane was all too cruelly aware that he owed his current plight to de Berenger. He must scarcely have been able to believe that the man who had caused his downfall was trying to extort money from him. He ignored the letter.

Shortly afterwards, de Berenger received a note from Cochrane Johnstone:

My dear Baron, I have been as Mr Tahourdin [his solicitor] will inform you, dreadfully low, *and have never been out of the house, when I do* I SHALL CALL ON YOU. An application will be made tomorrow for a new trial, what the result will be God knows – the prejudice is great in the public mind – my poor daughter is almost at death's door. Adieu. I am ever yours, A.C. Johnstone[17]

As with so many of his promises, Andrew Cochrane Johnstone merely said what he believed the other person wanted to hear. The ink had scarcely dried on his letter when he left England, never to return. Two more of his dupes, Donithorne and Tragear, who had been involved in another of his shady schemes, went to Calais to meet him, and bumping into him by chance were told to go to Paris, where he would join them. Naturally he did not appear there, and after some hardship they were obliged to return to England, sadder, wiser and very much poorer men.

De Berenger tried an old tactic to postpone being sentenced, his counsel claiming that his state of health made it impossible for him to attend. Lord Ellenborough had heard such ploys before. He said he had observed de Berenger after the long trial and remarked at the time that 'a more lively and active man he had never beheld'.[18] The application was refused.

Only six prisoners were brought for sentencing – Lord Cochrane, Butt, de Berenger, Holloway, Sandom and Lyte – since Cochrane Johnstone was nowhere to be found, and McRae had also absconded. Lord Cochrane and Butt were fined £1,000 each, and Holloway £500. All six were sent to prison for twelve months, and de Berenger, Cochrane and Butt were ordered to sit in the pillory opposite the Royal Exchange in the City of London for one hour between the hours of twelve noon and two in the afternoon. They were then committed to the custody of the Marshal of the Marshalsea Prison.

A few days after the sentence, the House of Commons took a vote on the expulsion of the Cochranes from parliament. A petition was presented on behalf of the recently recaptured McRae, who, grovelling with contrition, offered to make a statement to the House in which he would utterly exonerate Lord Cochrane. The House declined to receive the petition. Lord Cochrane then rose to speak in his defence, and perhaps did not help his case, if that were possible, by asserting that there had been a conspiracy to silence him. Andrew Cochrane Johnstone's expulsion was not opposed, but many of Lord Cochrane's fellow members had had another look at the evidence and were convinced that he was innocent. Despite many appeals made on his behalf, the final vote expelled him from the House. He was to be spared the disgrace of the pillory, however, as this part of the sentence was remitted for all three men. Soon afterwards he heard that he had been removed from the Navy lists and stripped of his Order of the Bath.

The public had no doubts about Cochrane's innocence. On 16 July, amid scenes of exuberant acclaim, he was re-elected as Member of Parliament for Westminster at an open hustings. Meanwhile, de Berenger, totally unaware of the reaction he was provoking, continued to write to Lord Cochrane asking for assistance, expressing increasing surprise that the noble Lord did not reply to his letters. To de Berenger's rage, Cochrane simply had the letters published. In time, pleading turned to threats, and de Berenger eventually took his revenge by publishing *The Noble Stock-jobber*, which gave a detailed account of how the fraud was carried out, and placed Lord Cochrane at the thick of the scheme. While conclusive proof of Cochrane's innocence is not available, his known behaviour on the day of the fraud strongly suggests that he knew nothing of the plot, and his presence at the meeting of 19 February is to be doubted, since he was later able to supply evidence that he had been visiting his wine merchant at the time.

Cochrane was to deny his guilt with anger and defiance for the rest of his life. He published *A Letter to Lord Ellenborough*, accusing the judge of misleading the jury, and tried unsuccessfully to have him impeached for 'Partiality, Misrepresentation, Injustice and Oppression'.[19] Cochrane's later career was one of courageous and distinguished service, but for official recognition that he was innocent of the fraud it was necessary for him to outlive the men of the Admiralty and politicians who had regarded him as such a dangerous rebel. In 1832, Cochrane, now the 10th Earl of Dundonald, was restored to the Navy list as Rear-Admiral of the Fleet, and in 1847 he was again awarded the Order of the Bath. He remained in active service well into his seventies, and the last years of his life saw many honours come to him, but he never, however hard he campaigned, managed to get the £1,000 fine repaid, or receive compensation for his years spent on half pay. His *Autobiography of a Seaman*, published in two volumes in 1859 and 1860, showed that even in old age the fires of indignation still burned brightly. He died in 1860, a few weeks short of his eighty-fifth birthday.

Andrew Cochrane Johnstone had apparently disappeared, but in 1826 the Audit Office, calculating that he owed the Government £600,000 on some bills of exchange drawn while he was Governor of Dominica, made efforts to discover his whereabouts. It was found that in either 1814 or 1815 he had arrived in Dominica, where he still owned some property, and remained there until 1819 or 1820, when he bought an estate in Demerara and settled there. In 1823, following a disagreement with his creditors, he was obliged to sell up and leave Demerara and move to Martinique, but after a few months he returned to Paris, where, realising that the Treasury was looking for its money, he wrote from an undisclosed address asking to be excused from his debts. The last known letter from him was written in 1828, and in the absence of any further correspondence on the matter it is to be assumed that he died not long afterwards. Holloway, Lyte, McRae and Sandom returned to that obscurity from which they had briefly emerged.

The actions of Richard Gaythorne Butt after his release from prison strongly suggest he had undergone severe mental suffering as a result of his conviction. On the advice of friends who thought it would be best if he left England, he voyaged to Dominica to find Cochrane Johnstone and recover

£4,800 he believed was owing to him, but returned empty-handed. He became obsessed with the idea that he had been found guilty solely so that Lord Ellenborough could pocket the £1,000 fine, and indeed that the noble judge had actually done so. All arguments to convince him that he was wrong were useless. When applying at Bow Street Magistrate's Court for a warrant to apprehend Lord Ellenborough, he became so violent that the magistrate threatened to commit him. Butt also accused Lord Castlereagh, leader of the House of Commons, of lying to the House in suggesting that he (Butt) had petitioned for mercy to have the sentence of the pillory removed. Butt wrote to the newspapers, which unsurprisingly refused to print his accusations, and neither could he find anyone willing to publish them in pamphlet form. He eventually had 200 posters printed and distributed. In March 1817, *The Times* commented: 'Yesterday, Mr R. G. Butt, who has for some time past taken singular pains to be prosecuted for libel, had at last his wish gratified . . . '.[20] When arrested it was found that he had prepared placards against other public figures that he was about to distribute. 'It is apprehended that Mr Butt is somewhat deranged in his mind but not in such a state as to be irresponsible for his actions,' it was observed. 'He is respectably connected but his relations have not thought fit to give bail for him and as he had dissipated all his property they are not inclined to issue a Commission of Lunacy against him.'[21] Butt was found guilty and sentenced to a total of fifteen months in prison. In 1821 he was writing almost daily letters about his case from White Cross Street debtors' prison. Like Cochrane, he maintained to the end of his life that he was innocent of any fraud. When Cochrane was eventually exonerated, Butt peppered parliament with petitions, demanding the same treatment. They were ignored. He died, aged 73, in 1849.

Charles Random de Berenger managed to put the whole affair behind him. Abandoning the idea of making his fortune in America, he married an Englishwoman and brought up a large family. He wrote a book on self-defence and invented a waterproof rifle. In 1831 he opened a sports club at Cremorne Gardens, Chelsea, where he taught shooting. He never recovered his lost inheritance, and died as he had lived, in debt, in 1845.

TWO

The Princess of Javasu

When Mary Willcocks was baptised in November 1791 in the isolated farming village of Witheridge, in Devonshire, her future must have seemed predetermined. The daughter of a cobbler who had fallen on hard times, she was one of eleven children, only four of whom lived to adulthood. Destined like her mother for a life of obscurity, worn by toil and childbearing, nevertheless Mary became, albeit briefly, the toast of Britain and the talk of two continents. The imposture that brought her lasting fame was not, however, a calculated deception, but evolved from Mary's character, skills and experiences. It was as if the first twenty-five years of her life were merely preparation for the greatest part she would ever play: Caraboo, the Princess of Javasu.

Restless and unsettled, Mary always seemed to be striving for something better in life, with a spirit of determination and self-reliance, as if she had something to prove. As a child she loved climbing trees, playing cricket and fishing. An excellent swimmer, she thought nothing of diving into the river. Although small and slightly built, she was strong for her size, and active. Her dexterous physicality lent her a feral and wayward charm, which was to be important later on when she would need to persuade her dupes that she was not an Englishwoman.

Receiving only the minimum of schooling, she reached adulthood barely able to read and write. Her wild and independent ways led some observers to conclude incorrectly that she was simple-minded, but Mary was both naturally bright and gifted with an extraordinarily retentive memory and considerable talent as a mimic. The one thing she lacked was creativity. Hers was the kind of mind that fed eagerly on facts and stimuli, quickly utilising them for her own purposes – so rapidly that it seemed to others as if her ideas were fresh and startling. She was capable of becoming what others wanted her to be, reinventing herself again and again as it suited her. At a time when many people rarely went beyond the bounds of their own village, she was unafraid of travelling long distances, often alone, and dreamed of going to America.

Sent to work on local farms weeding cornfields, she preferred to drive horses or try to prove to the farm boys that she could carry loads just as heavy as theirs. At the age of 15 she suffered a severe bout of rheumatic fever, which was to recur throughout her life. Later, her father, deeply embarrassed at her notoriety, was to suggest that she had never been quite right in the head ever since this illness.

At 16 she went to work as a nursemaid for a family called Moon who farmed at nearby Bradford Barton, but two years later, after asking for and being refused a pay rise, she walked out. Her next occupation was domestic service in Exeter, but only eight weeks later she decided the work was too hard, and left. This abandonment of positions which other girls might have thought acceptable was to be a feature of her life. Her restless nature preferred the stimulus of risky change to drab but safe certainty. Wandering the streets of Exeter with her wages in her pocket, she saw a beautiful white dress for sale, something so different from the plain working clothes she had always worn that, impulsively, she spent all her money on it. When she arrived home wearing it her outraged father thrashed her with his belt. Her family and friends, all convinced that she had come by the dress through theft or prostitution, regarded her with cold hostility. Mary was distraught, but by now she had perfected her strategy for dealing with situations she found unpleasant: she ran away.

Exhausted, ill and hungry, Mary arrived in London, where she was taken to a fever hospital. There she was given a treatment known as wet cupping. The back of her head was shaved and the skin scarified with an instrument set with a series of parallel blades. Hot glasses were then applied, which filled with blood. This treatment, intended to relieve the pressure on her overheated brain, left permanent scars, which gradually became hidden as her hair regrew. Once she was well, normal practice demanded she be sent back to Witheridge, but Mary was adept at finding sympathetic male protectors, who helped her to bend the rules and found ways of excusing her eccentricities. The first in this series of mildly besotted yet virtuously platonic admirers was the hospital clergyman, Mr Pattenden, who found her a job as a nursemaid with a family called Matthews early in 1811. Mrs Matthews, a worthy and religious lady, later commended Mary as a good servant whose conduct was always correct, 'except that she told terrible stories, yet after all they were such as did no injury to others, or good to herself. Her behaviour was always so strange and eccentric, and her ways so mysterious . . . that no–one who did not know the girl would believe them . . .'.[1] Mrs Matthews failed to elaborate, but it is very probable that Mary told stories of travel abroad, gypsies, highwaymen and dramatic adventures. She sometimes stopped eating for several consecutive days to prove how long she could go without food. After Mary had been with the family a year, Mrs Matthews asked Mr Pattenden to speak to her about her stories and pranks. Unable to face him, Mary ran away. Despite this, she was forgiven and allowed to return. Mrs Matthews and her daughter taught Mary to read and write, finding her quick to learn, and soon she was able to send letters home, enclosing money she had saved from her wages.

Mary also began to take an interest in the customs of the orthodox Jewish family who lived next door. The Devon girl who would later become an Eastern princess was fascinated by the prayers chanted in Hebrew, the extraordinary alphabet, the romance of ritual. She became friends with the Jewish family's cook, talking to her over the garden fence as she pegged washing on the line, and may have questioned her about the Jewish diet.

In 1813 a member of the Jewish family was to be married, and Mary was invited to the wedding. It was a promise of enchantment, like being transported to a strange, wonderful and unknown country. When she asked for permission to go, however, Mrs Matthews refused. Mary, not a girl to be thwarted, got a friend to write a letter inviting her to a christening. Permission was granted, but Mary went instead to the Jewish wedding. When Mrs Matthews found out the truth there was a bitter argument, and Mary packed her things and left. Staying briefly with a lady who made plumes for hats, she persuaded a friend to write to her parents saying she had left England.

Mary had in fact obtained admission to the Magdalen Hospital in London, a home for fallen women. She later claimed that she had mistaken the establishment for a nunnery, but it is obvious from the record of her admission that she knew the nature of the place and lied to get in, saying that she was an orphan and had led a loose life. She gave the name Ann Burgess, Ann being her middle name and Burgess her mother's maiden name. She was unsettled and restless from the start, and on being asked who her friends were said she would hang herself if it was discovered who she was. By July she was begging to be allowed to leave, and was eventually permitted to go.

For the next four years her story, as she later told it, is a fantastical traveller's tale. She claimed to have spent time disguised as a boy and to have fallen in with highwaymen, only narrowly escaping with her life after they suspected her of being a police spy. Much of the time she was actually in service, or on the road, taking lifts on carts or just walking. Begging, she knew, was fraught with risks. If caught, she could have been imprisoned, transported, or forcibly returned to her own parish and placed in a workhouse. She therefore developed a subtle technique, in which she never appeared to be directly soliciting money but presented herself as a forlorn and weary creature, tearing her clothes better to play the part, and was often assisted out of sympathy. The most momentous development was the liaison which led, in February 1816, to the birth of her son, John Edward Francis Baker. She was to give several conflicting accounts of both the identity of the father and the location of the birth. Mr Pattenden helped her have the child admitted to London's Foundling Hospital, where Mary gave the father's name as John Baker and his occupation as a bricklayer of Exeter. She next went into service with a family called Starling. Mrs Starling seemed to like Mary, although she, like so many, found her odd and eccentric to the extent that she sometimes thought the girl must be out of her mind.

She was very fond of the children, 'but told them such strange stories about gypsies and herself, that she frightened them out of their wits. She once came into the parlour, and had dressed herself up so like a gypsy, that the children did not know her.'[2]

Mary claimed that she had been to the East Indies and America, and that her child, whose father was a Frenchman, had been born in Philadelphia by the side of a river. At the end of October her son died. Mary soon lost whatever grip she had had on reason and began setting fire to the beds in the Starling home. She was sacked.

In February 1817 Mary returned to Devon, telling her parents she was about to depart for the Indies. She impressed them with her learning, and spent time with her younger sister, 15-year-old Susan, prattling away to her in a language which her father believed to be French. This was probably what she later referred to as her 'lingo',[3] a language she had made up, probably to amuse children, and lend her stories of foreign travel some verisimilitude. After ten days she sent a trunk of clothes to Bristol and set out on the road alone. She later claimed to have spent three days living with gypsies.

Arriving in Bristol on 10 March with enough money for cheap lodgings, Mary met Eleanor Joseph, a Jewish girl who was staying with a Mrs Neale and her two daughters and who let Mary share her room for a shilling a night. A ship was due to sail for America at the end of March, for which the cheapest fare was five guineas, providing she bought her own food.

To raise money for the fare, Mary and Eleanor went out begging together, but at first they were not successful. While on the road, Mary saw some French lace-makers from Normandy, and was fascinated by their high lace headdresses. More importantly, she saw that their unusual appearance was attracting attention. Mary was wearing a black shawl and Eleanor suggested she wear it as a turban. It took but a moment for Mary to 'outlandish'[4] her appearance, adding to the effect by talking in her lingo.

There was one drawback to the scheme, which Mary had not anticipated. French was not as exotic as she had supposed – there were many people in the city who spoke the language, and she was often obliged to be fast on her feet to avoid detection. One gentleman, eager to help her, wrote the name of the French consul on a sheet of paper for her. Still lacking the fare, Mary did what she was best at: on 1 April 1817 she abandoned her possessions and left Bristol. She may have reasoned that in the country she was far less likely to encounter people who spoke French. Three miles north-west of Bristol was the country home of Lord de Clifford, where the estate workers took pity on the poor lost foreign lady and gave her a dinner of roast veal, greens and potatoes. Assuming she was French, they decided to take her to see Lord de Clifford's French cook. Mary tried to get away, but was obliged to go in, where, confronted by the cook, addressed him in lingo. He asked if she was Spanish, and she quickly replied '*Sí*'. If he had been able to speak Spanish she would have been in some trouble, but he could not; however, one of the servants had some Spanish friends in Bristol and offered to take Mary there. At the very first opportunity, Mary bolted.

When she was able successfully to pull the wool over people's eyes, Mary regarded her escapades as a huge joke. Thus far, this was probably the most fun she had ever had. Begging a bed for the night at the cottage of a farm labourer named Yates, she was able to hear him talking to his wife in the next room. Having admitted her to their home, they were both now quaking with fear in case she should be a robber in disguise. Mary was obliged to stifle her fits of laughter.

The following day she met a man on the road, the son of a wheelwright, who, intrigued by her lingo, decided to attach himself to her. He introduced her to a French governess, when again Mary managed to convince her listeners that she was Spanish, and slipped away. The wheelwright's son was not to be eluded so easily though, and caught up with her as she was resting outside a public house. When he announced that he had been given money to look after her, the locals all gathered around Mary and started offering her things to eat and drink, which she declined. Told that she was

Spanish, they offered her brandy, which she refused, as she disliked alcoholic drinks. She finally accepted a little rum well diluted with water, and some biscuits. On the road again, the wheelwright's son doggedly by her side, she met two men, one of them claiming he could speak Spanish. By now Mary must have thought she could tough out anything and boldly spoke to him in lingo. He spoke back to her, neither of them understanding the other. Eventually the others asked him what she was saying. Having boasted he spoke Spanish, he was unwilling to admit he could not understand her and said that she was indeed Spanish, that she came from Madrid Hill and that her father and mother were following her.

Mary moved on, the wheelwright's son still trotting after her. She tried to discourage him by showing him the paper with the name and address of the French consul on it. Instead, after treating her to a beefsteak dinner, he took her back to the French governess, where she was shown off to some visitors, and it was suggested that he take her to a Spanish family. Mary had by now learned some valuable lessons: first of all that people were fascinated by foreigners, and anxious to help; and also that some would pretend to understand her lingo rather than admit ignorance. The last people she wanted to see, however, were the Spanish family, and on the way to see them Mary finally managed to give her unwanted companion the slip. On the following day she made her way along the road to the village of Almondsbury, some 7 miles north of Bristol.

This pretty village of just a few hundred inhabitants, its cottages nestling in the shelter of Almondsbury Hill, had for some years attracted the attention of wealthy merchants from Bristol, who built manor houses there. Of these, the finest was sixteenth-century Knole, with a distinctive octagonal stone tower, its magnificent hilltop location affording views across the Severn. The Knole estate covered 1,500 acres, and included a deer park, woodlands, dairy farms and cottages. It was an ideal setting in which a mysterious feral girl could wander at will.

On the evening of 3 April Mary arrived, tired, hungry and footsore, and knocked on the door of the first house she came to, the home of the village cobbler. Given some bread and milk, Mary mimed with folded hands against her cheek that she wanted to sleep, but the cobbler's wife was not happy about admitting her to the house, and took her to the overseer of the poor, Mr Hill, whose job it was to bring anyone suspected of vagrancy before the Justice of the Peace. Mary's foreign persona was the perfect defence. It was impossible to tell if she was a vagrant, and she could hardly be returned to her own parish. When Hill offered her a shilling from parish funds, she refused it, seeming not to understand what it was, and indicated again by a graceful and appealing gesture of her hands that she wanted to sleep.

Still puzzled, Hill took Mary to the home of the Reverend George Hunt, noted for both his learning and his benevolence. He was not at home, but his wife, who was not so noted, took one glance at the be-turbaned Mary, who was making gestures to a sofa, and said she didn't like the look of her. Hill then remembered that at Knole Park there was a Greek manservant who was much travelled and spoke several languages, and decided to take her there. To Mary, this was the de Clifford incident all over again. At the start, pretending to be French had seemed sufficient, as it had been for her father and sister, but so near to the great trading city of Bristol, she was hardly able to stir a step without encountering people fluent in European languages. As Hill drew her near to Knole, Mary tried to run away again, and only with difficulty could he persuade her to continue.

Knole was then leased by Samuel Worrall, a 63-year-old magistrate, Town Clerk of Bristol and co-director of the Tolzey Bank. He had earned himself the nickname of Devil Worrall, probably because of his bad temper, rude manners and bouts of hard drinking. His wife, Elizabeth, some fourteen years his junior, had been born in Massachusetts, the daughter of a distiller who, as a loyalist during the Revolution, had been obliged to flee to England with his family in the 1770s, after which all his American properties had been confiscated. Known for her interest in literature, she was regarded as something of an intellectual, and was also kind and sympathetic. Now that her two sons had grown to adulthood, her interest would almost certainly have been aroused by a new project.

Mary now came face to face with the Worralls for the first time. They noted her plain clothing and short, slight build. She was undoubtedly attractive, with dark hair, full lips, rosy cheeks and even white teeth. Despite her years of domestic service, her hands were clean, white and soft, another indication that she was no common vagrant. The only unusual aspect of her clothing was the black turban and a red and black shawl arranged loosely and tastefully around her shoulders in what they perceived as the Asiatic fashion. Her other clothing consisted of a black stuff gown with a muslin frill about the neck, black worsted stockings and leather shoes. She carried with her a small bundle, the contents of which they examined. It contained what was later described as 'a very few necessaries'[5] and a small piece of soap wrapped in linen. In her pockets were a few halfpennies and a 'bad'[6] (presumably counterfeit) sixpence.

The Greek manservant was summoned, and asked her questions in a number of languages. Mary decided not to make the same mistake as before when she had claimed to be Spanish. She reacted only with blank incomprehension. He gave his opinion that she must be a foreign gypsy.

It was obvious that Mary could not remain at Knole. She was a homeless girl with a counterfeit coin in her pocket, and it was out of the question for a man in Worrall's position to harbour someone who might be a criminal. But Mary had from the start worked her fascination on Elizabeth, who decided that she should be given a room at the local inn, the Bowl, some half a mile away, and ordered her maid and footman to accompany her there.

As Mary entered the comfortable parlour of the inn, she saw something that changed the whole direction of her imposture. On the wall was a picture of a pineapple. Botanical prints were then popular decorative items, and usually bore the name of the subject in Latin, which in the case of the pineapple was *Ananas*. Confident that she would not easily be confronted by someone fluent in the language of the land of the pineapple, Mary moved her origins eastward. She pointed to the picture, became very excited and managed by gestures to convince everyone present that the fruit was from her home country. The effect was electrifying. Doubts and puzzlement gave way to wonder. Having found a homeland, Mary plunged into her role and invented a solemn ritual. Accepting a cup of tea she first bowed her head as if in prayer before drinking it, no doubt inspired by memories of the Jewish practice of uttering blessings before food and drink. After drinking the tea, she insisted on carefully washing the cup before accepting more. So enthralled was her audience that she added more strangeness to her image. Having previously had no problem in identifying a sofa as somewhere to rest, when shown to her room Mary now pretended never to have seen a bed before, and lay down on the floor to sleep. The landlady's daughter was obliged to lie on the bed to demonstrate what it was for. Mary then knelt to say some prayers, and finally curled up and slept peacefully, leaving the whole village of Almondsbury in a ferment of speculation.

Early the next morning, Elizabeth Worrall hurried over to see Mary, with a bundle of clean linen. Mary was sitting despondently by the fire, probably wondering what to do next, and greeted Elizabeth with great delight. Soon afterwards, Reverend Hunt arrived with an armful of books. Guessing that the turbaned lady came from Asia, he had thought of showing her illustrations of far-away places in the hope of identifying her homeland. As the pages turned he watched her carefully, and then to his surprise saw a flicker of interest in pictures of China. Seeing a picture of a rowing boat, she mimed a much larger vessel, so they would understand she had come to England by ship.

Elizabeth was determined to bring Mary back to Knole, but to her surprise found the girl reluctant to accompany her. She had sensed the distrust of the Greek manservant and felt uncomfortable in his presence. On the walk back to Knole, Mary decided to impress her benefactress with her piety, and on passing the church, went up to the door and tried the handle, looking very disappointed when she was unable to go in. It was Good Friday and at Knole the servants were eating hot cross buns. Mary cut the cross from the top of a bun and held it to her heart. This only increased the mystery surrounding the girl.

Elizabeth, still unsure if the young woman was genuine, summoned Mary to her and expressed her fears that she was being imposed upon: 'if . . . distress has driven you to this expedient, make a friend of me; I am a female as yourself, and can feel for you, and will give you money and clothes, and will put you on your journey, without disclosing your conduct to anyone.'[7] She reminded Mary that if it was found that she was deceiving her, Mr Worrall had the power to send her to prison and commit her to hard labour. This was Mary's opportunity to come clean without penalty, but she did not take it. The chance of playing a part was too good to miss, and she greeted Elizabeth's address with no sign of understanding, responding in her own made-up language.

Elizabeth was convinced, and determined to find out the stranger's name. Time and again she pointed to herself, saying her own name. Mary, unsure what to do, did not respond at first. She was offered pen and ink, but hardly liking to risk producing convincing Asian writing, shrank away. Her mind was busy producing a delightfully mysterious and exotic name, a name like no other. Pretending to understand at last, she pointed to herself and spoke: 'Caraboo'. Elizabeth Worrall was enchanted. John Wells, author of *Princess Caraboo: Her True Story*, suggests that the name may have been inspired by 'King Caroo', an eighteenth-century gypsy king, born only 20 miles from Witheridge. A master of disguise, he too had had adventures in America, and Mary must surely have known of him. Caraboo was now shown around the house, where she demonstrated a great deal of interest in Chinese panelling and an oriental table. At supper, Mary, not exactly sure what a Chinese Christian actually ate, showed disgust for beer, cider and meat, and accepted only vegetables and water. That night she slept in the servants' quarters.

The vicar's theory of Mary being Chinese was about to take a knock, however, for when Elizabeth reported this to the Greek manservant he pointed out that the girl could not be Chinese, since her features were entirely European.

Samuel Worrall may not have known that his wife had brought the mysterious visitor to Knole, and it seems that he was displeased when he returned to find Caraboo in residence. On the day after her arrival Mary was taken to Bristol to appear before the Mayor, John Haythorne, at the Council House in the commercial heart of the city.

She had gone too far now to do anything but continue her imposture. Fortunately the Mayor was not immune to her attractions, and she spoke to him at length and convincingly in her lingo, with beautiful gestures of her white hands. He listened carefully and afterwards a magistrate present declared that 'her language and manners were such as he had never before heard or seen'.[8]

Elizabeth Worrall wanted to take her back home, but the Mayor agreed with her husband that the law must be observed. Mary was taken to St Peter's Hospital, a home for the poor and unemployed. Crowded, noisy, and dirty, with many of the inmates ill or mentally disturbed, this was no place for Caraboo, and Mary, retreating still further into her new persona, stopped eating and refused to sleep in a bed.

It did not take long for news of the attractive stranger to reach Bristol society, and before long, Caraboo was inundated with visitors. Many came just to see the latest curiosity. Some gentlemen, with a taste for eastern exoticism, were drawn to her air of mystery. Others were eager to discover where she was from, and brought with them any foreigners of their acquaintance to see if they could understand her language. A young Scotsman who had travelled in the East later wrote to Elizabeth to theorise that the foreigner was not called Caraboo at all, but came from a place called Karabouh on the shores of the Caspian Sea, and suggested she was shown a map of the area.

Elizabeth Worrall worried about Caraboo all weekend. Visiting Mary on Monday, and finding her tired, hungry and miserable, she at once discharged her and took her to Mr Worrall's apartment above the Tolzey Bank, leaving her in the charge of the housekeeper. The stream of gentlemen visitors continued, however, as Elizabeth was as anxious as anyone else to find out where Caraboo came from. At least Mary was able to hold court in some comfort. Just how long it would have taken for Samuel Worrall's patience to wear thin will never be known, for after ten days an unusual visitor arrived who was to change Mary's life for ever. A Portuguese familiar with Malaya and its languages, he was Manuel Eynesso, although this is not a Portuguese surname and may be a garbled version of the more likely Enes, or Ernesto. He listened to Caraboo's language, and, like the speaker of Spanish, claimed that he could interpret what she was saying. He told the astonished Worralls that 'she was a person of consequence in her own country, had been decoyed from an island in the East Indies, and brought to England against her consent, and deserted. That the language she spoke was not a pure dialect, but a mixture of languages used on the coast of Sumatra, and other islands in the East.'[9]

From that moment Mary was not simply Caraboo but Princess Caraboo. The means by which the Portuguese devised this story will never be known. It could have been something Eynesso fabricated himself either as a joke or out of his unwillingness to admit failure. He could also have taken cues from Mary's gestures and her ability to memorise and mimic back to him words and phrases he then recognised. It is worth knowing that the Portuguese for 'princess' is *princesa*. Having done his mischief, Eynesso departed abroad and was not heard of again.

So Caraboo was not a vagrant at all, but foreign royalty, cruelly abducted in the most dramatic circumstances and cast, as chance would have it, upon the charity of the Worralls. Mary was at once brought back to Knole. Elizabeth, beside herself with delight at the vindication of her charge, proceeded to make the girl the whole focus of her study. Everyone she knew who might have some story to tell of the East was invited to Knole to meet Caraboo and show her pictures, books and artefacts, from which Mary gained a great deal of useful information to make the imposture more convincing.

One of the books she was shown was Hager's *Elementary Characters of the Chinese*, which showed, among other things, how counting was done by means of tying knots in string. Realising that her claims to be Chinese were in doubt, Mary did not respond to anything in the book. She was more interested in the recently published book on Java by Stamford Raffles, and the alacrity with which she pointed to the illustrations made everyone sure that at last they had discovered her origins. The very first picture in the book was of a Javanese man wearing his dagger or *kris* at his right hip. Fry's *Pantographia*, a book illustrating the world's languages and scripts, also gave some vocabulary of each language, in English. Mary examined the pages carefully, realising that her choice could be crucial. Eventually she pointed to examples of the rare Sumatran dialects, Lampoon and Rejang, and the excited ladies and gentlemen suddenly found they could match words of Caraboo's spoken language to those in the book. Mary now had ways of saying words like 'father' and 'mother' and 'God', which was 'Allah Tallah'. She had had to go to the most obscure and little-known corners of the earth in order to make her imposture believable, but she had done it.

A gentleman who had made several voyages to the East Indies was determined to discover the story of Caraboo's life before arriving in England. He spent a great deal of time with her, and, enchanted by her rosy lips and white teeth, her glossy dark hair, animated expression and theatrical gestures, was able, without understanding a word she said, apart from the few she had learned from *Pantographia*, to compose the story. Caraboo came from an island she called Javasu. (Mary showed a constant tendency to add an 'oo' sound to the end of her made-up words.) Her father was a man of substance, a high-ranking white complexioned Chinese, called Jessu Mandu. Her Malay mother, who had blackened teeth and painted face and arms, had been killed in a war between the Malays and the cannibals or Boogoos. Her father, who had three more wives, travelled in a palanquin carried on the shoulders of 'macratoos' (common men) and wore a gold chain around his neck and a peacock-feather headdress. When people approached him they knelt and made a respectful *salaam*. Caraboo too had worn peacock feathers (Mary must have remembered the plume maker she had stayed with briefly). Her name, originally Sissu Mandu, had been changed to Caraboo to celebrate her father's great victory. She did not worship idols, indeed she was shocked at the suggestion, recoiling from pictures she was shown. She worshipped God, whom she called Allah Tallah.

Caraboo had been abducted by pirates while walking in her garden. She had been carrying a *kris*, with which she wounded two of her attackers, one of whom later died. Bound hand and foot, she was taken on board a ship commanded by a man called Chee-min, then sold to a Captain Tappa Boo. Her distress had made her ill, and she had been treated by a surgeon with cupping at the back of her neck. When the ship approached England, she escaped by jumping overboard and swimming ashore. At the time she had been wearing a gown and shawl worked with gold, which she later exchanged for the clothing in which she arrived at Almondsbury.

This account of her travels was swallowed with delight. Asked about the flags of the ports where she stopped during her journey, she mimed that she was below deck and saw nothing, which led the intellectual circle to excuse the fact that the map she drew of her travels made no geographical sense.

Elizabeth was eager to see an example of her visitor's native costume and provided her with fabric from which Mary, an accomplished seamstress, made a gown with long wide sleeves, embroidered around the waist and hem, and a daring mid-calf in length. She wore no stockings but leather sandals on her bare feet. Unsure of the correct diet to assume, she professed a preference for vegetables and rice, rather than meat or bread, and ate curry, which she prepared herself. Later she accepted fish, and once prepared a pigeon in the Asian style, which she called 'rampoo'.

Caraboo recognised many artefacts brought to her – a Chinese chain purse, a rose-coloured scarf, pierced ivory fans, a Chinese puzzle, Indian ink, satin stone, garnets, sugar candy and green tea, all of which she indicated came from her father's country. Cinnamon, cassia, white pepper, rice, mother of pearl, flying fish and a species of apple she identified as coming from Javasu, and coconut, long pepper and coral from her mother's land. Her listeners eagerly recorded all she said and began to create a vocabulary of her language in which she remained entirely consistent. They were puzzled at first when she used Romany expressions for English coins, such as 'tanner' and 'bob', but assumed that she had picked these up during her wanderings. One gentleman remarked in her hearing on the difference between the Indian and Malay *salaam*. Mary duly noted this and later adopted the Malay gesture.

Now that Mary had some examples of writing to follow she was happy to give the fascinated visitors some samples of her own and so produced specimens of graceful curving script. She was also able to read fluently from pages of obscure manuscripts that were placed before her, and since no one had ever translated these before, the readings added to the excitement of her audience. The act almost led to her discovery, however, as a visiting linguist observed in her hearing that the language she was reading was read from right to left. 'In a few minutes she had changed the mode of her pretending to read, and now traced the words from right to left.'[10] Knowing that she was supposed to be worshipping Allah Tallah, she set about doing this in the most theatrical way possible, climbing to the top of the tower early in the morning and disturbing the household with loud chanting.

For Mary the pleasure of duping so many bluestocking ladies and learned gentlemen was somewhat mitigated by being constantly under close scrutiny. Every gesture she made was watched and noted, and she was unable to resist giving them what they were looking for. Given the run of the house and grounds, she became a wild creature of the woods. Walking by the lake she would kneel and perform rituals, creating a prayer arbour which she splashed with water. She exercised with bow and arrows, showing great skill and dexterity, the quiver slung over her shoulder, firing arrows as she ran. She enjoyed rowing on the lake, plying the oars with great skill. Mischievously she tried to induce the Greek manservant to go rowing with her, with the idea of tipping him into the water, but he declined. As the days lengthened into summer, she often swam in the lake. Sometimes, when she was sure not to be observed, she dived in naked.

Mary used her expressive gestures to devise dances the like of which her admirers had never seen before. 'When dancing she would assume an infinite variety of attitudes, far from destitute of elegance; bend her body in numberless shapes, but never offensive to delicacy or propriety occasionally dropping on one knee, and then rising with uncommon agility, holding up one foot in a sling, and performing a species of waltz with the most singular twists and contortions.'[11] Her manners were a constant source of enchantment, especially to Elizabeth, on whom she waited at her toilette as a trusted confidante.

One visitor who had been to Malaya some years previously arrived with a *kris* which Caraboo at once recognised and placed at her right side: this clearly impressed the visitor. On another occasion Mary overheard a discussion that it was the custom in the East to anoint the point of a dagger with vegetable poison. Having stored this information, the next time she had a knife in her hands she rubbed some leaves between her fingers, applied the juice to her dagger and, touching it to her arm, mimed a swoon. One day she indicated that it was her father's birthday and was able to show everyone how old he was by means of a piece of knotted string. By then everyone had probably forgotten that Hager's book illustrated this practice, and so this was yet more proof that she was genuine.

Mary also delighted her observers by exercising with a sword in her right hand and a dagger in her left. Mr Worrall was persuaded to try his skill at fencing with her, as he was reputed to have had some skill with the sword in his youth. Perhaps feeling a little awkward at fencing with a glamorous princess less than half his age, he was frequently obliged to admit defeat, and her success merely added to her reputation.

No real attempt was made to learn about Caraboo by teaching her English. She was regarded as an object of interest to be studied, her language and handwriting carefully recorded. It was not thought odd that she made no attempt to learn the language, and achieved no great facility with it in the weeks she remained at Knole. Such communication as was possible was done through gesture, or by the use of her invented lingo and words she had acquired through reading.

The Worralls' servants were less easily duped and more suspicious than the ladies and gentlemen for whom Mary provided food for intellectual pretensions. Mary continued to share a bedroom with Elizabeth's housekeeper, who took care to listen for any inconsistency in her speech, but never once heard her speak in any language or tone but the one she had assumed. Some of the servants planned to lie awake and listen to see if she talked in her sleep, but Mary overheard their discussion and was able to feign sleep during which she talked her gibberish language. On one occasion two of the maids ran into the room shouting 'Fire!', but Mary showed no reaction.

Mary and Elizabeth regularly travelled to Bristol when the princess was sitting for a portrait by the artist Edward Bird. On one occasion Mary fell asleep in the carriage on the return journey, but on being awoken had the presence of mind not to give herself away. Even flattery could not move her. One gentleman, admiring her dark eyes and silky 'Asiatic' hair, drew his chair close to her, gazed into her face and declared: 'You are the most beautiful creature I ever beheld! You are an angel!'[12] She remained unmoved. This extraordinary self-control convinced many that it was impossible for her to be feigning. She did make one slip, however: when the Worrall's younger son, Frederick, accused her openly of being a cheat, she was stung into responding, 'Caraboo – no cheat!'[13] But by then she had been in the household long enough for the incident to be explained away by her picking up a few words of English.

The strain of constantly acting a role began to tell. One day Mary seemed to have disappeared and Elizabeth, searching for her, discovered her sitting high in the branches of a tree. Caraboo indicated that, as the female servants were away, she did not want to be contaminated by the men. It was probably one of the few places she could feel at peace and alone.

Whether it was Mary's natural restlessness or a fresh determination to go to America will never be known, but after three weeks at Knole she suddenly disappeared and was missing for a whole day. As Elizabeth sent servants hither and thither, Mary, fearful of pursuit, was cutting across country through hedges and ditches in the direction of Bristol. She took nothing with her, not even the presents she had been given. This is understandable, since the gifts, which included the Malay *kris*, would either have identified her or led to suspicion if she had tried to pawn them, and if she had stolen anything she would have been pursued as a thief. Mary later claimed she had been trying to get to America, had settled her account with Mrs Neale and sent her trunk to her parents; but she failed to explain where the means to do this came from. What is certain is that carrying a small bundle of clothes she walked back to Knole, arriving footsore, dirty and feverish. She explained that she had recovered the clothes (which were European) from where she had buried them to hide them from the 'macratoos'. Elizabeth put her to bed and called Dr William Mortimer of Bristol to attend her. He brought a colleague who devised a rather cruel test, stating in the princess's hearing that he thought she had only twenty-four hours to live. Mary controlled her expression, but her face flushed red. The doctor at once declared that this was proof she could understand what was being said, but the maid pointed out that the flushing was also a symptom of her fever. Those who wanted to believe in Caraboo continued to do so.

When Caraboo was recovered she wrote a letter of thanks to Dr Mortimer, copies of which were shown to oriental scholars in Bristol and Bath, and sent to East India House, from whence it was passed to Stamford Raffles himself. One visitor at Knole was a friend of Archbishop Richard Whateley, a tutor at the University of Oxford, and a copy of the letter was duly sent to him. 'On inspecting it,' wrote the Archbishop many years later 'I observed among many pot-hooks and unmeaning scrawls, several words and some half sentences in *Portuguese*. I had lately been in Portugal, and had learnt something of the language. I immediately wrote word to my friend that he had sent me a specimen of the Humbug language.'[14] Whateley showed the specimen to other scholars, who agreed with his judgement. The only Portuguese whom Mary is known to have spoken to was Eynesso, which suggests a remarkable talent for recall and mimicry.

This disturbing verdict on her writing may have caused some concern at Knole, but this was soon to be dispelled. It was inevitable that Mary should attract the attention of Charles Hunnings Wilkinson of Bath. Wilkinson, a member of the Royal College of Surgeons, who probably never achieved the MD which would have entitled him to make use of the title 'Dr' under which he was known, was a promoter of health cures such as galvanism and inhalations. He was also a self-professed expert in the many branches of science in which he gave lectures. His depth of knowledge may be questioned, but he had many friends and admirers who gained great enjoyment from his lectures and praised him as a man. If Mary had felt nervous about being presented to this notable polymath, she need not have worried, since he immediately fell victim to her charm: 'her manners are extremely graceful, her countenance surprisingly fascinating,' he later wrote. 'Such is the general effect on all who behold her, that, if before suspected as an impostor, the sight of her removes all doubt.'[15]

The words 'fascinating' and 'interesting' so frequently used of Mary have sexual connotations not apparent today. She was not conventionally pretty, but she had something about her of the wild creature only partly tamed which was bound to thrill. Mary always behaved with extraordinary modesty, shrinking away from even the most innocent male touch, yet it was known that she bathed naked. She had all the allure of a painted nude, a stimulation that was permissible in the name of Art.

Mary's imposture was greatly assisted by the fact that, for a variety of reasons, people wanted to believe in her. For some she provided the challenge of solving a puzzle, and the chance to make a public display of their erudition. For others, such as Dr Wilkinson, the prospect of a book, or even a lecture tour, must have beckoned. In Elizabeth, Mary appealed to sympathetic and charitable instincts, and brought much-needed excitement to her humdrum life. For a lady approaching fifty, with two sons, Mary may have supplied the place of the daughter she had never had. Samuel Worrall's motives are more difficult to decipher. No doubt pleased that his intellectual younger wife had something with which to occupy her mind, he may have thought that the presence in his home of foreign royalty might shore up confidence in the Tolzey Bank, the fortunes of which were in a highly precarious position.

Dr Wilkinson examined the marks of cupping on Mary's head and declared authoritatively that it had been done by no method used in Europe. To him, the inability of the Oxford scholars to identify her language only added to the mystery. Mary had now been the admired plaything of the cognoscenti for eight weeks, yet thus far nothing had appeared about her in the Bristol or Bath newspapers. This was to change. Dr Wilkinson, a lover of publicity, wrote a long letter to the *Bath Chronicle*, describing Caraboo and how she had appeared at Almondsbury, and asking if anyone had observed her so as to reveal the 'circumstances, which have placed a most interesting female in a situation truly distressing'.[16] It was usual practice for regional and national newspapers to copy articles from each other, and so before long Princess Caraboo was featured in newspapers all over Britain. Everywhere, people wondered about her and sent letters to Knole with their theories. Wilkinson also announced his intention of taking Caraboo to East India House in London, to be examined by experts.

Mary must have felt uneasy about this publicity. Not only did it increase her chances of making a mistake, but she was afraid that the descriptions of her in the newspapers might be seen by someone she knew. She was right.

Mr and Mrs Starling read about Caraboo with great interest, and had no difficulty in recognising their servant. They thought of writing to Mr Worrall, but decided against it. For all their later assertions that they were fond of her, they feared her eccentricity and were worried that if she found they had informed on her, she would waylay Mr Starling on his walks home. Therefore they said nothing. The wheelwright's son had no such concerns, however, and wrote to the Worralls with his suspicions. From that moment, Mary noticed a subtle change in her protectress, who 'would not be left alone with her; and every thing looked shy and suspicious'.[17] On 6 June Mary ran away again, and, as before, took nothing with her. Elizabeth, who was obviously still not convinced that her charge was an impostor, was frantic with worry and sent servants in all directions to search for her.

Obtaining a lift with a carrier, Mary arrived that evening at the Pack-Horse Inn, Bath. Had she really wanted to blend into the crowd, all she had to do was dress in European clothes and speak English, but she was still unable to let go of Caraboo. Her arrival at the inn and inability to speak English (she drew a picture of a tree to indicate she wanted a cup of tea) excited considerable attention, and it was only a matter of time before a gentleman realised who she was, and sent word to Dr Wilkinson. He arrived the following morning to find her at breakfast, and at once sent a message to Elizabeth. Another arrival was the gentleman who had so faithfully recorded Caraboo's adventures before reaching England. When Mary recognised her visitors she immediately concluded that the game was up, and burst into floods of tears, burying her face in a handkerchief. It would have been just like her to turn from tears to laughter as soon as she realised that they still believed in her. After breakfast she disappeared again, but Wilkinson discovered her walking in the street. He was concerned about her being mobbed, and to his relief two respectable ladies kindly agreed to take her under their protection, removing her to a house in Russell Street.

Caraboo adapted happily to her new situation and took her place in the fashionable drawing room as a pampered pet. Naturally her new benefactors could not keep this coup to themselves but had to display their exciting novelty to society. Ladies of fashion arrived at their door and crowded the room, all fawning on the princess. Banknotes were strewn before her, but she pretended not to know what they were. One lady, conscious that she was appearing before royalty, knelt at her feet, another took her delicately by the hand, and a third had the temerity to beg a kiss.

It was all Mary could do not to burst out laughing. It was as this delightful scene was being enacted that the door opened to admit Elizabeth Worrall.

As soon as she saw the lady whose kindness she had abused, Mary prostrated herself on the floor to ask her pardon. Her grace and obvious emotion had a melodramatic touch that the onlookers found deeply affecting. She explained, as best she was able, that she had only left Knole because she missed her homeland, especially her father, husband and child, the existence of the latter two having not been previously disclosed. Elizabeth's heart melted, and that evening they returned to Knole together.

Well aware that she would not be able to continue the imposture much longer, Mary determined to confess all. The next morning she followed Elizabeth into her dressing room, and to that lady's surprise turned the key in the lock. They were alone and uninterrupted, so this could have been the moment; but her courage failed her and she said nothing.

Mrs Neale, Mary's former landlady, having read about Caraboo in the newspapers, called that morning upon Dr Mortimer to voice her suspicions. She testified to Mary's remarkable memory, saying that after attending church together Mary had been able to repeat all the points of the sermon. In the evening Mortimer spoke to Elizabeth, and before he left the wheelwright's son also arrived at Knole. Elizabeth's distress and feeling of betrayal can only be imagined, yet she kept her head and decided to obtain firm proof of imposture before taking any action. It must have been an effort for her to behave as if all was well, but she did so, and the following morning announced that she was taking Caraboo to Bristol to finish the sitting for Edward Bird's portrait. Instead, the carriage took the ladies to the home of Dr Mortimer, where Mrs Neale and her daughters were waiting. Elizabeth chose not to confront Mary with the Neales but spoke to them herself, and having obtained the proof she needed, saw Mary alone.

When Elizabeth told Mary she knew she was an impostor, Mary, in a last-ditch attempt to convince her listener that she was genuine, switched continents again, and prattled in Romany, exclaiming 'Caraboo, Toddy Moddy (father mother) Irish',[18] but Mrs Worral had been cheated once too often and threatened to bring Mrs Neale into the room.

Mary finally admitted she was a fraud. She was at the mercy of Elizabeth's kindness and she knew it. She begged Elizabeth not to cast her off, and also that they would not send for her father. Elizabeth promised, but on condition that Mary at once give full details of her parentage and history.

Once Mrs Neale had departed, Mary told Dr Mortimer that she had learned about Eastern customs after living for four months in Bombay.

Unfortunately for her, Dr Mortimer was familiar with Bombay and knew that this was another lie. It says a great deal for the kindness of Elizabeth and the relationship that had grown up between the two women that she did not at once turn Mary onto the street to fend for herself.

Mary remained with Dr Mortimer and his wife, while Elizabeth, hoping to evoke signs of genuine contrition, arranged for her to receive prayers and sermons, but this made no impression on what one of the clergy called 'her impenetrable heart'.[19] So far from being penitent, Mary seemed proud of how many people she had duped and how long she had deceived them. When the imposture became public, there was a widespread Caraboo craze, and everyone, it seemed, wanted to meet her: 'natives and foreigners, linguists, painters, physiognomists, craniologists, and gypsies'[20] all came to see her, as well as nobility such as the Earl of Cork. The Marquess of Salisbury also requested an interview, but by then she had already left Bristol.

Few could condemn her, and many, like the editor of the *Bristol Mirror*, felt that 'this unfortunate girl seems to be as much an object of pity as of blame in this affair'.[21] The newspapers seemed to share her delight in exposing the pretensions of the self-appointed intelligentsia, and printed numerous poems to her charms and skill at deception. The Worralls must have despaired for their standing in society, and Mr Worrall especially for the fate of the Tolzey Bank, but most of the satire was aimed at Dr Wilkinson, who was nicknamed 'Dr Caraboo'.

Mary eventually told her full story to John Matthew Gutch, editor of *Felix Farley's Bristol Journal*. The father of her child, John Baker, the bricklayer of Exeter, had now become a handsome foreign gentleman called Bakerstendht or Beckerstein, and interspersed between the periods of domestic service were threads of fantasy and lies. Though Gutch was not immune to her charms, he instituted enquiries of his own. Having obtained corroboration of the more believable events in Mary's life from her parents and employers, and established that she had never been convicted of any crime, the Worralls generously agreed to provide her with money and clothing and pay for her passage to America. She sailed on the *Robert and Ann* on 28 June in the charge of three ladies of the Moravian Church who were going to Philadelphia to teach. It was anticipated that once in America Mary would find a respectable situation, and the three ladies were authorised to present her with further funds if she conducted herself satisfactorily. As the ship prepared to sail, Mary, who was able to see the far-off tower of Knole, thought of what she had lost, and wept.

Her fame was such that she was popularly linked to one of the great romantic figures of the age, Napoleon, then exiled to St Helena. It was widely rumoured that her ship, having been driven off course, approached the island and she 'conceived an ardent desire of seeing the man with whose future fortunes she was persuaded she was mysteriously connected'.[22] She was reported to have sprung into a rowing boat, cut it free with a large clasp knife, and rowed ashore, where her extensive knowledge of Asian languages and politics convinced everyone that she was no impostor, while she so raised the flagging sprits of Napoleon that he wanted to marry her. What Mary was actually doing on the way to America was enlivening a tedious voyage by unashamedly recounting her adventures as Caraboo to anyone who would listen.

By the time the ship arrived, the English newspapers and Mary's fame had preceded her, and the wharf was crowded with people eager to see Caraboo. A position as cook had been arranged for her, but she declined and succumbed instead to the offers of a showman who promised to put her on the stage. The Moravian ladies and the ship's captain begged her not to take this course, without effect. The American newspapers carried stories of her beauty and accomplishments, claiming that she would exhibit herself in the same dress she wore for the hoax. In the midst of all this enthusiasm, however, there was some hostility and anti-English prejudice. Given Mary's undoubted skills as a performer, she should have been a success, but her new patron failed to make the most of her true talents. Her debut, as part of a concert, involved no more than being conducted on stage as Caraboo and writing a letter in her feigned language. The audience was unimpressed, and a second performance was cancelled. By November her dream of fame was over.

What Mary did in the next seven years is unknown. She returned to England around 1824, setting herself up in a booth in New Bond Street London, exhibiting herself as Caraboo for a shilling a visit. When this failed, she tried the same thing in Bristol, but with similar result. She had been forgotten. She married a Robert Baker, ten years her senior, who was a dealer in leeches, a respectable trade that provided a comfortable income. Their daughter, Mary Ann, was born in about 1829, and when her husband died Mary continued the business. In later life she was ashamed of the Caraboo episode and refused to discuss it.

The Tolzey Bank foundered in 1819, and Samuel Worrall was declared bankrupt. He was obliged to resign as Town Clerk and died two years later, a forgotten man, whose passing did not merit an obituary in the Bristol newspapers even though he had served the city for thirty-two years. Elizabeth Worrall moved to Bristol, where she died in 1842. Whether she and Mary ever met again is not known. Dr Wilkinson managed to rise above the Caraboo debacle, and remained a well-respected man. He died in 1850, aged 87.

In 1864 Mary was living in Bedminster with her daughter, who was now carrying on the trade in leeches. Aged 75, Mary had been suffering from breathlessness and her doctor diagnosed asthma. Rebellious to the last, on being told her condition was incurable, she 'resolved to do without medical attendance'.[23] On Christmas Eve she went to bed as usual. The following morning, her daughter, unable to wake her, administered sherry, then sent for a doctor. By the time he arrived Princess Caraboo was no more.

THREE

The Viscount of Canada

In July 1831 the citizens of the United Kingdom were offered an exciting investment opportunity. The Lord Proprietor of Nova Scotia, New Brunswick and Canada, recently confirmed as heir to the 1st Earl of Stirling, announced that he was offering valuable tracts of unoccupied land for sale. There was an immediate and enthusiastic response. The only drawback, as investors were soon to discover, was that the British government did not recognise either the title of the seller or his ownership of the lands.

This was the latest act in a saga that had begun in 1621 when King James I granted the courtier poet Sir William Alexander the whole of the territory of Nova Scotia, with the object of encouraging colonisation. In 1624 Sir William was further empowered to divide the land into 16,000-acre tracts, which he could sell, granting each purchaser the rank of baronet. Charles I renewed the grant and in 1628 extended it to include the province of Canada. Sir William made valiant efforts to establish colonies there, but with limited success; in fact his industry placed him in considerable debt. Meanwhile, French claims to the lands had erupted into war. In 1631 a settlement was reached, in which the Crown, despite its prior agreement with Sir William, returned Nova Scotia to the French. Sir William was to be paid £10,000 for the cost of evacuating the Scottish settlers, but the money never appeared. He eventually sold his rights in Canada to a Monsieur de la Tour, a member of the small French colony there.

Sir William remained in favour, however. In 1635 he was granted most of New England and the whole of Long Island, and by then had amassed several titles: Earl of Stirling, Lord Alexander of Tullybody, Viscount of Canada and Earl of Dovan. Despite this impressive accumulation of honours, when he died in 1640 he was insolvent, and his Scottish holdings disappeared into the pockets of his creditors. Subsequent wars and treaties extinguished whatever rights Sir William had once had overseas, and the titles passed to his heirs; but with the death of his great-grandson, the 5th Earl of Stirling, in 1739, the peerage became extinct.

In 1759 an American, William Alexander, laid claim to the Stirling peerage on the grounds that he was descended from an uncle of the 1st Earl, but on 10 March 1762 the Lords Committee of Privileges ruled that he had failed to establish his claim. He returned to America and later became a general in the US Army, dying in 1783 without male issue.

The most persistent and ingenious claimant to the earldom was Alexander Humphrys. Born on 21 June 1783, he was the son of William Humphrys, a Birmingham merchant with substantial trading interests on the Continent. 'Nobody in Birmingham lived better,' said a family friend. 'They kept their carriage and a pair of fine grey horses, and had half a dozen of servants at least.'[1] From 1794 the family resided in a substantial country house called the Larches, and employed a solicitor, Josiah Corrie, to collect their rents. The wars in Europe were disastrous for trade, but following the Treaty of Amiens, peace between England and France enabled William and Alexander to go to Paris in 1802 to try to recover some business debts. They were still there on the outbreak of fresh hostilities in May 1803, and both were interned at Verdun. William died in 1807, but Alexander was obliged to remain in France until the peace of 1814, although he was permitted to live in Paris. His inheritance consisted mostly of bad debts, and he squandered much of the remainder in useless litigation to recover his fortunes. In 1812 he married Fortunata Bartoletti, a Neapolitan lady, and was introduced to her friend and confidante, Mademoiselle Marie Lenormand, one of the most notorious and successful fortune-tellers in France.

Born in 1772, Mlle Lenormand had shown an early talent for cartomancy and palmistry. The terror and uncertainty of the revolutionary period led to a great boom in the fortune-telling trade, and Mlle Lenormand, who was particularly in demand, included such notables as Marat and Robespierre among her clientele. During the First Empire she continued to prosper, and her most illustrious client was the Empress Josephine, much to the displeasure of Napoleon, who twice had 'the Sorceress', as she was known, imprisoned. After Napoleon's exile Mlle Lenormand set up a fashionable salon in the Rue de Tournon, and was the rage of Paris. It is tempting to suppose that the success and longevity of her career was a result of careful observation and a tendency to tell people what they wanted to hear: 'there was a cunning restlessness in her bright blue eye, which . . . lost no [sic] one peculiarity of the "consultant"; turning the blush of timidity, the stern gaze of defiance, or the smile of incredulity, equally to her own profit'.[2] When Alexander Humphrys first consulted Mlle Lenormand his family fortunes were in a state of decline.

Nevertheless, she had good news for him. It would take time, and he would experience many reverses, but eventually he would achieve high rank and great wealth.

In 1814 Alexander returned to England with his family, and both he and Fortunata remained in touch with Mlle Lenormand by letter. He settled in Worcester and took the post of assistant master at Netherton House School, but was well aware that this was not the way to make his fortune. The key to wealth, he believed, was already within him – a legend from his past, which had lain dormant and unrealised. His mother Hannah was the daughter of Reverend John Alexander of Londonderry, a minister of the Presbyterian church in Plunkett Street, Dublin, until his death in 1743. The Reverend's antecedents have never been confirmed, but he could have been the John Alexander, son of James, who was baptised in 1686 in Raphoe, near Londonderry,[3] while the chronicler of the Alexanders, the Reverend Charles Rogers, later stated that Hannah was descended from a Paisley branch of the family. Perhaps it was the coincidence of surname that led Hannah to tell her children that they had noble blood in their veins. Her father, she said, was a descendant of the 1st Earl of Stirling and, had he been inclined, might have made a claim not only to the title but to the substantial Stirling properties. Her husband often used to call Hannah 'the Countess', although whether this was an acknowledgement of her position or a term of indulgent affection was never revealed. Unlike her son, Hannah only hinted at great things, never trying to prove them. Both her brothers and her sister had died young without issue, so after her death in 1814, Alexander Humphrys was his mother's sole heir. He asked Josiah Corrie to act for him in making a claim to the earldom of Stirling on the basis that Hannah was the direct descendant of John Alexander, the fourth son of the 1st Earl. This son was known as John of Gartmore, since he had married Agnes Graham, the heiress of the Gartmore estate. He had left Scotland to settle in Ireland, where he died in 1666. Of this part of the family tree there was no doubt, but the remaining connections were less certain. Alexander claimed that John of Gartmore had a son, John of Antrim, who was born in Scotland and who accompanied his father to Ireland. John of Antrim was said to have married a Mary Hamilton in 1682, and died in 1712. According to Alexander, it was his son, born on 30 September 1686, who became the Reverend John, father of Hannah. There was no evidence that John of Antrim had ever existed, but to Alexander this was a minor difficulty. There was, however, another more serious obstacle to his claim. The earldom of Stirling had been granted to

Sir William and his male heirs only. Even if Hannah was his direct descendant, then the title could not pass to her son. Alexander's trump card was his claim that there was a Royal Charter, or novodamus, dated 7 December 1639, under which Charles I had granted permission for the peerage to pass through the female line if there was no male heir. No one had ever heard of such a charter, let alone seen it, but this did not deter Alexander, since it was known that some official records of that period were missing, rumoured to have been lost at sea. Furthermore, Alexander could blame the disappearance of any family papers in support of his theory on the American claimant. He was also unconcerned about the fact that the 1st Earl had died bankrupt. The original grant of Charles I had made over huge tracts of land to the Earl in perpetuity, and he was happy to ignore everything that had happened since. Should he be successful in his claim, he would gain enormous wealth, including possession of Nova Scotia, New Brunswick, Canada (which was then a separate province), parts of Wisconsin, Maine and Massachusetts, and a 300-mile-wide stretch of land reaching from the head waters of Lake Superior to California, with all the associated mines, woodlands and fisheries.

Mr Corrie, on finding that his client had no documents to prove his claim, declined to assist him. Alexander next attempted to enlist the aid of noble and powerful families, the very people to whose ranks he aspired, but to his great surprise found them hostile to his efforts. Another man might have given up the idea as an impossible fantasy, but Alexander Humphrys possessed extraordinary tenacity and determination, and was by now in the grip of an obsession that would dominate the rest of his life. From the outset he demonstrated an unshakeable confidence in the outcome of his claim, wildly exaggerated the importance of the evidence he used to maintain it and remained firmly blinkered against the weaknesses of his arguments. He considered any opposition as proof of an evil conspiracy of powerful men determined to deny him his inheritance. It would not have been surprising if a man so utterly convinced of his being right, but without material to prove this was so, had resorted to manufacturing the material he needed, deluding himself that he was only reconstructing papers that had once existed but had been stolen by his enemies.

In 1819 someone with the initials FD wrote to the *Gentleman's Magazine* asking for information about the Alexander family, and in particular wanting to know which descendants of the fourth, fifth and sixth sons were still alive in 1739, if there were any pedigrees of the family after that date, and if it was possible to examine the papers of successive claimants.

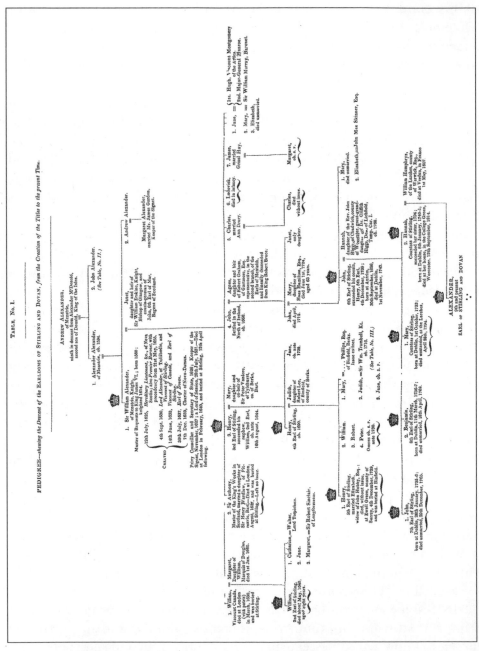

Pedigree provided by Alexander Alexander to prove his title to the Earldom of Stirling. *(The British Library)*

In April the same correspondent asked about the descent of the Reverend John Alexander, who was described as the nearest male heir to the earldom. The identity of FD is unknown, but may have been Alexander or an agent employed by him. The enquiry seems to have been unsuccessful.

A crucial step in the development of Alexander's case was the initiation of a correspondence in 1823 with Thomas Christopher Banks. Born in 1765, Banks was a member of the Inner Temple and a genealogist of some years experience, but what must have attracted him to Alexander's notice was his authorship of *Dormant and Extinct Baronage of England*. The Edinburgh advocate William Turnbull wrote of Banks in 1839: 'This is one of those busy, meddling, troublesome, and officious individuals, professing themselves "Genealogists", who tend so much to perpetuate blunders and misrepresentations in matters of general and family history, if indeed they do not *wittingly* aid and abet in the fabrication of impostures like the present.'[4] An anonymous pamphlet published in 1839 described Banks as 'a person of very low extraction, but of considerable ready talent and powerful memory'.[5]

Alexander had by now advanced substantial sums of money to counsel and an attorney to make searches for him, and while he had no more funds to pay Banks to act as his agent, he did have one bargaining counter, the immense wealth that would accrue to him when he established his right to the peerage; and he promised that, when this right was established, Banks would receive payment. Persuaded by Alexander's dynamic self-confidence, Banks agreed to act for him on this basis. First, however, there was a minor difficulty to be dealt with. The earldom could be vested only in someone of the surname Alexander, and so on 8 March 1824 Alexander Humphrys obtained a royal license to change his name to Alexander Humphrys Alexander, stating as his grounds that he was anxious to perpetuate the family surname of his maternal grandfather out of respect for his memory and at the wishes of his mother. No mention was made of his real motives. Alexander now assumed the title Earl of Stirling and Dovan, referring to his late mother as Countess, his grandfather as the 6th Earl, and conferring appropriate titles upon other members of his family. His next move was bold and controversial.

The death of the 6th Earl of Balcarres in 1825 had been followed by a proclamation calling upon the peers of Scotland to assemble at Holyrood House on 2 June to elect a peer to take his place as a representative in parliament. This was a chance for Alexander to demonstrate his position in public and before the men he regarded as his equals. Voting on such occasions was always preceded by the reading-out of names from the Roll of Peers for Scotland, which included the extinct peerages, and those gentlemen present answered when their names were called. When 'Earl of Stirling' was read out, Alexander answered. Surprised officials were in no position to challenge him, and both recorded his presence and registered his vote. He and Fortunata then proceeded to Stirling, where, prompted by his solicitor there, James Wright, the arrival of the 'Earl and Countess' was greeted by the ringing of the bells, and magistrates came to wait upon their noble visitors at the hotel and offer their congratulations. The couple made a visit to Stirling Castle and also to Argyll Lodge, the former residence of the Earls of Stirling. Before they departed, the town council met and elected the 'Earl' a burgess of the town.

Alexander's next act was to seek legal title to the earldom and its lands. In the 1820s the means by which entitlement to honours was established was in some disrepute, since it was recognised as being open to fraud and imposture. Evidence of any kind was admissible in court, and, if there was no counter-claim, the action would automatically succeed. The result of such a hearing remained open to challenge for twenty years, after which it could not be overturned. As a first step, on 7 February 1826 Alexander took his case to the court of Canongate, Edinburgh, where he proved himself heir to Hannah Alexander, presenting a pedigree that claimed his maternal grandfather was the great-grandson of the 1st Earl. The claim was duly ratified by a jury.

Returning to Worcester, Alexander plunged into an extensive correspondence, with the aim of finding evidence to support his claims and raising loans on the security of his assumed possessions. He remained in a state of buoyant, almost intoxicated optimism. In November 1826 he wrote to a friend that he had high hopes of his wishes being accomplished almost immediately. He anticipated being granted 'a location of *five millions of acres*, which is found to be not one *twentieth part* of the lands originally granted, all convertible at once, at common market price, into cash, and will be more than one million sterling'.[6] In July 1827 he wrote excitedly: 'By degrees, all the valuable papers of which my grandmother was robbed, about the time the General preferred his claims to the Earldom, are finding their way back to me.'[7] These letters, written with the intention of raising money, were either the outpourings of a man losing touch with reality or a deliberate attempt at deception, and possibly something of both. Mlle Lenormand gave the 'Earl' considerable encouragement. Having acquired a fortune during her heyday, she provided Alexander with loans amounting to 400,000 francs or £16,000 (about £1 million today) and was no doubt anxious to see her money and the interest thereon returned to her. In 1827 Banks was dispatched to America to find papers that, he was told, had been stolen by agents of the American claimant. While Banks was away, Alexander continued to incur vast expenses and tried to raise loans to pay them off; but all his attempts failed, probably for lack of security. Matters were not eased when Banks returned empty-handed. In April 1828 Alexander engaged the Edinburgh solicitor Ephraim Lockhart as his legal adviser, while Banks was sent to Ireland to trace the elusive novodamus. Banks wrote to Lockhart for advice on the style of a novodamus – he said he wanted to sure of what he was searching for – and Lockhart obligingly sent him a draft. Banks also obtained some copies of genuine charters from the period. By 1829 it seemed that Banks's efforts had been crowned with success: from Carlow he wrote that on his return to Dublin he found a parcel had arrived from an unknown sender containing an old document – not the hoped-for charter but a contemporary excerpt, witnessed by John Spottiswoode, Archbishop of St Andrews and Chancellor of Scotland in the 1630s.

Alexander was by now Headmaster of Netherton House, but, probably because of his legal expenses, the family were reduced to extreme financial distress and he was unable to pay the rent of his lodgings. The excerpt was just what he needed, a tangible document he could use to raise money. When Lockhart was shown the excerpt, he was surprised to find that it was identical word for word with the draft he had sent Banks; nevertheless, he did not raise any queries and, as instructed, commenced legal proceedings to prove the validity of the document. He also took action against John Watts of New York and William Duer of Albany, the grandsons of the American claimant, alleging that the excerpt had been stolen from the claimant's grandmother at the general's instigation. Neither Watts nor Duer was able to take the charge seriously, and, as there was no proof of the allegation, the action was dismissed on 4 March 1830. Another action attempting to use the excerpt to prove the existence of the novodamus of 1639 also failed.

In October 1829, abandoning his school and indeed his butcher to whom he owed money, Alexander moved his family to London, taking apartments at the corner of Regent Street and Jermyn Street. He was introduced to the financial agent John Tyrrell, to whom he described his 11 million acres in Maine. Part of the land was occupied, and the occupiers were to give him a quarter of a dollar an acre to be confirmed in their titles, while his title to the unoccupied part was, he said, beyond doubt. He needed only to raise money for the legal expenses and the cost of sending someone out to Maine to take possession of the estates. If he could also raise money to prosecute his claims in Scotland, he added, he would then obtain possession of the estates of Gartmore, Tullybody, Tillicoultry and Menstry. Tyrrell took Alexander at his word and negotiated a number of loans, one of which was from Admiral Sir Henry Digby. Before long the sum of £13,000 was lodged in Alexander's bank account, in return for which he signed a promissory note for £50,000. Moving to 20 Baker Street, he kept a carriage and lived in style. Despite the close professional relationship between Alexander and Banks, Tyrrell was instructed to say nothing to Banks about the loans he was raising. Alexander was considerably indebted to Banks, and probably wanted him to know as little about his current solvency as possible.

Alexander did not personally attend the next peers' election on 2 September 1830 but applied for, and was granted, permission to submit a signed list of the candidates for whom he wished to vote. When the name of Earl of Stirling was read out at the election, the Earl of Rosebery registered a protest, expressing the opinion that 'it would be far more consistent with regularity and propriety, were those individuals who conceived they were entitled to dormant peerages, to make good their claims to them before the House of Lords, previous to taking the titles and exercising the privileges attached to them'.[8]

Two days later Alexander launched an action in the Supreme Court of Scotland against Mr Graham of Gartmore, claiming the Gartmore lands for himself on the basis of the marriage of John of Gartmore. This was not to be resolved for two and half years, but while it was proceeding his efforts to establish himself as nearest heir to the titles of William,1st Earl of Stirling, remained unchallenged and thus met with the approval of the courts on 11 October 1830 and 30 May 1831. Once again, the proofs he supplied were not subjected to enquiry. Among the documents he produced was a deposition said to have been made in 1722 by Sara Lyner, an 84-year-old widow, stating that her mother had seen John of Gartmore together with his only son, the alleged John of Antrim. The Lyner document also attested that the widow had been present at John of Antrim's marriage and had looked after his son. Another affidavit, dated 16 July 1723, had been sworn by a Henry Hovenden, declaring that the Reverend John Alexander of Londonderry was the grandson of John of Gartmore and that he had personally seen the novodamus which had granted the earldom to William Alexander 'and the heirs male of his bodye, which failing, to the eldest heirs female'.[9] Why these people should have felt it necessary to make such affidavits was not clear at the time, and was only recognised as important with the hindsight of over a century.

In January 1831 Alexander addressed a memorial to King William IV asking for a royal audience. This was refused: the Lord Chancellor replied that Alexander's pretensions were untenable. The 'Earl' attended Holyrood to vote in the peers' election on 3 June 1831, and this time the Duke of Buccleuch and the Earl of Lauderdale registered a formal protest at his vote being accepted, stating that 'we have great reason to suspect the authenticity of the documents, such as they are, on which the claimant is said to rest his assumption of that title'.[10]

On 2 July 1831 a final court action under the same uncritical system as before established Alexander's rights to the 1st Earl's inheritance. Lockhart was instructed to issue a proclamation titled *Notice to the Baronets of Nova Scotia*, addressed to the heirs of the original baronets created by the 1st Earl, advising them of their rights.

An office was opened at 53 Parliament Street for the sale of land and debentures on the American possessions, and on 12 July 1831, describing himself as 'Lord Proprietor of the Province of Nova Scotia, New Brunswick and the adjacent Islands',[11] Alexander issued a prospectus to proposed investors, with details of the court actions that had ratified him as heir to the 1st Earl: 'He is now desirous that the waste lands within his said territories should be settled and appropriated . . . . Either for absolute purchase or lease for a term of years,'[12] estimating the value of the land at between 2s and 20s per acre depending on the quality of the soil and local advantages. As to the original grants made by Sir William, he declared that the crown was obliged to confirm these free of all expense, but large tracts of land remained unallotted. 'At this time there is a particularly fine district of 1,000,000 acres of most excellent land in New Brunswick, comprehending every attribute of climate and soil to render settlements in entirety or in subdivisions according to the inclinations or capabilities of persons to take the whole or only proportions.'[13] He also encouraged those who might wish to form a company, in which case he would take a tenth of the shares, the company having the exclusive rights of working any such mines that might be found. His prospectuses and advertisements were widely circulated in Britain, the United States and Canada. How many people were duped into investing and how much money he made from them has never been quantified.

On 14 July 1831 Alexander decided to reward the efforts of Mr Banks, not with the money he undoubtedly owed him, but by granting 16,000 acres of land in Nova Scotia and creating him a baronet. A Mr Philippart (probably the historian John Philippart with whom the Alexanders are known to have corresponded) received a similar honour. In August 1831 Alexander wrote to the King once more, asking to be permitted to render homage at the forthcoming coronation. He was ignored.

For the previous eighteen months John Tyrrell had been successfully raising money for Alexander on the basis of the charter, but in 1831, during a conversation with Banks, he received a considerable shock: the document that he had been led to believe was an original charter was in fact only an excerpt, and, moreover, had not been ratified as genuine. Despite Alexander's confident assertions that the charter existed, it could not be produced. There was an abrupt termination of the business relationship. Tyrrell was later reticent in giving the reasons, perhaps concerned that he might be liable for prosecution, stating only that it happened because Alexander had said that others might do better for him. Banks alleged that it was because of the way Tyrrell conducted himself in business. The most likely reason was Tyrrell's discovery that he had been induced to obtain loans under false pretences.

It can hardly have been a coincidence that, soon after Tyrrell's split from Alexander, Sir Henry Digby took legal action to recover his money, giving instructions that Alexander be arrested as a commoner under the surname Humphrys. Digby said he had lent the money believing Alexander to be a peer and that he would be repaid at some future date. When the case appeared before Chief Justice Tindal at the Court of Common Pleas on 22 November 1831, Alexander claimed that as a peer of Scotland he was in a privileged position and could not be arrested. Tindal declined to comment on the validity of the peerage claim, which was not a matter for that court, but based his judgment on whether 'he is in the eyes of the world appearing and acting as a Peer of Scotland'.[14] Since Alexander had by then voted three times as a peer, Tindal judged that the defendant had acted as a peer and was thus privileged to avoid arrest.

Alexander's attempts to interest potential purchasers of land were not meeting with success. Those who made enquiries were advised to steer clear of any deal, which made Alexander rage against officialdom. Matters were exacerbated by the recent boom in the settlement of Canada and the exploitation of its natural resources, which had given rise to the formation of companies to acquire the lands Alexander believed to be his own. Convinced that there was a government plot to block him from access to his established rights, he later wrote 'an unparalleled system of injustice and persecution was organised, for the tyrannical purpose of overpowering me'.[15] His complaints to the authorities became more frequent and more persistent, and were, in the end, his undoing. In October 1831 he wrote to Earl Grey, First Lord of the Treasury, claiming his legal right of inheritance to the lands and lordships of Nova Scotia and Canada and protesting against the exercise of any rights over the lands by any other person. He also sent a manifesto to the public authorities of Nova Scotia refusing to recognise any allotment of territory made other than by his ancestor, but generously allowing 'the Native inhabitants of Nova Scotia or Canada every preference over persons emigrating from Great Britain'.[16] Despite these setbacks, his agents were instructed to offer the lands for auction at the next opportunity.

In preparation for the sale, his solicitor wrote to Lord Goderich, Secretary for War and the Colonies, in December 1831, asking to open negotiations with the government to obtain 'a full and satisfactory adjustment of claims and titles'.[17] Prime Minister Lord Howick replied the following month, stating that the government declined to enter into negotiations on the subject of the claims and suggested that Alexander 'should be distinctly apprised that they are, and will be, altogether denied and resisted'.[18] When Alexander's solicitor wrote again, Howick replied that the title could not be recognised until established to the satisfaction of His Majesty or the House of Peers. Even Alexander must have known that this requirement was impossible, and he never attempted it.

In 1832 the Marchioness-Dowager of Downshire, a genuine heir of the 4th Earl, complained to the House of Lords about Alexander, pointing out that if the novodamus did exist (and she nowhere claimed that it did) then the earldom would be vested in her. On 19 March her memorial was referred to a select committee of the House of Lords, which had been appointed on a motion of the Earl of Rosebery to consider the subject of persons claiming dormant peerages voting at elections, to prevent, as Lord Rosebery put it, 'the facility with which persons can assume a title without authority, and thus lessen the character and respectability of the peerage in the eyes of the public'.[19] Alexander naturally wrote a letter of protest to the committee, and on 7 May the committee reported its decision: in any case where there had been an objection to a vote on the grounds that the person was not entitled to the peerage, that person should not be permitted to vote again until he had established his right before the House of Lords. It was also decided that a new Roll of Peers should be drawn up, the names to consist only of those entitled to vote.

Alexander had more pressing things to worry about. On 15 June 1832 he presented a petition to the House of Commons against the application of the New Brunswick and Nova Scotia Land Company for a charter of incorporation and protested against the acquisition of land by the Nova Scotia Mining Company, alleging that any occupation of the land by another party was an usurpation of his rights. He demanded compensation for the portion of his lands to be assigned, and objected to all pending applications.

From 4 April to 21 August 1832 a series of letters in Alexander's favour by a correspondent signing himself AB appeared in the *Morning Post* and *The Times*. Since one quoted the letter from Lord Howick, the writer was probably either Alexander or his solicitor.

In October and November 1832 advertisements appeared in the newspapers headed 'Nova Scotia New Brunswick, and Canada', proposing that a joint stock company be formed for locating the unappropriated lands in those places and giving notice that Alexander was the proprietor, warning that no grants of those lands could be made by any other person. The auction of the 'increasingly valuable and important Freehold Property',[20] with cultivable land, timber, and mining and fishing rights, was fixed for 7 November; but it never took place.

A paragraph appeared in *The Times* of November 6 1832, presumably from the editor:

We observe an advertisement for the sale of sixty-three thousand acres of land in the province of New Brunswick at the auction mart tomorrow, the 7th instant, on behalf of the 'Earl of Stirling'. It may not be improper to state, that on enquiry at the Colonial Department, we find that the Government do not recognise the claims which the gentleman assuming that title makes to the unoccupied land in the province; but have, on the contrary, directed the local authorities to oppose any entry which may be made on any such lands by persons deriving title from grants made by the 'Earl of Stirling'.[21]

This effectively stopped the sale, and Alexander later complained bitterly that *The Times* had also refused to insert another advertisement he had sent.

Parliament was dissolved in December 1832, but Alexander did not attempt to vote at the ensuing general election. Instead, he wrote a long letter to the peers of Scotland, explaining that he would not be appearing to vote as it was incompatible with his dignity to submit to derogatory treatment and also, since he did not have the support of the other peers, he was unconcerned as to the result of the vote. He concluded: 'The day of retribution, I feel, is not far off, and then I may act a part which I have no doubt will cause me to be differently respected and considered by those who are now pleased to cavil about straws . . .'.[22]

Alexander's protests, petitions and attempt to auction land that was not his property were causing some irritation in government circles and led to a serious reconsideration of his case, in particular the court actions by which he had established his claims to the title and land. In 1833 the Officers of State for Scotland commenced an action to reverse his legal proofs. On 2 March of that year Alexander's action against Mr Graham was dismissed, and as a result some information emerged that was fatal to his case: Alexander had claimed to be the descendant of John of Antrim, son of John of Gartmore, but the defence produced a charter showing that Gartmore's legal heir was his daughter, proving that John of Gartmore had never had a son. This disclosure should have been the end of Alexander's pretensions, but the 'Earl' was nothing if not obstinate, and this only led him to try another tack – to show that John of Gartmore had married a second time, to a Miss Elizabeth Maxwell of Londonderry, and that it was the second marriage that had produced a son. The fact that there was no trace of either the marriage or the son was not for Alexander the obstacle it might have been to others.

Throughout this time Mr Banks had been one of Alexander's busiest representatives and strongest allies. Now signing himself Sir Thomas C. Banks, Bart. N.S., he had been confident that the Crown would recognise him as Baronet of Nova Scotia, but his claims were ignored and consequently he took legal action. In 1834 he produced a pamphlet in his defence, in which he denounced the Scottish Officers of State as 'Satanites' and 'imps of the fallen angel', who 'worshipped the golden calf' and wrote 'as the lowest English scribbler in Grub Street'.[23]

Only a few weeks later Banks and Alexander had a serious quarrel. Banks ceased to act for Alexander, abandoned his legal actions, withdrew his pamphlet and renounced his title. From that moment on the two men were bitter enemies. Banks made no public statement as to the reasons for this breach, but Alexander later denounced his former confidante as a 'traitor . . . an impostor . . . an extortioner . . . a detractor . . . a low-minded ruffian . . . a companion of the foul fiend',[24] asserting that it was all about money. Money may well have been involved, as Banks's letters to

Alexander had often mentioned the expense he had incurred during his research, which he was confident would be ultimately worthwhile. But it is possible to speculate about other reasons. When action was commenced to reverse the proofs of Alexander's peerage, he made great efforts to delay the proceedings for as long as possible, saying that he was looking for new evidence; and when the case was finally heard, one item was very noticeable by its absence – the charter excerpt. Alexander had instructed his counsel not to make use of it, which suggests that, by the time of his split with Banks, he may have known that the excerpt was a forgery. If Banks had demanded to know when he was going to be paid, he may well have told Alexander that he had forged the excerpt. Each man had the ability to drag the other down, but both remained silent. Perhaps, after more than ten years without result, Banks had concluded that the claims were specious and his client a fraud. Alexander dared not use the excerpt again and remained terrified that the man who knew most of his secrets had defected to the side of his enemies. His only recourse was to denounce his former ally as 'a malevolent and mercenary agent' and 'a vindictive and treacherous being'.[25]

It was not until December 1836 that the action to reverse Alexander's proofs was heard. In the interim Alexander continued to write to government ministers, including Colonial Secretary Lord Aberdeen, and successive Prime Ministers Lord Melbourne and Robert Peel, and on 6 January 1834 registered a strong protest at a grant of 500,000 acres of Canadian land to the Irish Colonial Association.

Shortly before the new hearing Alexander published a book, which was little more than a paranoical complaint that the government was attempting to subvert his lawful rights. 'I must see whether, by boldly exposing the villainy and dark intrigue of my enemies, it is possible to open the eyes of the British public, who are not wilfully blind, to the existence of the foulest conspiracy against an individual that ever disgraced this country.'[26]

He remained unswervingly confident of ultimate triumph, stating that he had recently discovered another important document. Although he had still not traced the elusive charter, he claimed that *the evidence respecting it is complete*[27] and that it had been ascertained that authenticated copies existed but 'have been purposely withheld by persons who have them in their keeping'.[28] Everywhere he saw enemies, plotters and schemers whom he supposed were dedicated to denying him his rights from motives of personal hatred. They were 'malignant beings and the arch-traitor with whom they are leagued'[29] – undoubtedly a reference to Banks – 'ever on the watch for new opportunities for doing mischief'.[30] The court action was a 'shameful attempt to rob me of the whole advantages of my situation . . . for corrupt and abominable motives',[31] and he railed at 'the combined attacks of swindlers, bill-brokers, pettifogging lawyers, and other unprincipled persons'.[32]

As ever, the complete proofs that Alexander claimed to possess looked much less convincing when examined with a critical eye. The documents he presented in court were a deposition from his sister, Mrs Eliza Pountney, who called herself Lady Eliza and who described her mother's belief in her descent from the Earls of Stirling; a deposition from a William Trumbull, which showed only that the 5th Earl's sons had died without issue; the affidavits of Sara Lyner and Henry Hovenden; and a paper alleged to be a page from a family Bible, giving the inscription on the tomb of the elusive John of Antrim, who was said to have been buried at Newtownards, near Belfast, in 1712, showing his descent from John of Gartmore. Unfortunately, the Bible itself was not available.

Piece by piece, Alexander's proofs were demolished. The Pountney and Trumbull affidavits made no mention of the supposed Gartmore connection, and proved nothing, the page said to be from a Bible was worthless without the original book and, still worse, expert testimony suggested that the Lyner and Hovenden documents were recent forgeries. Two stone-cutters from Newtownards who had worked in the old church there and knew it well testified that they had never seen a tombstone with the alleged inscription.

On 10 December 1836 Lord Cockburn delivered a devastating judgement. While there was no doubt that the claimant was the son of Hannah Humphrys (née Alexander), he had failed to prove the alleged connection between her father and John of Antrim and John of Gartmore. The Lyner and Hovenden statements were probably forgeries, but even if they had been genuine, they were just hearsay and insufficient for proving the existence of an individual, while convincing proof did exist that John of Gartmore had had no sons.

A few days later, Alexander, terrified of being arrested for forgery and debt, fled to France under an assumed name, leaving his family to do the best they could without him. He arrived in Paris on 21 December. One of the first people he contacted was Mlle Lenormand, who was living in an apartment at 5 Rue de Tournon. On a sign above her door she was described as a bookseller and author, but although she had published books on cartomancy and a memoir of the Empress Josephine, the only business she was known to conduct there was fortune-telling, assisted by a private secretary, Monsieur Triboul.

Alexander remained in France for several months and called upon Mlle Lenormand almost daily, arriving at about 8 p.m. and usually staying at least two hours on each occasion. If he did not go in, he left her a note: neither what they discussed nor the contents of the notes were ever revealed. In April 1837 one of Alexander's sons, Eugene, received a sealed packet through the post containing a number of documents. A note on the parchment cover stated simply 'some of my wife's family papers' in writing that was identified by several people, including Mr Corrie, as that of William Humphrys. The packet was impressed with three seals. Realising the importance of this item, Eugene had the packet opened in the presence of witnesses, including a public notary. In an unsigned note dated 17 April 1837 the sender said the papers had been stolen from the house of William Humphrys and had been sent anonymously to avoid disgrace. Among the documents was a family tree showing that John of Gartmore had had a son, John, by his second wife Elizabeth Maxwell of Londonderry. A letter from a lawyer signing himself WG, dated 14 January 1723, referred to the charter of novodamus and suggested that though it was not in the official registers of Scotland it may have occupied a portion of volume 57 from which several leaves were missing. Further letters dated 1765 and 1766 stated that the family tombstone at Newtownards had been destroyed by the American claimant. Alexander later identified the seals as those of his family, which, he said, he had not seen since 1825.

This was exciting enough, but in July an extraordinary new document came to light in Paris. Mlle Lenormand claimed it had been left in her rooms by two anonymous but fashionably dressed ladies who were merely delivering it for an individual who declined to give his name, 'being of such exalted rank as to make such a declaration on his part unsafe and improper without positive proof'.[33] The document was a map of Canada dated 1703, printed from a copper engraving of Guillaume Delisle (a prominent cartographer of the period) and on the back were written or pasted several messages, all of which supported Alexander's claims. There was a letter dated 4 August 1706 from a Philippe Mallet claiming he had seen the original novodamus, and a marginal note (apparently written by King Louis XV) declaring Mallet's letter to be worthy of notice. Caron St Etienne, in another note dated 6 April 1707, also claimed to have read the charter, which was said to be nearly fifty pages long. Esprit Flechier, Bishop of Nimes, stated in a letter dated 3 June 1707 that he too had seen the charter.

Another letter, dated 25 August 1707, appeared to be from John of Antrim. It referred to the charter and stated the writer's belief that the register in which it had been included had been lost at sea and claiming that he (the writer) was the son of John of Gartmore by a second marriage. This letter was vouched for by a statement of Archbishop Fenelon of Cambray dated 16 October 1707. Pasted on the back of the map was the inscription from the tombstone of John of Antrim in Newtownards, confirming his descent. The whole was finished with a family seal.

Armed with this new evidence, Alexander returned to England. On 25 November, assisted by Lockhart, he appealed against the decision of Lord Cockburn and produced his new papers in evidence. Suspicion was immediately aroused concerning the validity of the documents, and a commission of enquiry was appointed, which took almost fifteen months to complete its investigation. While these matters were pending Alexander continued to make protests about government measures affecting what he claimed were his lands, and raised an objection to the appointment of Lord Durham to the governorship of Canada. On 27 January 1838 he asked for an immediate confidential interview with Lord Melbourne. Neither this interview, nor his petition to attend the coronation of Queen Victoria, was granted.

In April 1838 Mlle Lenormand was summoned to the Prefecture of Police in Paris and asked to state how the map came into her possession. She reiterated her story that the map had been sent to her by a person of whom she either could not or would not give any account. According to a report in *The Times*,[34] she admitted having been paid for the map, a fact which was later hotly denied by Alexander's son Charles.

British Government agents were sent to France, where Mlle Lenormand was able to follow the steps of the investigation and write regularly to both Alexander and Fortunata, advising them of what witnesses had been asked to go to Scotland to give evidence. The enquiries ultimately discovered a Monsieur Leguix, who in 1836 had sold maps and prints on the Quai Voltaire. He remembered selling a 1703 map of Canada, which then had no writing on the back, to an Englishman, and he was willing to give evidence. On 8 January 1839, in some alarm, Mlle Lenormand wrote to Alexander: 'They have found out the man on the Quay. They wish him to go to Scotland.'[35] Both she and Alexander were clearly well aware of the significance of this discovery.

On 14 February 1839 officers were sent to Alexander's house in Edinburgh to arrest him. As they burst through the door he seized a sword and locked himself in his room, while his distraught wife sent for Lockhart, who examined the warrants, found them to be legal and advised his client to give himself up. Alexander was taken into custody and charged with forgery. When his house was searched for documents, the letters from Mlle Lenormand were found, together with a deed acknowledging that he was indebted to her to the sum of 400,000 francs, received in cash. The loan bore interest at 5 per cent, and he had agreed to pay her in full after the recovery of his property.

Under questioning, Alexander denied knowing Monsieur Leguix and said he had visited Mlle Lenormand only very occasionally. He stated that she was a writer by profession, and it took some very determined questioning to get him to admit that she was a fortune-teller and that he had consulted her in that capacity. He claimed that he had been in Paris on literary pursuits, though he declined to say for whom, and eventually he refused to answer any more questions.

The trial opened in Edinburgh on 29 April 1839 and lasted for five days, 'during which time every cranny of the court was occupied by the rank and fashion of Edinburgh. The number of ladies present gave an air of brilliancy to the assemblage, which resembled the audience of a theatre rather than of a hall of judgement.'[36] Alexander pleaded not guilty. The defence, led by Mr Robertson, had a difficult task, but was assisted by the fact that proof of guilt rested on three heads. The prosecution first had to show that the documents were forgeries, secondly that Alexander had 'uttered' them, that is, used them in evidence, and thirdly that he knew them to be forgeries. Robertson was not confident he could do more than cast doubts on the prosecution's proofs of forgery. That Alexander had uttered the documents was incontestable, but the third head of proof was something he could exploit to the full.

The prosecution first turned its attention to the charter excerpt. Although it was supposed to date from 1639, expert witnesses unanimously stated that it appeared to be less than a hundred years old. The paper was brown and looked aged, but under the stitching it was the same shade of brown, whereas in a genuine old document this area would have been lighter. The edges of the pages seemed to have been recently cut and the writing did not look especially old. Dr Andrew Fyfe, a chemistry lecturer, said that in his opinion the paper had been artificially coloured with some organic matter.

This evidence might have been dismissed by a clever counsel, but the forger, in claiming that the charter was witnessed by Chancellor of Scotland Archbishop Spottiswoode, had made a crucial error. The official list of

Scottish Chancellors, which the forger had presumably consulted, showed that Spottiswoode had been succeeded as Chancellor in 1641, but omitted the important facts that he had been deposed from the Chancellorship in 1638 and had died on 26 November 1639, eleven days before the date of the charter. Experts also testified that reference marks made on the excerpt were of a kind not seen on documents earlier than 1806.

The forger had relied upon the fact that there was a gap in the official records where the original charter might have been located, but had reckoned without the existence of indexes that revealed exactly what the missing items were. George Robertson, a Keeper of the Records for Scotland, had consulted the indexes and testified that none of the missing items was a charter, and none referred in any way to the Earl of Stirling. The rumour that some documents had been lost at sea was an exaggeration. The only missing items of the period were twelve leaves from Book 57, and there was hardly room for a document nearly fifty pages long, as referred to on the back of the map.

The map of Canada, although dated 1703, had not been printed on that date. The French archivist Theulet, an expert in the works of Delisle, pointed out that, while the map was a print from the original engraving of 1703, the original imprint had been changed. The map produced in evidence gave Delisle the title of 'Premier Géographe du Roi', a title he was awarded on 24 August 1718; the map was dated 1703, not because it was printed then, but to fix the date of commencement of copyright. Since this particular copy of the map could not have been printed before 24 August 1718, it was impossible for the writings on the back of the map, said to have been made before that date, to be genuine. Archbishop Fenelon and Bishop Flechier had both died before 1718. Theulet gave the opinion that all the writings on the back of the map were false.

When Pierre Joseph Leguix took the stand there was some consternation in the defence team. If it could be shown that Alexander had bought the map without the writing on it, it would be impossible to maintain that he knew nothing about the forgery. Alexander's counsel, Mr Robertson, questioned the map-seller, Leguix, closely and extensively about how much he was receiving in expenses, to suggest that his evidence was tainted, and then objected to the admissibility of the witness. Their Lordships observed that Leguix was receiving no more than was necessary and proper for him to receive, and the award of such expenses was quite common. They allowed the evidence. Leguix testified that in the winter of 1836 to 1837 an Englishman frequently came to his shop in search of maps of Canada.

Several maps had been sold to the man, but the one he especially wanted eluded him, a map dated 1703. Leguix made considerable searches for such a document, and eventually located one. The man bought the map, and did not come to his shop again. Shown the map produced in evidence at court, Leguix agreed that the one he had sold was similar but that it had then had no writing on the back. The moment came that Robertson had been dreading. Leguix came down from the witness box to look at the defendant, and was asked if this was the Englishman who had bought the map. To the astonishment of the court, he said: 'No, sir.'[37] The prosecution had more luck with Huges Beaubis, the porter at 5 Rue de Tournon. Not only did he recall the frequent visits to Mlle Lenormand of a man the servants referred to as 'the Englishman', but he confidently identified Alexander as the man.

Mr Robertson put up a spirited defence for his client, and his address to the jury was a masterpiece. 'In your countenances I already see the cheering light of an acquittal,' he said optimistically.[38] He did his best to cast doubt on the evidence of forgery, especially that of the scientists. 'I hate all the trickery of science. A plain man judges for himself whether a document be a forgery or not. Look at Flechier and Fenelon's signatures for yourselves. You are as good judges, in my opinion, as any engraver that ever scratched on copper.'[39] In any case, he suggested to the jury that the defendant did not have the knowledge or skill to commit forgery.

The crux of the defence was the character of the defendant. No witness could have been more instrumental in determining Alexander's fate than his lifelong friend, Colonel George Charles D'Aguilar, head of the Adjutant General's staff in Ireland, who refused to enter the witness box but stood resolutely by Alexander's side in the dock. 'Nothing on earth could have induced me to take the part I have taken, to stand before the Court where I do if did not think Lord Stirling to be incapable of a dishonourable action,' he declared.[40] He had, said Robertson, rushed to the aid of his friend 'with the spirit of a British officer, and the pride and generosity of a British gentleman'.[41]

Robertson next played on the sympathy of his listeners. He described Alexander's past life as 'anxious days of heart-sickening hope, and sleepless nights of feverish rest', and referred to his 'rising family . . . seeing nothing but penury and distress before them'.[42] For the future he trusted that 'his mind shall be directed to pursuits more solid, and to the attainment of objects more consolatory and enduring'.[43]

Finally, he made an emotional appeal: 'Let the visionary coronet be plucked from his bewildered brow – let the prospects of wealth and of courtly titles and honours vanish into air; but, oh, gentlemen, leave him that best and highest title of nobility – his good name . . . . Do not, gentlemen, – do not add to the pangs of this man more than he deserves. . . . For in my conscience I believe him innocent of the crimes here charged, and to have been merely the dupe of the designing, and the prey of the unworthy.'[44]

Lord Meadowbank's drier summing-up stuck strictly to the facts, but was undoubtedly in favour of a guilty verdict. He pointed out that Alexander had borrowed large sums of money on the basis of assurances that he owned property to which he had no title, and it could be proven that he had lied about his frequent visits to Mlle Lenormand, 'a person obviously of the worst character, and who, although she says that a lie never passed her lips, is proved to you to have had no profession but that of fortune telling – no means of subsistence but that of imposture, and telling falsehoods from morning to night'.[45]

He also commented on a point the prosecution had not raised, that it appeared to him that the seals on the packet of letters sent to Eugene corresponded exactly with the supposedly much older seal on the back of the map of Canada. The facts of the case, he concluded, showed that the whole thing was done for the ultimate benefit of the prisoner, and so he believed that the jury could conclude that Alexander had full knowledge of the forgeries.

The jury retired at 11 a.m. and were absent five hours. They unanimously found that both the excerpt and the documents on the map were forgeries, but it was not proven that Alexander forged them or uttered them knowing them to be forged. They unanimously found it not proven that the documents in the packet sent to Eugene Alexander were forged.

The announcement of the verdict was received with a burst of stamping and shouting from the gallery, which was cleared by order of the judges. Alexander fainted into the arms of Colonel D'Aguilar, and had to be carried out of the court into an adjoining room. When he had recovered enough to depart, he was greeted by a huge ovation from the crowds waiting outside.

Despite Robertson's fondly expressed hopes, Alexander, who went to live first in Paris and then in Brussels, did not move on to more attainable projects. He continued to call himself the Earl of Stirling and pursued his case with the same energy and anger as before. He appealed against the official dismissal of his proofs, but any hold he may once have had upon reality had long gone when he accused the government of having employed 'rogues . . . intriguers and spies', who, assuming 'every variety of character, got admission into my house and society',[46] and claimed that agents had been secretly sent abroad to find archive copies of the proofs of his pedigree and rights, that registers were either taken away or had leaves torn out, and that his family tombstones had been destroyed.

Mlle Lenormand continued to practise her profession, depite her ebbing fame. A visitor in these later years braved the damp courtyard off the Rue de Tournon, its dim uneven staircase with slimy walls, finding her apartments 'of somber and faded aspect, bearing evidence of past grandeur'. She sat in a high-backed leather chair, shrouded in deep shadow, but when his eyes grew used to the gloom he saw 'a person of short stature and of immense bulk . . . Her face was round and fat, yet full of meaning . . . I shall never forget the impression conveyed by that deep voice as she spoke, in low, whispering words, rapid and monotonous, the decrees of fate which stood revealed in the painted pictures she fingered with such marvellous dexterity.'[47] After her death in 1843, it was rumoured that she had left an immense fortune to her nephew, but her 1911 biographer Alfred Marquiset states that she left 120,000 francs (about £300,000 today).

In 1845 Alexander was still writing to Lord Chief Justice Denman complaining of 'the system of persecution and violence of which I am a victim'[48] and 'the hostility of the government',[49] which he attributed to their not having all the facts, and asserting that the map and the writing on it were all genuine. He denied that he had founded his case on the excerpt, stating that once its authenticity had been questioned he had withdrawn it. He added that he had a list of all the people who were correspondents of Mlle Lenormand, hinting that they were English, Scottish and Irish people of high rank. If this was a subtle attempt at blackmail, it produced no response.

He appealed to the House of Lords, but the legal process finally halted in 1846 when proceedings were officially shelved. He then moved to the United States and settled at 11th Street, Washington, where he continued the battle. Every so often the case was resurrected and briefly filled the newspapers. An American supporter, John Hayes of Washington, wrote in 1853 claiming that the map of Canada and its inscriptions were genuine. He believed that Delisle had added the title 'Premier Géographe' at a later date, and that while the document was in official hands Lord Stirling's enemies had made alterations to the writing to make it look like a forgery. Alexander died in Washington on 4 May 1854 aged 76. His former confidante and adversary Thomas Banks died the following September in Greenwich.

Two of Alexander's five sons continued to pursue their father's interests. On 11 February 1864 his eldest son, Alexander William Francis Alexander, established himself as heir to his father and revived the proceedings. The case was eventually heard by the House of Lords, who delivered judgment on 3 April 1868, in which it was declared that the evidence rested solely on forged documents.

On 15 April 1872 the second son, Charles Louis Alexander, made a claim to Congress on behalf of his brother as Earl of Stirling, in which, among other points, he claimed that the original map of Canada and its writings had been genuine but that it had been stolen and a copy substituted. Needless to say, he failed.

FOUR

The Sting

On 18 May 1840 Andrew O'Reilly, Paris correspondent of *The Times*, wrote an article whose consequences were far wider that he could have imagined. Then aged 57, O'Reilly had served the paper for many years, acting as a hub of foreign news, assembling information from continental newspapers, editing stories and passing them on to *The Times* offices in Printing House Square. He also organised the dispatch of documents by fast courier and cross-channel steamer. On this occasion, O'Reilly recognised a story that had recently appeared in Belgian and French newspapers as a substantial scoop; and so before composing his dispatch he spent some days investigating the details and obtaining supporting evidence. Entitled 'Extraordinary and Extensive Forgery and Swindling Conspiracy on the Continent', the piece appeared in *The Times* of 26 May, and, sensational as it was, the headline was no exaggeration.

The principal instrument of the fraud was the circular letter of credit, the forerunner of the modern-day travellers' cheque, devised some seventy years earlier to assist gentlemen travelling on the Continent. The purchaser deposited a sum of money with a bank in London, whereupon he was provided with an engraved document that enabled him to visit specified continental banks to draw on his funds while abroad. Each letter of credit was stamped with the initials of the issuing bank and signed by a senior partner. There were blank spaces left for the number of the letter, the name of the bearer and the amount of credit, which could be from £100 to £10,000. As money was drawn, so it was noted on the letter until the full amount had been issued. Most banks wrote to their foreign counterparts to advise them of any letters of credit they had issued, but one bank was an exception, Messrs Glyn, Hallifax, Mills and Co. The letters issued by Glyn's included, usefully, a list of the principal towns in Europe, beginning with Abbeville and ending with Zante, and for each one gave the names of the banks where money could be drawn. These banks, asked to provide money on a letter of credit from Glyn's, would have no written advice with which to verify the document and would therefore have to rely on the banker's experience to decide if the letter appeared genuine and his judgement as to whether the bearer looked honest.

The mastermind behind the plan to swindle continental banks using forged letters of credit was Auguste Harold, Marquis de Bourbel, a rogue who left a trail of misery and scandal wherever he went. He claimed to come from a family 'old as the rocks of Provence',[1] and indeed the de Bourbels of Montpinçon in Normandy had first been ennobled in the year 936. Born on 30 January 1804,[2] as a young man he was employed in a junior post by Monsieur Hyde de Neuville, the French ambassador to Portugal. The date and circumstances of his departure from that post are unknown, but it was sudden, and at de Neuville's particular request. He was later attached to the French embassy at Copenhagen, and from there went to Paris, where he became a member of the Secret Police. Known as a gambler, duellist and roué, he was handsome and well mannered, with a plausible and insinuating charm. In 1841 he was described as having 'light hair, fine stature, wears a great coat of kid skin, his complexion pale, and of agreeable physiognomy'.[3] He was at home in the very best society, with a wide knowledge of both the fashionable world and its leading figures; he spoke four European languages fluently and was an amusing raconteur. He was also known for his good taste in the arts, was a skilled painter in oils and, more dangerously, a caricaturist, while he 'rode, danced, fenced and wielded the broadsword with uncommon dexterity'.[4] Not lacking in physical courage, early in his career he fought a duel with a M. Haidé, said to be a Greek gentleman, whom he fatally wounded.

On 28 March 1828 at the British embassy chapel in Paris, de Bourbel married 21-year-old Constance Cecilia Bulkely, a lady of fortune from a respectable Berkshire family; soon afterwards, however, his scandalous behaviour made even Paris too hot to hold him. He sold the family seat at Montpinçon and spent the next two years in England. In the 1830s he moved his family (there were now two or three children) to Florence, where he 'entered very generally into the dissipations and intrigues of Florence, and was universally looked upon as a specious, agreeable, but thoroughly *mauvais sujet*'[5] – in other words, an unprincipled reprobate.

In 1838, when his unfortunate wife was in the last month of another pregnancy, he abandoned her to run away with a young woman who has been described as either his wife's maid or an opera dancer. Mme de Bourbel did not recover from the shock and died in childbirth on 9 April 1838. Public outrage at de Bourbel's behaviour forced him to remove his family to the Villa Micali, near Leghorn. There he was frequently visited by an acquaintance who was probably no less a villain than himself.

William Cunninghame-Graham, sometimes known as Wicked William, was born on 16 August 1775, the son of the poet and politician Robert Cunninghame-Graham of Gartmore. His father had taken great care over his education, but young Graham, though talented, was a sad disappointment. During 1792 and 1793, when Graham was at university in Glasgow, his father was obliged to write to him frequently, complaining about his idleness, extravagance and inattention to his studies. After completing his education at Neuchâtel, Graham entered politics and became Member of Parliament for Dumbarton, and Lieutenant-Colonel of that county's militia.

In 1798 Graham married Anna Dickson, who bore him two daughters, but in 1816, after Anna's death, he married Janet Bogle (née Hunter), the widow of Allan Bogle, a Glasgow merchant who had traded with the West Indies, by whom she had a son, Allan George Bogle. On 16 March 1818 she gave birth to another son, Alexander Spiers Graham, who took after his father in his fondness for a life of idleness, to which he added two other vices, debauchery and drink. Both sons would eventually be involved in their father's plan.

Like de Bourbel, William Cunninghame-Graham had an interest in the fine arts and was an excellent mathematician, but his main talents were mechanical, and he was especially adept at wood turning and the construction of tools and machines. He had invented and constructed a tracing machine probably similar to the pantograph, a device invented in the seventeenth century to make copies of fine art engravings. The movement of a pencil at the bottom of the machine caused another pencil at the top to move in the same way, and could either reproduce an exact copy of the original pencil marks, or, by adjustments, create larger or smaller copies.

By nature Graham was 'cool, crafty, designing and thoroughly unprincipled'.[6] A dedicated gambler, after squandering his inheritance (he lost the family seat of Finlaystone in a card game) he was obliged to flee Scotland in 1828 to avoid his creditors. By 1833 he was living in Florence, where he first became acquainted with the Marquis de Bourbel.

Despite the difference in age, de Bourbel and Graham had much in common and as time passed spent increasing amounts of time in each other's company. De Bourbel was also a keen gambler and made use of Graham's mathematical talents in calculating odds, seemingly undeterred by the Scot's disastrous record in that field. By the end of 1838 the frequent absence of Graham from society and his preoccupied air when in company excited no little comment among his acquaintances. Unsuspected by friends and family, the two now virtually inseparable men had been devising a complex and daring plot which, if successful, would make them immensely rich. De Bourbel had been looking for a large coup to make his fortune, and being a man of imagination it had occurred to him that his organisational abilities, Graham's mechanical talents and the connections of his son Allan George Bogle, partner in a prosperous Florence banking business with Messrs Kerrich and MacCarthy, provided the perfect combination. The plan was to forge letters of credit, those of Glyn's being the obvious choice. They were simpler to produce than a banknote, but even so presented a number of challenges. First of all there was the engraving and printing of the document itself, a process that could take several weeks and which would be regarded with suspicion by anyone employed in the undertaking. Secondly, they had to make a facsimile of the signature of the banker that would fool those who were familiar with it. Thirdly, they needed to manufacture a stamp bearing the initials of the firm, 'G. H. M. and Co.', and, finally, Glyn's letters used a distinctive, unusually thick paper unobtainable on the Continent. It was a complex operation that would hardly be worth attempting unless the reward was very great. Even if they overcame all the difficulties and produced a perfect forgery, a letter of credit of substantial value could excite suspicion, and once the money had been drawn, it would be a matter of days before details of the payments were transmitted from the European banks to Glyn's in England and checked against customers' accounts. De Bourbel considered the difficulties and had a masterstroke of inspiration. The key to success was to forge a large number of letters of credit in relatively modest sums, and employ a team of agents working for commission who would go to banks in different countries and present the forgeries at the same time. Their work done, they would then depart, using false passports, to America, India, Algiers or Egypt, and would be long gone by the time the fraud was discovered. De Bourbel calculated that the gang could make £1 million (some £65 million today), most of which would go into his own pocket.

De Bourbel spent a great deal of time in Graham's workshop, and soon both men were satisfied that the tracing machine could turn out good fac-similes of signatures. To establish an alibi, it was important that de Bourbel should be a familiar face to Bogle Kerrich and Co., and early in March 1839 he was introduced to the firm by Allan Bogle, and opened an account.

It seemed to Kerrich in hindsight that from then on de Bourbel was a regular visitor to the bank even when he had no actual business to transact.

De Bourbel also needed the cooperation of an agent to whom he could entrust his new wealth and who would not ask too many questions about a sudden acquisition of funds that coincided with a gigantic fraud. He was able to secure the loyalty of a Florentine called Freppa, stating that he anticipated receiving some money following success in some speculations, on which Freppa would, for his services, personally receive the sum of 50,000 francs.

The next step was to obtain a genuine Glyn and Co. letter of credit in order to copy the signature. These letters were not usually kept by banks but remained in the custody of the account holder, but it so happened that Robert Nicholson, who lived in Florence, had deposited his letter of credit with Bogle Kerrich and Co., where it was kept by Mr Kerrich in a tin box. This letter was signed by Mr Hallifax, one of the senior partners of the bank. When Nicholson wished to draw upon the letter, he would apply to the bank, Kerrich would take the letter from its box and hand it to Bogle, who would make the payment and then immediately return the document to Kerrich. In December 1839, therefore, it excited no comment when Allan Bogle asked Kerrich for Nicholson's letter of credit. It was in his possession for three hours before it was returned to Kerrich. At the time, Kerrich assumed that a payment had been made, and had no reason to check up on his partner. It was only later that he discovered that no payment had been made to Nicholson in that month, and suspected that Bogle had passed the letter to Graham, who had copied the signature with his tracing machine.

Satisfied with the success of the first part of the plan, de Bourbel set out for London, taking an apartment above a hairdresser's shop at 100, the Quadrant, Regent Street, the beautiful (then colonnaded) sweep of buildings just north of Piccadilly Circus. In London he encountered an old friend, the Baron Louis D'Arjuzon, 'son of a distinguished General of the Empire and a Peer of France',[7] who had an uncontrollable addiction to gambling that made him a ripe candidate for any money-making scheme. As anticipated, D'Arjuzon joined in the conspiracy with enthusiasm. It was now necessary to purchase a letter of credit from which to make the engraving, and on 7 January 1840 D'Arjuzon, given £150 by de Bourbel, deposited the funds with Glyn's and obtained a genuine letter, which, coincidentally, had also been signed by Mr Hallifax. Being of an economical turn of mind, de Bourbel later made sure that most of the outstanding sum on this letter was recovered from the bank.

If villainy is attracted to villainy, then when the Marquis de Bourbel first met the lovely Angelina he must have known that she would be a valuable member of the gang. She claimed to be a native of Jersey and to have completed her education in Boulogne. She certainly spoke fluent French. Angelina was bold, beautiful, cared only for money and was no stranger to crime. She had married Thomas Davidson Pow, a young man of fortune so addicted to drink that he regularly consumed a pint and a half of gin a day. Pow had made a will leaving all his property to his wife, but he had a strong constitution and Angelina was not prepared to wait until he drank himself to death. In 1838 the couple were living in a lodging house at 31 Queen Street, Lambeth. Both the landlady and the occupants were careful not to notice what went on around them, and in consequence the house was considered to be little better than a brothel. The only person who did observe and make a note of events was Frederick Pipe, who had known Pow for two years. Pipe claimed to be a veterinary surgeon, although he has also been described as a footman. He was owed money by Pow and was anxious to collect it. On 5 July he set out for Westminster Hospital, where he knew that Pow had been admitted, but was surprised to find that Angelina and a medical attendant, Henry Myers, had been there two days previously and abruptly removed her husband from the hospital. Pipe thought this highly inadvisable, and began to follow Angelina and Myers. On more than one occasion he saw them entering a house together and stay there for some hours. Making enquiries, he discovered that the house was a brothel. It was obvious to Pipe that Angelina (who was later described as a woman of loose morals and little better than a common prostitute) was having an affair with Myers, a married man. The two were holding Pow in a lodging house where they administered large quantities of gin and bled him to an extent which even in 1838 was deemed excessive, until he finally succumbed, at the age of 24. The inquest held on 23 July found a verdict of wilful murder against Angelina and Myers, and at a later hearing Frederick Pipe appeared in court to give evidence of his investigations and suspicions.

The case came to trial in September, but it was felt that there were insufficient grounds for the charge, and both were acquitted. In all probability, the persistent Frederick Pipe, having failed to secure the conviction of the woman he thought had murdered his friend, now began to pursue Angelina for payment of his debts. What followed was not perhaps entirely inexplicable: Angelina Pow was young, attractive and wealthy; in January 1839 she and Frederick Pipe were married.

A year later, Frederick Pipe met de Bourbel though his connection with some of the gambling houses at the Quadrant, and introduced him to Edward Gullan, an engraver of Windmill Street, Haymarket. Having engaged Gullan to make the copper plate from which to print the forgeries, de Bourbel became concerned that if Gullan were presented with a complete letter of credit as the basis for his task he might suspect that he was being asked to participate in a serious crime. To conceal the nature of the document he cut it into a number of slips – Gullan later estimated there were twelve to eighteen – which were handed to him individually over a period of two months. Gullan never saw more than one slip at a time, and the pieces, apart from the one he was working on, were always kept locked up at de Bourbel's apartments. It was a curious way of proceeding and Gullan, who later claimed that he had never seen a letter of credit, did become suspicious, especially as he was advised by de Bourbel to do his work without asking any questions. He was well paid, however, and probably took the view that he would be able to plead ignorance if necessary. Initially, Gullan worked at his own premises, but de Bourbel became unhappy about other visitors to the shop seeing what was being done and insisted that Gullan come to his apartments and complete the work there. The stamp with the initials of Glyn and Co. was an easier proposition, and de Bourbel employed a man called Palmer to produce one. It was Frederick Pipe who approached Morbey and Co., the manufacturers of the paper on which the Glyn and Co. letters were printed, to obtain a supply.

The printing was carried out by a friend of Edward Gullan who was sufficiently impoverished not to ask any questions. Thomas Perry, also known as Ireland, was 30 and lived with his wife, Anne, and four children at 5 Upper Rupert Street, Haymarket. His business was run from 88 Oxford Street. In February he printed over 200 of the letters of credit, some of the work being carried out at Pipe's house in Lisson Grove and some at the Quadrant. The copies were then transmitted to Graham in Florence, who was delighted with them, and used his tracing machine to add Mr Hallifax's signature.

While all this was happening de Bourbel was assembling a gang of agents, since he had no intention of presenting any of the forged documents himself. The agents included D'Arjuzon, who would travel under the name of Castel, and his mistress, Marie Rosalie Desjardins, who obtained a passport as the Countess de Vandec. Frederick Pipe travelled as Dr Coulson, which was thought to be the name of a former employer, and

Angelina adopted the name of Lenoi. Alexander Graham took the name of Robert Nicholson, the man whose letter of credit Bogle had borrowed. Although Alexander had been assigned an important role in the operation, his debaucheries soon caught up with him and he was ultimately too ill to take much part.

Little is known about Charles Gerard de Pindray (sometimes spelt Praindry), another member of the gang. He claimed to be a count, but his title does not appear in the dictionary of French noble houses; he may have been an adventurer who travelled under assumed titles looking for ways of making money without the tedious necessity of work. Thomas Perry the engraver was also admitted to the gang, although he spoke no French and it was decided he should travel with Angelina Pipe. These agents were to receive 20 per cent of any sums they obtained from the banks. Quite what Graham and Bogle were to get was never discovered, but Perry overheard Graham tell Bogle that he would earn his share very easily as he had so little to do.

De Bourbel planned that the operation would commence on 21 April, simultaneously in Belgium, the Rhinelands and Italy. At the end of March he, Perry and Mrs Pipe travelled to Calais, arriving on 28 March, and from there went to Ostend, which they reached the following day, taking rooms in the Hotel d'Allemagne. There they met up with D'Arjuzon and his mistress, who were travelling together with a little girl, and Frederick Pipe. On 1 April this party, apart from de Bourbel and Pipe, travelled in a splendid carriage with two servants to Aix-la-Chapelle, where Alexander Graham was waiting for them. The travellers took rooms at the Hotel Bellevue and remained there, living in style, until 19 April. D'Arjuzon took the opportunity of further lining his pockets by visiting a jeweller and taking away a pair of diamond earrings, saying he would show them to an Italian princess who would pay 3,600 francs for them. He did not return.

On their way to Italy de Bourbel and Pipe stopped at Nice, where by prior arrangement they met Graham on 14 April. De Bourbel was concerned that by associating with villains he was in danger of being robbed by his own agents, and had attempted to reduce the chances of this happening by putting men he trusted in charge of those sections of the operation he could not personally supervise. Graham was to accompany Frederick Pipe as one of the supervisors and D'Arjuzon would travel with Perry as another, but it was not possible to control the whole gang, and great anxiety remained about subsidiary agents who were acting alone. De Bourbel wrote to D'Arjuzon from Nice. His letters are a mixture of detailed instructions, confidence-boosting, flattery and pathetic appeals for loyalty. 'The banker at Florence says he is certain that all will go on perfectly well. . . . Everything at this moment appears to me *couleur de rose*.' He assured D'Arjuzon that he was the only man he could really trust, denouncing de Pindray as 'an infamous scoundrel', adding that 'without you . . . I should despair for I am afraid of being robbed by Alexander', and ending with the last plea of the confirmed trickster: 'Adieu dear Louis, I write to you no more. On my knees I implore you to take care of me and my children.'[8] Cunninghame-Graham wrote to his son on the same day, and clearly there were some concerns about Alexander's ability to play his part: 'you must pay the greatest attention to the orders which are given to you . . . especially avoid drink during business time, or you are sure to spoil all, for I am convinced that unless you are under the influence of wine you will act suitably in all this affair.'[9]

De Bourbel also wrote to Alexander: 'Bogle and your father are convinced that all will go on well . . .'.[10] He then listed the dates and places on which Alexander was to present his forged letters of credit, up to and including 29 April, since he was aware that the information would not reach the London bankers until the following day.

De Bourbel proceeded to Florence, arriving on 18 April. He was present at the bank of Bogle Kerrich and Co. two days later, where he drew a small amount on a cheque through Bogle, who completed the paperwork in a tremulous hand. De Bourbel did not, it was later established, arrive with the cheque and neither did anyone else bring one on his behalf, an incident which Bogle left unexplained. De Bourbel returned to the bank on the following day for a very curious appointment. This was the day on which the operation was to commence, and, anxious to have a good alibi, he was happy to draw attention to himself.

Bogle had a private room at the bank that contained cash and securities. It was divided by a glass partition, in which there was a hole through which money could be passed to customers and placed on a marble slab when required. Normally the public had no access to the part of the room where the money was kept. At 10 a.m. on 21 April Mr Kerrich arrived at the bank and saw de Bourbel in the open part of Bogle's room, transacting business with Bogle. Kerrich went to his own room but half an hour later saw that de Bourbel was still with Bogle but in the private section. Kerrich decided to investigate, but on trying the door handle found that the room was locked. He was able to see de Bourbel and Bogle clearly through the glass, so left them there and returned to his own room, coming back later to find, much to his astonishment and concern, that the door was still locked. In all, de Bourbel was closeted with Bogle for two or three hours. What they discussed during that time has never been revealed.

Shortly after de Bourbel's departure, the 'Count de Pindray' appeared at Bogle Kerrich and Co. and presented his forged letter of credit; although the letter was good for £2,000, he asked only for £200. As was usual, when a new letter was received it was examined by Mr Kerrich, who was satisfied that it was genuine. De Pindray received £200 in gold. No doubt the modest plundering of Bogle's own firm was designed to remove suspicion of any involvement.

On the same day, Frederick Pipe, who was in Genoa with Graham, obtained £1,500 from the bank of Gibbs and Co., saying that he needed the funds to purchase works of art. He received the money in gold without any difficulty, and Graham took charge of it.

After his successful extraction of money from Bogle Kerrich and Co., de Pindray next went to a Florentine shopkeeper called Phillipson to take up some more money on the letter of credit. The letter was left with Phillipson, but that that evening Phillipson returned the letter to de Pindray saying he had some doubts as to its genuineness. De Pindray was in a difficult position. The operation had only just begun and already suspicions had been aroused. After banking closed that afternoon (the bank's hours were 10 a.m. to 3 p.m.) MacCarthy, one of Bogle's partners, met Phillipson, who, while not able directly to prove his suspicions, left MacCarthy with a very uncomfortable impression. He decided to speak to Bogle about it, but search as he might, he could not find him. Eventually, between 4 and 5 p.m., he left a letter at Bogle's lodgings stating his suspicions and asking to see him; but Bogle did not respond. MacCarthy did not see Bogle until the following morning, when he simply said that the note had spoiled his appetite but that he was not inclined to discuss it further.

Who should then arrive at the bank but de Pindray, who explained that having heard about the doubts and as 'it is a point which touches my honour',[11] he was returning the £200. Moved by his frank and open manner, his defiance of all suspicion and an exquisite sensitivity that had led him to return money he might have retained, the bank agreed to take back the £200 and wrote on the circular letter that the payment had been cancelled at the desire of the bearer. Not only had de Pindray established his reputation but the annotation on the letter gave it a further stamp of genuineness. Where Bogle had been on the evening of 21 April was never discovered, but he might have been with de Pindray persuading him to defuse suspicion by returning to the bank.

Meanwhile, the other conspirators were having better luck. On 22 April Frederick Pipe obtained £600 from Nigra and Son of Turin, on the 23rd £800 from Pasteur Girod and Co. of Milan, and on the 24th £800 from Louis Laurent at Parma. From there he and Graham took a steamer to Leghorn and arrived at the Villa Micali to report their progress to de Bourbel and hand over the money to him, retaining some as their share. On 28 April de Bourbel was in Florence, where he deposited 1,700 gold napoleons with the accommodating Freppa.

Since the fraud had not yet been detected it was considered safe to continue, and Pipe and Graham proceeded to Rome, where on 28 April they obtained another £200 from Monsieur Le Mesurier. So easy was this transaction that Pipe returned and asked for another £1,300. At this, Le Mesurier hesitated, recalling that he had never honoured a Glyn's letter before. Pipe pretended great indignation. He said he had been sent out by his father to purchase some pictures and that if he did not receive the £1,300 he would return the £200, and once back in England commence an action against Glyn's, claiming the expenses of his wasted trip and damages at being prevented from fulfilling his engagement. He must have been convincing. Le Mesurier gave the matter further thought, consulted the English consul, and paid up. Alexander Graham obtained only £150 in Aix-la-Chapelle before becoming too ill to continue.

De Pindray left Florence with his letter of credit soon after the scene at Bogle Kerrich and Co. and proceeded to Venice, where he obtained £347 from Landi and Roncadelli and £40 from the brothers Dubois. On 29 April he was in Trieste, where he received £1,612 6s from Mr Richard Routh. This gentleman found de Pindray's manners so pleasing that on that very night he invited him to share his box at the opera and later take supper at his house. So friendly and trusting were the two by then that de Pindray left Routh his carriage to dispose of, asking him to remit the proceeds to him in Greece or Egypt. From there de Pindray, who may never have had any intention of surrendering most of his gains to de Bourbel, decamped with the whole of the money. What became of the carriage was never reported, but, according to *The Times*, Routh was ruined.

Marie Desjardins, disarmingly accompanied by a little girl and travelling in a private carriage with a courier, was finding that the fraud was running smoothly in the cities of the Rhine. She received £500 from Messrs Oppenheim and Co. in Cologne, £500 from Messrs Deinhard and Jordan of Coblenz, a further £520 from Gogel Koch and Co. of Frankfurt, and

£500 from Humann and Mappes Fils in Mayence. She then proceeded in elegant triumph to Paris.

Perry, accompanied by D'Arjuzon, had difficulties from the start. In Liège Perry asked for the sum of £550 from the bankers Nagelmackers and Co. but was refused because he did not have a proper passport. Obliged to go to Brussels to obtain one, on the following day he returned and was able to draw £100, of which D'Arjuzon took charge of £80. In Brussels they did better with a fresh letter of credit, obtaining £750 from Engler and Co., of which Perry got £250. In Ghent Perry presented the letter on which he had received £100 at Liège to de Meulemeester and Son, but that firm, not having a letter of advice from Glyn's, declined to make a payment.

On 23 April Perry went to Antwerp, where he asked a Monsieur Agié for £750 on the same letter he had presented to Engler and Co. Agié was suspicious. He could see, as it was noted on the letter, that Perry had obtained £750 only the previous day, and he was surprised that a man of Perry's appearance (presumably a reference to Perry not being dressed as a gentleman) should require so much money. Perry had revealed that he was soon returning to England, and the banker thought it strange that he should be drawing money abroad so shortly before his return, when he could obtain the sum in England without paying commission. Agié smelt fraud. He refused payment, stating that he did not have the necessary advice from Glyn's, and after Perry had departed he wrote to Engler, who contacted the police. Perry was so rattled by the experience that he burned the incriminating document. On 25 April he was on board the Ostend steamer bound for London accompanied by Angelina Pipe when they were both arrested and questioned by the Belgian police. Angelina, while admitting she knew de Bourbel, D'Arjuzon and his mistress, Perry and Alexander, denied all knowledge of the fraud, but Perry, perhaps hoping for clemency, made a full statement of his part in the affair and openly named the other conspirators, including Allan Bogle.

The game was up, and it was clear that de Bourbel had greatly overestimated the potential rewards, since the gang made in total only £10,700 (about £700,000 today), excluding the £2,000 de Pindray had absconded with. The news first broke in the Brussels newspapers and then in *Galignani's Messenger* in Paris, but it was to be some weeks before the case became an international sensation.

Since the events of 21 April, things had been going on as usual at Bogle Kerrich and Co.; however, matters were about to take a serious turn for Allan Bogle. On 9 May the bank received a letter from Messrs Oppenheim and Co. of Cologne warning that forged letters of credit from Glyn's were in circulation, and there were rumours that Graham and de Bourbel were involved. That same evening a packet of papers arrived at the bank from Mr Fox (later Lord Holland), the English *chargé d'affaires* at Florence. Fox had received a copy of Perry's deposition from the Belgian authorities, and sent copies both to the Tuscan government and to Mr Kerrich. Kerrich, who had thus far entertained no suspicions of his partner, was appalled. As soon as the bank closed for the day he looked for Bogle in all his usual haunts and eventually that evening found him at his lodgings, where he confronted him with the documents. 'He appeared greatly distressed,' Kerrich said later, 'so much so that it was painful to witness.'[12] Still wanting to believe in his partner's innocence, Kerrich waited for Bogle to say that he was not involved in the conspiracy, but he did not, and neither did he confess; he could only moan that he was ruined. Kerrich stayed with him for some time, and possibly afraid that his partner and friend would do something desperate, decided it was best not to leave him alone. He took Bogle to his mother's house, and left him there, that unfortunate lady and her two daughters 'in a most painful state of distress'.[13] Graham, who had returned to Florence to be with his family, departed in secret as soon as he realised he was under suspicion.

There were a number of courses open to Allan Bogle. He could have made a complete denial of the charges; he could have gone to the English ambassador and lodged a protest; or he could have consulted a solicitor. It is tempting to suppose that an innocent man would have done all three. Instead, he returned home, took to his bed and despite all entreaties to come out and make a formal denial, did neither. On the following day, Kerrich sought out MacCarthy and told him about Bogle's situation. The two men went to see Bogle at his lodgings on 11 May between 11 and 12 in the morning, and found him still in bed. When he saw his two partners he became agitated and declared that he would never enter the bank again. Kerrich implored him to reconsider, but Bogle would not be moved and told the men to take away his keys. Kerrich urged him to get out of bed and show himself at his 'usual places of resort',[14] but Bogle could only whimper 'I cannot. I have not the spirits.'[15] Reluctantly, at Bogle's request, MacCarthy prepared a notice of dissolution of the partnership, which was duly signed. During the next few days Bogle left his lodgings only once a day to travel to his mother's house in a closed carriage, to dine.

By 10 May de Bourbel realised he must make his escape, but his name was too well known and to travel under his own passport would invite

Letter of 5 May 1840 from M. Barry to Andrew O'Reilly about letters sent to *The Times* from the Continent. *(*The Times *International Archive)* arrest. He was staying in Empoli, near Florence, from where he wrote to Freppa, imploring him to obtain a passport in Freppa's name, or if he could not, to supply him with the means to erase his name from his own passport so that he could substitute another. In due course he obtained what he needed and departed for Spain.

On 22 May Bogle unexpectedly arrived at the bank in great distress, saying he had been served with a signed order from the government of Tuscany to leave the Duchy in five days' time. He begged the partners to intercede on his behalf, and MacCarthy obligingly accompanied him to see Mr Fox, but all appeals were in vain. Bogle decided to go to England, despite anxiety about travelling through France, where he thought he might be arrested. Before he left, a packet, probably of letters, arrived at the bank from Algiers, addressed to Bogle, and Kerrich took it to him. Bogle retained the packet but did not open or refer to it. When he left Florence on 28 May he took it away with him.

On 23 May William Cunninghame-Graham, who had been living at Marseilles, returned to Leghorn on a steamer via Genoa, not suspecting that he was being closely watched by the Genoese banker who had been robbed of £1,500. On arrival Graham was denounced to the authorities, detained on board ship and questioned for three hours. He was carrying a great deal of money, and in his trunk were found four stamps for forging bills, including one for the firm of Glyn and Co.'s letters of credit. Despite these finds, it was felt that there was insufficient proof to identify him as one of the fraudsters, and the banker withdrew the charges. The stamps were returned to Graham before he was escorted over the Tuscan frontier and ordered never to return.

O'Reilly's article appeared in *The Times* on 26 May: it was explosive, naming all the members of the gang and quoting Perry's statement and de Bourbel's letters.

Graham's wife and daughters were ordered to leave Tuscany at the end of March, but before they did so they sent some of Graham's possessions, including his lathe, tools and machines, to the bank, asking that they be looked after. Kerrich had the items placed in a store-room, and for some months did not give the matter further thought.

On 8 June another packet from Algiers arrived at the bank, addressed to Bogle, and on 17 June a third. Mr Kerrich retained the papers but did not feel justified in opening them until 29 June, when Le Mesurier of Rome visited Florence. Under a growing conviction of Bogle's guilt, Kerrich showed the packets to Le Mesurier, who at once said: 'That paper is in the handwriting of the man who swindled me.'[16] The handwriting was later confirmed to be that of Frederick Pipe. The packets were opened in the presence of the English ambassador, and they contained letters, some of which were addressed to the Marquis de Bourbel and others to Charles Smith, poste restante, Florence, advising the recipients that the writer had arrived in Algiers and was planning to go from there to Marseilles and then Paris, and from there to London, and asking that his wife be advised to meet him at a pre-arranged place on 17 June. He further instructed that any letters should be sent to him under the name of Mr Lamont, General Post Office, London (Lamont was the maiden name of Mrs Pipe). It was thought that Charles Smith was in fact Bogle, although this could never be proven. This aside, the mere existence of the correspondence addressed to Bogle was highly incriminating.

Bogle arrived in London in June 1840. He took lodgings in Bridge Street, Westminster, and commenced an action against *The Times* for libel. On 22 June the solicitor Samuel Fyson, at Bogle's instruction, wrote a letter to John Joseph Lawson, *The Times*'s printer, advising him that he had been instructed to commence an action for 'a libel so utterly destructive of all reputation, that before admitting it to a place in your journal, you were bound to satisfy yourself that it did not implicate a perfectly innocent individual'.[17] The case was taken up by *The Times*'s solicitor Alexander Dobie. If Bogle was hoping for an apology and compensation, he was to be disappointed. *The Times* stood by its correspondent and allowed the action to proceed. Fifteen separate applications were made to examine witnesses on the Continent, of which Bogle, who probably did not want his actions exposed in open court, opposed all but two. His opposition was eventually overruled, but had meanwhile led to considerable delay.

On 30 June and 3 July Bogle wrote to Kerrich, who, now sadly disillusioned with his erstwhile partner, did not reply. The exact contents of these communications were never reported but it appears that Bogle begged Kerrich to come to England and give evidence in his favour. He also expressed some concern about the items left by Graham's family in Kerrich's charge, which he wanted forwarded to him. Kerrich, realising that they could be of some importance, called on a man named Roster to assist him in examining the articles. They met in Kerrich's office, where Roster happened to see a letter of credit of Glyn and Co. lying on the table and exclaimed: 'I have seen that before, in Mr Graham's hands.'

'That', said Mr Kerrich, 'is impossible, as it has never been out of mine. Examine the signature closely, as you labour under a mistake.'

Roster examined the letter carefully. This was a genuine letter of Glyn's with the bank's signature in the handwriting of Mr Mills. 'No,' he said, 'it is not exactly the one I have seen, though very similar to it.'

Kerrich then took Robert Nicholson's letter from his tin box and showed it to Roster, who immediately recognised it. 'That is the one I have seen before now in Mr Graham's hands, tracing it in a machine invented by him which took off facsimiles of drawings or writings of any kind.'

'Did you ever see this machine at work?' asked Kerrich.

'Yes,' said Roster, 'once in particular, I perfectly recollect being with Mr Graham when he showed me a paper exactly similar to the one now in my hand, having the signature in the front or face of it, and he requested me to 'try the copying of the signature in the machine, as his own hand trembled that morning, and he had only the power of possessing the paper for a short time.'[18] Roster then described the machine to Kerrich, adding that while at the time he could not understand why Graham was tracing the signature, having heard about the recent forgeries he was satisfied that his object was anything but a proper one. The two men then entered the bank's store-room, where Roster was at once able to identify Graham's tracing machine and show Kerrich how it worked. He then recalled that Graham had given him a piece of paper to demonstrate how accurately anything could be copied by the machine. A few days later he returned to the bank and showed Kerrich the paper, which had on one side a picture copied from an original in the public gallery of Florence and on the other two facsimiles of Glyn and Co.'s signature in the handwriting of Mr Hallifax. Kerrich, recalling Bogle's borrowing of Robert Nicholson's letter of credit, was now left in no doubt as to how the forgery had occurred.

In August Dobie travelled to the Continent, bearing a letter from Foreign Secretary Lord Palmerston to the British Ambassador Lord Granville asking him to provide all the assistance he required. In Florence, Dobie visited Kerrich and Co., had a copy of the tracing machine made, which he later produced in court, and gave notice to the firm that they were not to part with any items of Graham's in their possession. Dobie visited the defrauded bankers all over Europe and returned in December confident that he had sufficient evidence to plead justification, the perfect defence for an accusation of libel being that the story was true.

Bogle was asked to produce the papers he had taken with him from Florence, but failed to do so. Given the incriminating nature of the later items it is probable that the earlier letters were destroyed. In August 1841 the libel case of *Bogle* v. *Lawson* was heard at the Surrey summer assizes in

Croydon. Mr Thesiger, for Allan Bogle, advised the jury that their verdict would decide 'whether the plaintiff is hereafter to hold up his head in society . . . or . . . struggle through a miserable and shameful existence'.[19]

The facts of the conspiracy itself as presented to the court were beyond doubt, but in his summing-up to the jury Mr Justice Tindal advised that they should consider their verdict without the statement of Perry and the letters of de Bourbel and Graham, which referred to Bogle. If they felt that, 'though there was suspicion attaching to Bogle, yet that the evidence did not amount to proof that he was a conspirator, then the verdict must be for the plaintiff'.[20] If they did find for him, then it was up to them to decide what damages would be 'a fair and reasonable compensation'.[21]

The jury retired for only half an hour and returned with a verdict for Allan Bogle, awarding him damages of one farthing. As this was announced, an audible titter ran through the court. Despite the best efforts of Mr Thesiger, Bogle was ordered to pay his own costs.

The total cost of the action to *The Times* was about £5,000, and on 1 October 1841 a group of bankers met at the Mansion House to discuss how to thank the newspaper for the exposure of the fraud. A fund was commenced to defray the paper's legal costs, and this eventually reached £2,700. *The Times*, however, declined to accept the money and instead used it to create scholarships for boys to attend Oxford and Cambridge universities. Part of the money was used to create commemorative plaques, one over the main entrance to the paper's premises in Printing House Square and one at the Royal Exchange.

In a Belgian court on 19 February 1841 Perry and Angelina Pipe were found guilty of fraud and were sentenced to be branded and to serve fifteen and twelve years in prison respectively, with hard labour. Frederick Pipe, having passed through Naples and Algiers, is said to have returned to England by way of Marseilles, but was not heard of thereafter.

On 31 May 1840 de Bourbel wrote to Freppa from Valencia asking him to remit him the balance of his funds. At the time of the libel trial he was rumoured to be in London, helping Bogle. He was never brought to justice. It is believed that he ultimately went to America, dying in Texas in 1845.[22] Where Graham went after being ejected from Tuscany is unknown. He died, probably on the Continent, in November 1845.[23]

In July 1840 de Pindray was overtaken at Iaşi in what is now Romania, but after giving his captors 1,000 francs, was set at liberty. He was later placed under the surveillance of the police at Constantinople, and was, by order of the French police, transferred to Marseilles and later to Aix, but the court there 'declared its incompetence to take cognizance of the affair'.[24] He slipped away and was not heard of again.

Alexander Graham, worn out by disease, was unable to travel. He was taken to a hospital in Paris, where he died in 'great want and misery'[25] not long before the libel trial.

Justice finally caught up with D'Arjuzon and Marie Desjardins. They had been living in Paris under the name of Bernardi but departed on 5 May in a private carriage, and it was believed, from letters seized at the post office, that they were on the way to join de Bourbel and share the booty. Arrested and accused of forgery, they stood trial at the Paris Assizes in July 1840. Marie had been convicted a few days previously and sentenced to four years in prison for passing off the child who travelled with her as her own. D'Arjuzon had promised to marry her if she had a child, and as none was forthcoming, she procured one from a midwife and convinced her lover that it was theirs. At the forgery trial she protected him by confessing that she alone was guilty and that he knew nothing of the forged letter of credit. De Bourbel's letter to D'Arjuzon was read out in court, but he denied that he had received it, and the defence claimed successfully that it could not be put in evidence against him. He was acquitted and Marie was found guilty and sentenced to five years to run concurrently with her previous sentence. In 1842 it was stated in the French newspapers that Marie had escaped custody and been recaptured in Paris. When arrested she had in her possession a false passport in the name of a commercial traveller of Marseilles, which it was believed she had been intending to pass to D'Arjuzon so that he could make his escape as he was due to be tried on further charges. Their subsequent fate is unknown.

Allan George Bogle remained in England, where he lodged above a public house at 26 Bridge Street, Westminster. The business was run by a Mr and Mrs Blake, but was funded by Bogle, who gave the Blakes £1,000. When they went bankrupt in 1842 he refused to say where he had obtained the money. The matter was never resolved, since Bogle died of pneumonia on 13 March 1843. He was 36 years old.

In 1847 *The Times* appointed a new manager, Mowbray Morris, who was unhappy about the level of expenditure by foreign correspondents. In 1848 Andrew O'Reilly was reprimanded for his extravagance, and later that year Morris went to Paris to dismiss him. O'Reilly was left with the unhappy impression that his fate was the result of personal ill-feeling. He died in 1862, aged 79.

FIVE

The Bank with No Scruples

On the morning of Sunday 17 February 1856 a labourer walking on Hampstead Heath discovered the body of a smartly dressed man lying on the grass behind the historic inn known as Jack Straw's Castle. The cause of death was not difficult to guess. By the side of the body was a half-pint bottle labelled Essential Oil of Bitter Almonds – Poison. Very little of the liquid remained, and there were traces of it in a silver cream jug that lay nearby and from which the deceased had obviously taken his final draught. A case of razors was beside him, no doubt for the unlikely contingency of the poison not being effective. The body, which was cold and stiff, was removed to the mortuary of Hampstead Workhouse, where a post-mortem was performed. When the stomach was opened, the scent of almonds was so powerful it filled the room.

The identity of this determined suicide was revealed in a handwritten note found in his pocket, which revealed him to be 42-year-old John Sadleir, Member of Parliament, a substantial property owner and founder of the Tipperary Bank. His death was a huge shock in both political and commercial circles, where for a time the talk was of little else. With no obviously pressing reason why Sadleir should have taken his life, it was rumoured 'that the unfortunate man's brain had become over-excited by the multiplicity and extent of his speculations'.[1]

'Mr Sadleir was no common man,' observed the *Cork Daily Reporter*, 'but possessed abilities of a very high order, and an inflexibility of temperament that could only be shaken by something of unusual magnitude. . . . His death . . . is indeed a deplorable event, and we record it with very deep regret.'[2] *Freeman's Journal* was quick to express 'deepest sympathy' and pronounced Sadleir's death to be a 'melancholy catastrophe'.[3] He was, said the *Morning Advertiser*, 'greatly respected . . . esteemed and admired'.[4] His 'untimely end', said the *Morning Chronicle*, which revealed that Sadleir's unwise speculations had resulted in personal losses of £200,000, 'has cast a gloom over many a circle'.[5] Sympathy was also extended to the companies that would 'lose the benefit of his counsel and services'.[6]

87

It was true that the Bank of Ireland had recently refused to cash Tipperary Bank drafts, but investors had been assured that any problems were the result of Mr Sadleir having forgotten to pay in the money required. Depositors who had hurried to withdraw their funds had found the branches open, and discovered that they paid out promptly. A Thomastown gentleman who asked to withdraw his savings of £800 was told that if he did not give the requisite notice he would forfeit interest. He decided to lodge the notice and leave his money where it was, confident that it would be safe for a few days at least.

When news of Sadleir's death reached Ireland on 18 February, branches of the Tipperary Bank were again besieged by anxious depositors, many of whom were small tenant farmers who had entrusted their life savings to its care. At Nenagh the manager declined to make payments, though the crowds were somewhat appeased by the bank remaining open to record claims, but in Thurles the surging mob was so disorderly that the police were called to protect the premises.

Not everyone took the bank's difficulties seriously. 'There has been a kind of petty run on the three bank offices in our city,' stated the *Kilkenny Monitor*. 'The more ignorant portion of the country people who had small sums deposited, or who held notes of any kind, at once took the alarm, and commenced looking for gold immediately. It is unnecessary to say that this trifling panic altogether confined to a very few of the lower order of the people, caused no inconvenience to any of the establishments here, and it has now almost ceased.'[7]

A reporter from the *Limerick Chronicle* visited Tipperary on 19 February and found local farmers gathering in small groups on pathways and at shop doors, viewing their deposit receipts with gloomy expressions. On entering the bank he found it packed with customers, most of them farmers with savings of £300 to £1,000, being told by manager Michael Dillon that they could not be paid until 29 February, but that they need not worry as the assets of the bank were more than sufficient to meet any losses. Knowing that the Sadleir family owned a large amount of landed property, many customers were confident that the bank would, in time, be able to pay its investors.

When the inquest opened on the same day it provided very few clues as to the reasons for Sadleir's suicide. A relative, solicitor Anthony Norris, testified that in the last week Sadleir, who was usually 'cool and collected', had been haggard, restless and depressed. Calling on him unexpectedly on Saturday evening, he found Sadleir walking distractedly about the room and noticed 'a very great redness and peculiarity about the eyes as if he had been weeping'.[8] The coroner was about to close the inquiry when it was revealed that before Sadleir had departed for Hampstead Heath he had asked for a letter to be sent to his sister-in-law, and left three others on the hall table, instructing his manservant that they should be delivered the following morning if he did not return. Two were addressed to his cousin, Robert Keating MP, and one to Norris, who said he had forgotten to bring it. After some deliberation the jury agreed unanimously that all these letters should be produced, and the inquest was adjourned for a week. On the following day the Tipperary Bank closed its doors and went into receivership.

Sadleir's last letters were more explosive than anyone could have anticipated. Only gradually did the financial world appreciate the scale of his criminality. *The Times* judged him a 'national calamity'[9] who had brought shame on his family and ruin to thousands. He was, quite possibly, the greatest swindler of the nineteenth century.

John Sadleir was born on 17 November 1813 at Shrone Hill near Tipperary. His father, Clement, was a landowner, and his maternal uncle, James Scully, had for some years run a small private bank, which, unusually for the time, had been solvent when it finally closed in 1827. Sadleir was educated at Clongowes Wood College, an institution that provided a broad syllabus, combining scholarship, religious observance and discipline with healthy recreation. The intention was to turn out well-rounded individuals who would be useful and worthy members of society. It was not apparent for some years that John Sadleir was one of its failures.

His public face, that of an austere gentleman of quiet dignity, concealed a chillingly callous nature: he was selfish, secretive and cunning. Unlike so many fraudsters who entice their dupes with lavish display and bumptious self-promotion, 'in no respect had he the pretentious bearing of an habitual and dashing swindler'.[10]

Sadleir qualified as a solicitor in 1837, and practised first in Tipperary, then Dublin. In 1838, together with his older brother James, who was manager of the National Bank in Ireland, and younger brother Clement jnr, an accountant, he founded the Tipperary Joint Stock Bank. James Sadleir was appointed director and manager, while the respected James Scully became chairman. This pedigree was vital to the success of the bank. The shareholders of joint stock companies took a far greater risk than investors in the limited liability companies of today. If the company became insolvent, they not only stood to lose their initial investment, but would be called upon to pay the company's debts. No part of their personal property was immune from forfeit. In Sadleir's own words, spoken to the Annual General Meeting of the London and County Joint Stock Bank only nine days before his death, the prosperity of such banks 'mainly depended on the ability and efficiency of their officers and the integrity of their directors'.[11]

The early years of the Tipperary Bank were marked by healthy expansion as it opened new branches and acquired investors. In some towns it was the only available bank. Insidiously, however, the rise of the Tipperary Bank masked the growing powers of John Sadleir. Over the years, direct supervision of the bank's affairs gradually moved away from the Scully family and into the hands of the Sadleirs, with James the nominal manager, but the quiet and unassuming John brought matters increasingly under his personal control.

At first, the Scullys did not object to the transfer of influence, but in time Sadleir's first cousin, Vincent Scully QC, who owned 700 shares, became alarmed at the bank's regular failure to carry out an annual audit. Nevertheless, the bank was clearly prospering.

Sadleir's experience as a solicitor and control over the funds of a successful bank gave him ample opportunity to take advantage of the misfortunes of others, which he had no hesitation in doing. The Earl of Kingston was one such disorganised dupe whose extravagances had led him to the brink of ruin. To the desperate Earl, John Sadleir's expertise seemed like the answer to a prayer. In 1845 Kingston was persuaded to apply for a £50,000 mortgage from the Tipperary Bank, but though the papers were signed, the money was never paid to him. Eventually he was obliged to take out another deed pledging his plate and furniture, for which he received less than £17,000. Forced to take out a life policy with the Albion Insurance Company, the Earl was promised an annuity of £4,000, but in the next eleven years he received only £8,000. When the Albion paid £50,000 to the Tipperary Bank to fund the Earl's mortgage, Sadleir calmly pocketed the money and supplied a forged receipt. Sadleir then persuaded Thomas Eyre, Vincent Scully's wealthy uncle, to advance a £40,000 loan to Kingston, with an annual repayment of £3,000. The loan was paid into Scully's account at the Tipperary Bank; only £7,000 ever reached Kingston. John and his solicitor cousin, Nicholas Sadleir, were appointed agents for Kingston's estates and collected the rents, which were intended to pay off the mortgage. Over the next few years Sadleir increased his hold on these estates. He issued understated receipts for the rents and appropriated the difference. The Earl, unaware that Sadleir was using his money for land speculation, slid ever more deeply into debt.

In 1846, greedy for richer pickings, Sadleir sailed for London and took an apartment in the fashionable West End. He was 32 years old, tall, with black curling hair and dark eyes, good-looking, wealthy, well mannered and single. For most men in his position the next step was a suitable marriage. The ideal of the Victorian man of business was to return from his daily toil to a comfortable home, a faithful wife and a brood of well-behaved children, yet Sadleir never showed any inclination to marry. Such liaisons as are attributed to him suggest he courted a beautiful dancer from the Haymarket Theatre, or formed an attachment to either the widow or the neglected wife of a member of parliament. If this is true, then it seems he deliberately chose relationships which could never lead to marriage. He was generally noted for his sober habits and, according to the *Observer*, 'lived plainly and entertained sparingly, if he entertained at all'[12] and 'appeared a clear-headed active man of business without pretensions to high breeding, but not deficient in proper courtesy. His habits were very moderate; and his residence was rather well than handsomely furnished.'[13] His only personal extravagance was the keeping of a small stud of horses for hunting with the Gunnersbury Hounds.

The only thing that motivated John Sadleir was the chance of making money, and accordingly he arrived at the financial centre of Britain at the height of the railway speculation boom. He became a shareholder in several continental concerns and chairman of the Royal Swedish Railway Company. His extensive knowledge of the legal complexities of land ownership and transfer made him sought after as an agent or receiver for estates. Anxious to extend his power and influence, in July 1847 he stood for election as Member of Parliament for Carlow. His connection with the town, through a branch of the Tipperary Bank, and reputation as a businessman of integrity swept him into parliament with a substantial majority. He served as a Liberal Independent and, although 'deficient in the heartiness and buoyant vivacity of an agitator',[14] he joined a small but noisy and influential party of Irish MPs popularly known as the Irish Brigade. In the following year the London and County Joint Stock Bank was delighted to appoint him as its chairman.

Even at a distance he was able to exercise a firm grip on the affairs of the Tipperary Bank, depending on his trusting brother James. When Vincent Scully became a director following the death of chairman James Scully, and expressed his worries about the continued lack of an annual audit, he received only a soothing letter about the success of the bank's business.

The year 1849 saw the foundation of the Incumbered Estates Court of Ireland, a means of simplifying the transfer of lands. To a man of Sadleir's experience this was an ideal opportunity to enrich himself further, and over the next six years he purchased lands worth £233,000 (about £14 million at today's values). One valuable acquisition was an estate of the hapless Earl of Kingston, for whose mounting debts Sadleir was partly responsible. Public concern about this case had not gone away, and, when Scully referred to it in a letter to his cousin, Sadleir replied: 'It is one of the ugliest cases we have – that is to say, it is one that your profession exaggerate and make a handle of to endeavour to injure the credit of the bank in Dublin; but the bank defies any report.'[15]

In 1850 Sadleir was sufficiently distinguished for his portrait to appear in the *Illustrated London News*. In that year, however, his greed caused him to overreach himself and as a result he made an enemy who was to have a profound effect on his career. With Sadleir pressurising Kingston to sell his remaining estates, the Earl was forced to seek legal advice, the first wise decision he had made for some time. His new representative, John McNamara Cantwell, discovered that John and James Sadleir were selling off some of the Earl's furniture and plate and at once prevented the sale with an injunction. Examining the accounts of the estate, which was under Sadleir's receivership, Cantwell was unable to discover what had happened to the rents, which amounted to £19,000 per annum (over £1.1 million today). Cantwell regarded Sadleir with dislike and deep distrust. His efforts to recover Kingston's money were to lead to a protracted legal battle, which was to dog the fortunes of the Tipperary Bank for many years.

One reason for Sadleir's keenness to make money from investments was the expense of electioneering, both his own and that of relatives, including his brother James, who also successfully stood for parliament. Press opinion is a vital matter for a politician and Sadleir had tried unsuccessfully to buy the popular *Freeman's Journal*. He decided instead to found and finance a new paper, the Dublin-based *Telegraph*, appointing James Kennedy, a solicitor he had known since his Dublin days, as a front to conceal the paper's true ownership. Launched in January 1852, the paper immediately offered serious opposition to its rivals by selling at 3*d* a copy, to their 6*d*, and quickly achieved a large circulation, forcing its rivals to lower their prices.

Sadleir's slide into political and financial ruin (and the two went hand in hand) was set in motion by the general election of 1852. The tide of enthusiasm that had swept him into parliament in 1847 was on the wane.

His Conservative opponent was a local landlord, and it would be a close-run contest, as Carlow was a small constituency and every vote counted. Sadleir was especially anxious to secure the support of Edward Dowling, who controlled the votes of several sub-tenants, and had since 1847 switched his allegiance to Sadleir's opponent. Simple canvassing did not sway him, but it was known that Dowling owed money both to the Tipperary Bank and a Sadleir supporter, Daniel Crotty. To protect himself against non-payment of the debt, Crotty had obtained a bond of indemnity from Dowling and he also had a warrant to enable him to obtain speedy judgement if required. With these things weighing on his mind, Dowling might have seemed vulnerable, yet when Sadleir, his relative Thaddeus O'Shea (who was the manager of the Carlow branch of the Tipperary bank) and Crotty offered both money and a release of part of his bank debts if he would vote for Sadleir, Dowling still stood firm. Reaching Carlow to place his vote, Dowling was astonished to be arrested for debt and taken to prison, where he no doubt protested that his repayment to the bank had not yet fallen due. Sadleir was returned to parliament with a reduced majority. Ironically, he would just have scraped home even if Dowling had voted.

In August came the first act seriously to undermine Sadleir's reputation, when Edward Dowling sued Crotty for false arrest and Sadleir's part in the plot was publicly revealed. It was alleged in court that Sadleir had visited Crotty and obtained possession of the bond, and that Crotty expected him to reimburse his expenses. Sadleir, who did not give evidence at the trial, made a statement in which he denied everything – and once he had denied something he tended to put it out of his mind. He often tried to avoid conflict by delaying facing facts for as long as possible in the hope that, if he forgot them, everyone else would too. In the Dowling case, as with that of the Earl of Kingston, this was a serious mistake. Both these issues would return to trouble him and both would be instrumental in his downfall. In 1852, however, no action could be taken against him, although the affair had branded him as untrustworthy. The aggrieved Dowling was released in August, but while he had been in prison his debts had fallen due and in October he was arrested again and lodged in the Marshalsea debtors' prison in Dublin.

At the end of 1852 Sadleir was offered his first political appointment, as Irish Lord of the Treasury in Lord Aberdeen's coalition government. He was just 39 years old, had been in London for only six years and in parliament for five, yet he had already taken his first step towards a career of distinction; but if Aberdeen was prepared to ignore the doubts raised by the Dowling case, others were not. Three days after his appointment Aberdeen received a letter deploring Sadleir's treatment of Dowling and asking for the removal of 'this unfortunate blot' from the cabinet.[16] Aberdeen did not comply, and passed the letter to Sadleir as an 'act of friendship'.[17]

There was more serious opposition from unexpected quarters. Sadleir and those of his political associates who had also accepted appointments had completely underestimated the reaction of the Irish voters, the clergy and the Liberal press, who saw the taking of government office by prominent members of the Irish Brigade as selling out to the establishment. *The Nation* described Sadleir and his friend and supporter William Keogh, who had become Solicitor General, as having committed 'one of the most flagrant derelictions of public honour ever beheld. . . . That Mr John Sadleir should go straight over to any party conducive to his own personal interests does not surprise us very much,' continued the article, referring to Sadleir's 'intricate and plotting intellect', adding 'Mr John Sadleir is a clever man. Inside that sallow and wrinkled face of his ever play schemes and intrigues by the score.'[18] Either the 1850 portrait was unusually flattering or Sadleir's cares had weighed heavily upon him. Someone who knew him well commented that 'his figure was youthful, but his face – that was indeed remarkable. Strongly marked, sallow, eyes and hair intensely black, and the lines of the mouth worn into deep channels.'[19]

The new officers were obliged to submit themselves for re-election, and in January 1853 the combined effect of what was seen as his defection from the Irish cause and the rumblings of doubt about Dowling's imprisonment eroded Sadleir's vote and he was defeated. The Dowling case must have been particularly damaging, for he was the only defector who was not returned.

While waiting for a new seat to be found he occupied himself with his business life. The *Telegraph* had not maintained its popularity, and would eventually become a weekly paper. It was and remained a huge financial drain. In July 1853 he was back in parliament, winning Sligo by just eight votes. It was not a happy victory, since it was immediately followed by two petitions against him on the grounds of bribery. Once again, he managed to cover his tracks. Sadleir denied the accusations as usual, and there was insufficient evidence to take matters further.

In November 1853 Dowling's second action came before the courts. Crotty had died some months before and an examination of his papers had uncovered a devious scheme in which a number of dupes had been used as intermediaries to conceal both the 1852 plot to entrap Dowling and Sadleir's part in it. Dowling took action against one of the dupes, the blacksmith Edward Lawler, in a case that caused a sensation in both London and Dublin. Acting for Dowling was John McNamara Cantwell, who at last, after his involvement in the Earl of Kingston's affairs, had the opportunity to expose Sadleir.

Sadleir, who had earlier denied he had taken possession of the bond, was now obliged to admit that he had done so, but claimed that the only reason was to help Crotty. He made every effort to distance himself from all the other proceedings against Dowling, but was forced to admit under questioning that he had wanted to prevent Dowling voting against him. The jury found for Dowling, which effectively meant they believed Sadleir to be guilty of corruption and perjury. Sadleir left the court in disgrace, his political career in ruins. Shortly afterwards he submitted his resignation as Irish Lord of the Treasury. He was still MP for Sligo, but thereafter he never again spoke in parliament or sought public office. 'He seemed oppressed with care, and walked the lobbies like a fallen statesman, who had no longer patronage to dispense.'[20] In the following year Dowling took an action against him for damages, and won £1,100.

The Dowling scandal had caused some uneasiness among the shareholders of the Tipperary Bank, who began to offload their shares. Sadleir's old ally James Kennedy sold his shares in November, which were eventually taken up by James Sadleir. Vincent Scully had been trying to disassociate himself from the bank for some time. Unwilling to make a public fuss, which might damage the family business, he voiced his concerns in private letters. In September 1853 he wrote to Sadleir asking him to make all necessary arrangements for 'winding up all dealings between us. I am particular anxious to leave the Tipperary Bank, being entirely ignorant of its affairs, and having lost all confidence in its management.'[21] In January 1854 he wrote to James, pointing out that he had repeatedly expressed his dissatisfaction at the absence of an audit, and this had now led to 'the secession of some of its best shareholders, besides injuring the bank in other respects'.[22]

James responded that he personally had never objected to holding an audit but that at every meeting the accounts had been gone into most carefully and to the satisfaction of everyone. He believed that public confidence had increased in the last year 'notwithstanding the conspiracy got up by a portion of the press to injure the credit of the Tipperary Bank, and the number of times that the Kingston Trustees account case has been before the public'.[23]

An agreement was finally drawn up in August 1854 for the sale of Vincent Scully's shares to Robert Keating, as trustee for John Sadleir, but when the company report was published in February 1855 Scully discovered that the transfer had not taken place and that he was still on the list of shareholders. Thoroughly irritated by the delay, he immediately wrote to Sadleir: 'How on earth do you get on at all with others if this is your way of managing serious business?'[24] Despite further letters and promises from Sadleir affairs had still not been settled by 24 March when Scully wrote: 'It is monstrous to have to write so repeatedly about so simple a matter.'[25] The transfer was ultimately made in April.

When the affairs of the Tipperary Bank finally came under public scrutiny it was thought that it had only recently come into difficulty and that it was probably the years 1854 and 1855 that were crucial. What private despair Sadleir suffered as a result of the virtual extinguishing of his political life will never be known, but his desperate and disastrous borrowings bolstered by major fraud and forgery seem to date from this time, when he callously began to use the Tipperary funds and the resources of his relatives as his own personal money boxes. Also at this time, his speculations on the Stock Exchange became wilder. He played the commodities market, with notable lack of success. It was later alleged that he lost £120,000 on sugar in the course of a single day in the autumn of 1855, and at other times he lost £35,000 on hemp and £50,000 on iron.

While Sadleir owned a substantial amount of property, most of it was encumbered by loans. As founder and chairman of the Carson's Creek Gold Mining Company, he had no difficulty in obtaining a large loan from its coffers, which was due for repayment in January 1855. When he was unable to repay, he offered as security the deeds of an estate in Limerick. The deed was lodged in the London and County Bank. He later removed it without anyone's knowledge or agreement, and used it as a security for another loan.

The Public Officer of the Tipperary Bank, Wilson Kennedy, who was also well aware of Vincent Scully's concerns, had watched in dismay as Sadleir became more and more indebted to the bank. James, who was initially confident that his brother's properties could cover the loans, also became deeply concerned, especially in view of mounting evidence of dishonest transactions. In March 1855 Sadleir had approached the London and County asking them for an advance of £20,000 on a Tipperary Bank bill of exchange, but had not consulted James about it first. James was furious with his brother and on 7 March 1855 he wrote: 'I would not be burthened with your constant lies any longer. You may provide for the credit or let it alone. Until I see the money ordered lodged I will not accept the £20,000 or move in it. Your constant lying is worse than anything else . . . In fact your doings and impertinence beat anything.'[26]

Sadleir continued to ask for loans, protesting that without them he would be ruined, to which James responded: 'I consider your ruin, as you call it, of very little consequence,' and demanded full legal authority to sell his brother's properties, 'as I consider you quite incapable and quite unfit. . . . I am certain you bungled every property you had to do with.'[27]

On 15 March an agreement was drawn up, granting James and Robert Keating the power to dispose of Sadleir's lands, but, against the advice of the solicitor James Kennedy, it was never registered or acted upon. James Sadleir, well aware of the fact that the financial fortunes of his brother and the Tipperary Bank were now almost one and the same, was worried that registering the agreement would expose Sadleir's desperate position. Sadleir held onto his properties, obtained further advances, and plunged still deeper into debt, while Keating washed his hands of him in disgust.

That April Sadleir concocted his most audacious money-making scheme to date. The Tipperary Bank had authorised the issue of 10,000 shares, of which only 4,055 had been taken up, at £10 each. He now proposed to offer the remainder for purchase by English shareholders through the London and County Bank. The difficulty was that the thousands of new shares would dilute the value of established holdings and reduce the amount of dividends. As soon as shareholders realised this, they would sell their holdings, and confidence in the bank would plummet. For the scheme to work, it would have to look as if the shares on offer were not new ones, but transfers from an existing shareholder. Sadleir already had a dupe to hand, an old school friend called Austen Ferrall. In 1846 Sadleir had asked Ferrall to hold shares in trust for a lady cousin who did not want her name to appear as an investor. Ferrall, unaware that the lady did not exist, agreed. Quite what duplicitous scheme Sadleir had in mind on that occasion is unknown, but eleven years later he still had permission to use Ferrall's name. Large numbers of blank share certificates were prepared and assigned to Ferrall, who, still under the impression that he was helping Sadleir's lady relative, was happy to agree to their transfer.

English investors were now made an extraordinarily exciting offer. The shares were offered to them at 25 per cent above par, which was only tenable if the Bank was very prosperous indeed, and to show just how solid the investment really was a prospectus was produced, together with the accounts for 1854, which were said to have been approved by the directors at the annual general meeting of 1 February 1855. The figures were, of course, false and showed a profit of double the true value, while vastly overstating the company's assets. Most of the bank's assets were in fact the debt owed by Sadleir.

The false certificates were passed to a London and County director, Farmery John Law, who, unaware of the fraud, passed them on to his branch managers, inviting them to sell the shares to their customers. With a commission of ten shillings for each share they sold, they plunged into the task with enthusiasm.

In June 1855 Wilson Kennedy, after protesting against the loans being made to Sadleir, decided that he wanted to have no more to do with the Tipperary Bank and offered his shares to James Sadleir. James, realising that the bank could be damaged if his brother's overdraft was made public, agreed to purchase the shares. That month another spectre from the past reared its head as the Earl of Kingston obtained a court decree demanding that both Thomas Eyre, who was supposed to have lent him £40,000, and the Tipperary Bank account for the rents received from his estate.

Sadleir did not want to sell his lands, but the prospect that he might do so was a valuable commodity to him, and on the basis of this, in June he obtained £20,000 from the London and County Bank. A month later this had been sucked into the whirlpool of his financial affairs, and he asked for another £15,000. Fortunately for that bank, the directors were not so trusting as his friends and relatives in the Tipperary. Recognising that he was in financial difficulties, they refused the loan and froze his account.

In the meantime James was taking desperate measures to try to save the bank. He arranged a special meeting of the directors in July, and asked for an advance of £95,000 on the security of his brother's lands, informing them that Sadleir's overdraft amounted to £40,000 (the figure was far higher, but James knew that if he told the truth not only would he not receive the director's agreement, but his gross mismanagement would cost him his position). Sadleir's properties, valued by James at between £450,000 and £480,000, were, he said, to be held by trustees and used to discharge his debts. Trustingly, the directors agreed that the Tipperary Bank would act as guarantor for Sadleir's debts at the London and County Bank. James was paid the first instalment of the £95,000, which he banked immediately. This kept the Tipperary Bank afloat for a little longer, but when it came to registering the deeds to assign Sadleir's estates to the trustees, there was a snag: a number of estates had already been assigned to Thomas Eyre as security for earlier loans. The second instalment of the £95,000 was stopped.

In order to release the securities Sadleir embarked on a scheme to defraud the Royal Swedish Railway Company and the by now 75-year-old Eyre. The Royal Swedish required capital to expand, which was to be raised by selling debentures on the Stock Exchange. Sadleir carried out the sale and pocketed the money. He then wrote to Eyre on 13 August offering him shares in the Royal Swedish for the release of his properties, representing the exchange as a valuable opportunity that should be taken advantage of immediately. As an inducement, he stated that under the new arrangement Eyre would receive an annual income of £5,000. Eyre replied that he would agree to the exchange only if advised to do so by James Kennedy. Sadleir immediately telegraphed Kennedy to tell him that Eyre had made a favourable response, and informed Josiah Wilkinson his solicitor that Eyre had agreed to the arrangement. Wilkinson took Sadleir at his word and obligingly released the remainder of the advance. Sadleir now had to move fast, and wrote to Eyre to close the deal, advising him that 'whatever serves me in this respect, cannot, I believe damage you'.[28] He was still concealing from Eyre the fact that the £40,000 loan to the Earl of Kingston had never reached its intended recipient, and even as these letters went back and forth the Earl filed his decree and waited for judgment.

James Kennedy was sent to negotiate the deal. He had told Sadleir that in order to secure an annual income of £5,000, 20,000 Royal Swedish shares would be required. Sadleir replied that this was no problem, and indeed it was not, because he had forged them. He also told Kennedy that the £5,000 annual income could be guaranteed by his brother James, and offered another security, a promissory note of £12,000. This too was a forgery.

The unsuspecting Kennedy carried out the negotiations as required, and the lands were released. They were transferred in trust to the London and County Bank by a deed dated 7 September, which ensured that after their sale any surplus was to go to the Tipperary Bank. The deed was duly sent to the Tipperary Bank board of directors. In due course, minutes of a board meeting approving the deed were available for inspection.

The forged shares were transferred to Eyre, together with a forged statement from the company certifying that they carried 5 per cent annual interest, and the forged promissory note. The package also included the conveyance of part of an estate. This too was a forgery, and in any case, the property in question was already mortgaged for more than its value.

In October Josiah Wilkinson spotted a good investment opportunity. The Newcastle-upon-Tyne Commercial Banking Company was up for sale, following the illness of its managing director. James Sadleir and others purchased it as a going concern, dismissed the manager and appointed Thaddeus O'Shea in his place. The directors were replaced with new men who included James Sadleir, Robert Keating and Farmery John Law. A month later £59,000 was transferred to the London and County Bank, of which £52,000 helped ease the position of the ailing Tipperary Bank.

In the previous few months, London and County Bank managers in Chelmsford, Peterborough, Uxbridge, Luton and Leighton Buzzard had been busily selling the Tipperary Bank shares to their customers at £12 10s apiece – but the sales were not going fast enough for Sadleir. He decided to offer a further inducement, with a falsified balance sheet for 1855, for the benefit of the English market alone. Proposing to 'shove the customers' balances up', he claimed: 'I know many of the English Joint-stock Banks, in order to give a good appearance to their balance, have constantly trebled the amount of their balances, &c., &c., by making a series of entries. Whereby they appeared to have assets and liabilities to four times the amount they really possessed or had. This has always been kept very quiet, and what at first was a kind of fiction became gradually to be bona fide.'[29]

The fraudulent balance sheet showed the issue to him of deposit receipts for sums up to £500,000, supposed to have been received from companies in which he had an interest, balanced by an account in his name as trustee. Despite the now desperate financial state of the Tipperary Bank, he still hoped to adjust the figures to show a profit.

The scheme was not as successful as expected. Seventy English investors bought shares, paying a total of over £15,000, which was not nearly enough to avert disaster. Many were small investors, such as farmers, ministers of religion, doctors, a draper, a miller and several spinsters.

By the end of 1855 John Sadleir's overdraft with the Tipperary Bank was £247,000 (about £15 million at today's values). It had been permitted to rocket to that figure only because he was supplying James with figures that showed he had sufficient investments to cover his liabilities. James later claimed that his brother had told him that the worst was over and that he was confident that after paying all his debts he would have a considerable surplus. The truth was that Sadleir's finances were in a desperate state, of which only he knew the full enormity, and were recoverable only by an amazing stroke of unanticipated good fortune. If he hoped for good luck on the Stock Exchange, he was to be disappointed. He made further losses in January 1856, and the Tipperary Bank was obliged to loan him a further £41,000. By now his total losses from all sources amounted to £1,500,000, of which about two-thirds was probably a result of his speculations on the stock market.

On 1 February 1856 it was necessary to delay disaster by producing, for the benefit of the Irish shareholders, a set of false accounts which showed the hopelessly insolvent Tipperary Bank to be a profitable and valuable concern and declaring a dividend of 6 per cent with a 3 per cent bonus. The list of directors mentioned in the document were no longer with the company; in fact, the only one remaining was James Sadleir. The fraud worked and the 'unfortunate traders and farmers . . . deluded by this proclamation of prosperity, deposited their hard earnings in this voracious pit with increased confidence'.[30]

Sadleir was by now facing inevitable ruin. An order had been served upon him to lodge £6,000 as receiver of the Earl of Kingston, and all his usual sources of money were vanishing. The coffers of the London and County, which had taken away his chequebook, were closed to him, and the Tipperary could scarcely advance him any more without precipitating a disastrous crash. He was reduced to approaching individuals for private loans, on the strength of hastily forged deeds, and misappropriating the funds of a marriage settlement that he was holding in trust. As a last ditch measure he sought out suitable heiresses and proposed marriage. His air of frantic desperation cannot have helped him, and they turned him down.

While many people knew about the perilous position of the Tipperary Bank, it is unlikely that they realised the scale of the crash that was to come. When the London clearing house began to refuse Tipperary drafts, the claim that non-payment was the result of an error bought only a day or two of time.

On 15 February things went from bad to worse. The secretary of the Royal Swedish had spotted something very amiss in the company's books, and confronted Sadleir, who promised to make a full report in three days' time. On the morning of Saturday 16 February Sadleir received a telegraph from James, optimistically stating 'all right at the branches – only a few small things refused here. If from twenty to thirty thousand over here on Monday morning all is safe.'[31] Since Sadleir did not have the money or any hope of raising it, this did not have the soothing effect James might have anticipated. Soon afterwards Sadleir arrived at the office of

Josiah Wilkinson in a very excited state, where he paced restlessly about the room, begging for help to save the bank. He showed Wilkinson the telegraph, and proposed a number of desperate schemes to raise loans to save the bank, all of which Wilkinson said he could neither recommend nor adopt. He was in any case extremely loath to loan Sadleir anything. The previous November James had come to see him, asking for £15,000 for his brother, saying that he would not be able to meet his engagements without the money. Although James had claimed that his brother had assets to cover the loan, Wilkinson felt sure that Sadleir's debts were far greater than he admitted. He had refused the loan, and now, hard as it seemed, he refused again. Sadleir clapped his hand to his head and exclaimed: 'Good God, if the Tipperary Bank should fail, the fault will be entirely mine, and I shall have been the ruin of hundreds and thousands.'[32] On being told that a deed he had given as security for an earlier loan was about to be registered, he became even more agitated. Wilkinson's firm had previously advanced large sums to Sadleir, but the balances had become so large that they had asked for security. This had been supplied six weeks previously in the form of a deed for the purchase of a property at the Incumbered Estates Court, but the firm had not yet registered the deed. Wilkinson was now so alarmed by the behaviour of his client that he at once dispatched his partner to Dublin to register the deed.

Sadleir spent the rest of the day in the city meeting friends and relatives in a last frantic attempt to raise funds. With all hope gone, he sent his butler to a nearby chemist's shop for a bottle of Essential Oil of Bitter Almonds. After going to his club that evening, he returned home, where he wrote four letters. At midnight he walked to Hampstead Heath.

The contents of Sadleir's last four letters were a matter of intense public speculation, and details were released long before they were read at the resumed inquest. When the *Morning Advertiser* of 23 February carried an article headed 'Astounding Disclosures' alleging that the frauds and forgeries of John Sadleir would not be under £1 million, copies of the newspaper were changing hands for 5s (£14 at today's values).

'I cannot live,' Sadleir had written to Norris, apparently overcome by a long belated sense of remorse. 'I have injured many. I committed abominable crimes, unknown to any human being that will now appear to light, bringing my family and others to distress.'[33] 'Oh how I feel for those on whom all this ruin must fall!' he wrote to Keating. 'I could bear all punishment, but I could never bear to witness the sufferings of those on whom I have brought ruin. It must be better that I should not live. No-one has been privy to my crimes. They sprung from my own cursed brain alone.'[34] To James's wife, Emma, he wrote: 'James is not to blame. I have caused all this dreadful ruin. James was to me too fond a brother, but was not to blame for being deceived, and led astray by my diabolical sin.'[35]

At the inquest, which resumed on 26 February, and at which the letters were read, the questions arose of whether Sadleir was sane at the time he wrote them, and was the disaster really as bad as he supposed? Despite the best efforts of Sadleir's friends and family, who strove to obtain a verdict of insanity, the court eventually brought in a verdict of wilful self-murder. The family had already anticipated this finding, for Sadleir had been buried in a quiet private ceremony early on the morning of 21 February in Highgate Cemetery in an unconsecrated plot, as was appropriate for a suicide. A Roman Catholic clergyman officiated, and only a few immediate family and close friends were present.

Great sympathy was felt for James Sadleir, who was, said the *Carlow Sentinel*, 'up to the last moment of the existence of his unfortunate brother, ignorant of the wicked career he had pursued, or of the enormous nature of the terrible speculations he had been engaged in'.[36] 'There is a widespread feeling of pity for the position of Mr James Sadleir the chief victim of his brother's frauds, and upon whose shoulders will fall the full weight of the suicide's transgressions,' said *The Times*. 'The member for Tipperary is, in fact, a ruined man, and it is said that he has already broken up his establishment, parted with servants, equipage, &c., and is prepared to meet with becoming fortitude the sad reverse which has cruelly crushed his worldly prospects.'[37] At the time of the crash James Sadleir was by far the largest shareholder in the Tipperary Bank, with 1,838 shares, and in time court judgments totalling over £34,000 would be made against him (approximately £2 million today).

The Royal Swedish Railway Company collapsed amid claims by angry investors. Its directors worked round the clock without remuneration to avoid bankruptcy, but to no avail. A committee of investigation finally reported that Sadleir's liabilities to the company were in excess of £350,000 (about £19 million today). The Carson's Creek Gold Mining Company, which had been under Sadleir's total control, was unable to find any trace of its securities, while the angry and dismayed shareholders of the Newcastle Bank were told that it had been emptied of funds.

As the winding-up proceeded, so there were more shocks. When a London solicitor arrived at the Dublin registry offices with a bundle of conveyances of properties sold to Sadleir which had been used as security for loans, all but one were shown to be forgeries, and the only genuine one had had the amount changed from £2,000 to £5,000. Wilkinson's partner found that the deed Sadleir had given him bore forged signatures, and the seal, while genuine, had been transferred from another document. It was only later that he discovered that Sadleir had forged his signature on a cheque.

'Every hour since he expired reveals some fresh and more flagrant swindle,' commented *The Nation*: 'the evidence of a wholesale, reckless and desperate system of fraud, accumulate on every mail. For months to come we may expect to see revealed its debris bit by bit.'[38]

The greatest tragedies resulted from the failure of the Tipperary Bank, which produced widespread hardship and distress. Ordinary working people, seeking to avoid penury in old age, had entrusted the bank with their life savings. Many had lodged every shilling they possessed.

There was alarm in London; there was wild panic in Ireland. The Tipperary Bank closed its doors; the country people flocked into the towns. They surrounded and attacked the branches; the poor victims imagined their money must be within, and they got crowbars, picks and spades to force the walls and 'dig it out'. The scenes of mad despair which the streets of Thurles and Tipperary saw that day would melt a heart of adamant. Old men went about like maniacs, confused and hysterical; widows knelt in the street, and aloud, asked God was it true they were beggared for ever.[39]

One poor woman lost the £100 she had scraped together to send to her stepson in America. A publican had saved £500, a schoolteacher £200, while a Tipperary police constable had savings of £300 and another just £100. A farmer who had sold his entire crop some weeks before had received a letter of credit which he was intending to take to the Bank of Ireland on his next visit. The delay had ruined him. A boatman, who had over many years accumulated £100 to support an aged parent, appeared at his bank and, refusing to believe that the money could not be paid to him, took out a cord and threatened to hang himself on the spot if it was not forthcoming. All advice and remonstration proving of no avail, a constable was called in to remove him. A farmer had deposited £300, and had intended to take the money out, but had been dissuaded from doing so by his wife. When he learned of the crash, he beat her to death. The bank also held many deposits of public and charitable funds. The parish priest of Tipperary had lodged £2,400 towards the building of a new chapel, and asking for £200 to start the work, found it could not be paid. At Nenagh there was a meeting of the Poor Law Board who had over £1,200 in rates at the Tipperary Bank. A cheque was hurriedly drawn up and a clerk dispatched to withdraw the funds. He returned empty-handed. The Board of Guardians of the Thomastown Poor Law Union had deposited £1,600. They and the Roscrea, Donaghmore and Athy Unions suddenly found their funds unobtainable and the ratepayers now faced being taxed a second time. In the short term many of the unions found they had no funds to pay for the paupers' dinners. £500 of the Thomastown 'cess', a local land tax, was also in the Tipperary Bank.

Depositors who assumed that the overdraft from the Tipperary Bank was covered by Sadleir's landed property were dismayed to discover that Sadleir had lodged the property deeds with the London and County Bank, which was not about to give them up; indeed, it had already started to sell them to meet the loans it had made to Sadleir. That company survived, but its reputation suffered by association with Sadleir and there was an 'extraordinary mania' among shareholders to sell their holdings, while the 'evil notoriety attached to Mr Sadleir's name rendered the retirement from the board of those directors who were in any way personally connected with him imperative'.[40] The Tipperary Bank laid claim to Sadleir's properties, but it was not until December 1858 that judgment was finally given in favour of the London bank.

The Tipperary Bank was eventually shown to have liabilities of £430,000, with total realisable assets of £50,000. The entire responsibility to meet the differential fell upon the shareholders, not only those who held shares at the time of the crash, but those who had held shares at any time during the three years prior to the crash. The efforts of some individuals to be removed from the list of liable shareholders resulted in legal battles that in some cases went on for years. Vincent Scully, who had been furious at the delays in selling his shares, was held liable and lost £8,000. His personal reputation remained unblemished and he was returned to Parliament in 1859, but the scandal was the end of political ambition for the Sadleirs. Frank and John, the sons of James Scully, had been left their shareholdings by their father. John, who was a farmer, was obliged to sell the lands and cattle he had inherited and lost in total £20,000. Frank fled to Paris, where the family disgrace continued to weigh heavily upon him and he was eventually placed in an asylum. Robert Keating asked to be removed from the list of those liable, saying he only held the shares in trust for Sadleir, but eventually judgment was made against him and he had to sell his family home to pay the debt. His political career was over, and the London and County Bank insisted he resign solely because he was John Sadleir's cousin. As the full details of Sadleir's depredations were made public, so rifts appeared between the Sadleirs and the Scullys that were never healed, and some branches of the families severed connections.

Wilson Kennedy's career was also shattered, and he was forced to emigrate. Farmery John Law, another innocent man tainted by his association with Sadleir, resigned his post and fled abroad. Thomas Eyre, who had loaned a total of £52,000 (over £3 million today), spent years of litigation to recover his money and was only partially successful. Smaller investors, the widows, spinsters and half-pay officers unable to meet the calls upon their property, were stripped of every farthing they owned, and many of the claims made by creditors against shareholders were never satisfied. The manager of the winding-up proceedings was eventually able to pay depositors two shillings in the pound.

Particularly aggrieved were the English shareholders who had been duped into buying at a premium. The optimists among them banded together, started a collection for a defence fund and took legal advice. The realists fled abroad. Judgment was finally delivered in May, and it was ruled that, despite Sadleir's frauds, the people he had imposed upon had become genuine shareholders in the company, entitled to share any profits of the concern, and therefore also responsible for the losses. Pursued by the lawsuits of attorneys who had bought up debts due to the company, many had to declare bankruptcy.

'It is probable that the conduct of no private individual has been productive of a larger amount of social misery than that of the unhappy man who has now terminated a career of deliberate and deep-laid swindling by a deliberate and well-timed suicide,'[41] commented the *Annual Register*. The Reverend Thomas of Melbourne cannot have been the only clergyman to preach a sermon on Sadleir as a terrible warning to young men.

The man best placed to throw light on the financial minefield that was the affairs of the Tipperary Bank was James Sadleir, who willingly submitted to questioning. As this proceeded, however, public sympathy gradually gave way to disquiet. James was clearly guilty of neglecting his duties to the bank in order to help his beleaguered brother, but had he really, as Sadleir had declared in his suicide letters, had no hand in the frauds? James, it was revealed, had deliberately concealed the agreement made on 15 March from the bank's directors, and lied to the July meeting, telling the directors that Sadleir's overdraft was £40,000 when he must have known it was nearer £200,000. The deed of 7 September had never been seen by the Tipperary Bank directors. False names for the directors had been entered on the minutes of a meeting that never took place – and those minutes had been written up by James. Letters were produced from Sadleir to his brother showing that James had full knowledge of the plan to produce false accounts, although James denied personal involvement. Most damaging, however, were documents showing that James had colluded in the fraud on the English shareholders. He had also been responsible for the preparation of false accounts in January 1856, which had been submitted to and approved by a fictitious meeting.

As concern became outright agitation for his arrest, James removed all doubt by fleeing abroad. His wife, Emma, declined to accompany him, and he settled in Zurich, where he was able to live modestly on a small annuity provided by her family. In the following year he was formally expelled from the House of Commons. He may have retained an air of prosperity: on the afternoon of 4 June 1881 he was enjoying a pleasant stroll when he was shot dead by a robber, who took his gold watch.

SIX

A Racing Certainty

On the evening of 30 November 1871 a warder at Newgate Gaol heard moans of pain coming from the cell of Harry Benson, who was awaiting trial on charges of fraud and forgery. The prisoner was found lying on his bed, his legs terribly burnt. In a desperate attempt at suicide, he had set fire to his straw mattress, and then lain determinedly in the flames. He survived, but was too ill to be tried until the following July, when he had to be carried into court.

Harry Benson was the 24-year-old French-born son of a respectable Jewish merchant. Educated in London and Paris, he was well dressed, spoke several languages and was an accomplished musician and composer. The previous October he had called on Sir Thomas Dakin, the Lord Mayor of London, claiming to be the Marquis de Morancy, Mayor of Châteaudun, and bearing a letter of introduction from Monsieur Léon Say, the Prefect of the Seine. The Mansion House Fund for relief of the French had been set up during the recent Franco-Prussian War, and the Mayor was happy to give the Marquis a cheque for £1,000. It wasn't until the following month that the visit was mentioned to Monsieur Say, who replied that he knew nothing of the Marquis and had not written the letter in question. The culprit was traced to his hotel and arrested. In his possession were address cards showing that he had been masquerading under several different names, and three passports. He had cashed the cheque, and all but £70 of the money was found on his person. His distraught father offered to make up the loss.

Benson was released from prison in July 1873, still unable to walk. An aunt and uncle paid for his lodgings in Helena Road, Dalston, with Henry Avis, a 62-year-old customs officer, and his wife Ann, aged 52. Assuming the name of G.H. Yonge, he told them he was recovering from a railway accident. At first he had to be carried up and down stairs, but as time passed he was able to get about on crutches and eventually to walk with the aid of two sticks. His family paid for his accommodation, but, unable to live in the style he felt he deserved, he was obliged, much against his inclination, to look for work. In February 1874 he answered a newspaper advertisement placed by a William Kurr who wished to employ a man to write articles. Kurr, born in October 1850, was the son of a master baker and lived with his family – including two brothers and two sisters – in the Caledonian Road. The boys, and especially William, 'were known among the neighbours as shrewd, quick-witted and "able to take care of themselves"'. As children, they did not use these considerable talents for crime, but after the early death of their mother, 'the want of a mother's training hand, a wretched home, and a money grubbing father, soon alienated the youths from the path of rectitude'.[1] They were educated at Messrs Burbidge and Ridgeway's academy at Pentonville Hill, where the members of what was later to be a betting fraud gang first met. When William Kurr left school, his father sent him to work as a clerk, but the boy's experience of honest toil was a brief one, which held no appeal. From the age of 15 he preferred to live on his wits. The experience of his eldest brother, Louis, who became a heavy gambler and died aged 26 in 1873, should have warned him of the dangers of a misspent life, but he was not deterred.

Unlike the small, frail Benson, William Kurr was a large, ruddy-faced man, who might have been taken for a farmer. To begin with, Kurr viewed Benson as just another employee, whom he paid five guineas per week, but in time the two men began to know and understand each other and to recognise that they were both rogues with very special talents. If they had never met, it is probable that they would have continued their lives of relatively minor crime. As a team, however, they could achieve very much more. Kurr lacked subtlety but had energy, determination, an abundance of nerve and was adept at directing a team of loyal confederates. Benson had polish, education, an air of refinement and a flair for smooth persuasion. It was the perfect combination.

Kurr's area of expertise was the racing and betting world. The Betting House Act of 1853 had made the running and advertising of bookmakers' shops illegal, but by an oversight that was widely exploited this prohibition did not apply in Scotland, where such businesses became common. Kurr was not, however, content to make money from bookmaking in the usual way, since he could make far more by operating fraudulent schemes that offered customers a system in which purportedly they could not lose. There is never a shortage of dupes who want to believe in a sure thing, but Kurr's idea had two drawbacks: he was never able to attract those with the most money to lose, and his businesses hardly got going before angry punters became suspicious and he was obliged to shut up shop and move on to avoid arrest. This was a trouble and expense he wanted to avoid.

There was another part of Kurr's business essential to his continued success: he needed early warning of when the police had become alerted to his latest scheme so that he could be sure to depart before he was arrested. The best possible source of information was, as he soon discovered, the police themselves.

In November 1872 Kurr had been enjoying a drink at the Angel Hotel Islington with one of his associates, Edwin Murray, when a stranger joined their conversation. Kurr revealed that he was a bookmaker, and his new acquaintance introduced himself as Sergeant John Meiklejohn, of the plain clothes detective division of Scotland Yard. Meiklejohn was anxious to find opportunities of augmenting his modest police salary by whatever means were available, and it was soon apparent to the two men that they could be useful to each other.

In February 1873 Kurr started a new business in Edinburgh, Phillip Gardner and Co., but when one of his men was arrested he was obliged to return to London. There he again met Meiklejohn, who hinted that he thought Kurr might know something of the Gardner business. With things looking a little warm, Kurr decided to spend six months in America, which gave him just enough time to promote another swindle. This was unsuccessful, and on his return to London Kurr received a message from Meiklejohn suggesting that he could get Kurr off the hook on the Gardner case. The offer was accepted, the policeman received £100, a letter was sent to the Edinburgh police and Kurr found that he was no longer a suspect. Other transactions of a similar nature were to follow, but by now Kurr was dreaming of bigger things. To give his business the look of quality it required, however, he needed a man of education to write his promotional material.

Harry Benson was a vital component of Kurr's plan to move into the big time. Benson dealt with correspondence and prepared circulars, his literary abilities giving the operation a veneer of quality and respectability. New legislation in 1874 extended the provisions of the Betting House Act to Scotland, so Kurr decided to look further afield, advertising his schemes in foreign newspapers. In July 1874 the two men were operating in London under the name of Archer and Co., with the Systematic Investment Society – yet another betting swindle – concentrating on attracting business from France. Money poured in, and was collected from an accommodation address by Harry Street, one of Kurr's messengers. They made £4,000

(£240,000 at today's values) in just six days, but then the scheme suddenly collapsed when Street was arrested by Chief Detective Inspector Nathaniel Druscovich, considered one of the best men in Scotland Yard and responsible for the investigation of foreign frauds. Kurr was obliged to close down the London operation and move to Glasgow, where the business continued as the Paris Discretionary. Before long the gang had made another £8,000.

Kurr was now a well-to-do young man, partly because of a legacy from his father, who had died in 1873 unaware both of William's illegal activities and the fact that he had brought his younger brother, Frederick, into the business. Kurr soon acquired a home at Marquess Road, Canonbury, a public house – the Oxford Arms, in Islington – and two racehorses.

Benson, too, was at last able to live in the luxurious style he craved. He took Rosebank house in Shanklin, in the Isle of Wight, where he kept two carriages and employed his former landlady, the recently widowed Mrs Avis, as his housekeeper, and a French valet. He also bought and edited a local newspaper and moved in the best society. Although he still called himself Yonge, he let it be known that he was a French nobleman and an intimate friend of the Empress of Austria. Most people took him at his own report, but when a Captain Harvey decided to check his antecedents, Benson was obliged to change his story, claiming to be an agent of the French government entrusted with handling large sums of money. Mrs Avis remained discreetly silent about his impoverished past.

Meanwhile, the Glasgow operation was doing well, when in November 1874 Kurr received a letter from Meiklejohn addressing him familiarly as 'Dear Bill' and warning him that it might be necessary for the gang to 'scamper out of the way'. He asked for an early meeting: 'I fancy the brief [i.e. a warrant] is out for some of you. If not it will be. So you must keep a sharp look-out.'[2] Kurr took the hint and shut down the operation. Meiklejohn received £500 for the tip-off, and used the money to buy a house in the South Lambeth Road.

Returning to London in 1875, Kurr and Benson, together with Murray and a publican, Henry Walters, started yet another business, the Society for Insurance against Losses on the Turf, which was widely advertised in France, Germany, Italy, Switzerland and Russia and claimed, falsely, to have a number of eminent men as its directors. Swindling foreigners meant that it was much easier to keep the dupes in the dark. Only the larger British race meetings were reported in the continental papers, so the Society claimed that the secret of success on the turf was to bet on the smaller meetings. This promising enterprise collapsed almost immediately after the arrest of Murray and Walters. A warrant was also issued for Kurr's arrest.

Kurr was beginning to realise that it was not sufficient to have just one detective in his pocket. Fortunately for his plans, there were at the time only fifteen detectives in Scotland Yard, and Kurr was well aware of the men he needed to cultivate and those who could not be bought. In 1875 the Detective Division was headed by the supremely incorruptible 45-year-old Superintendent Algernon Frederick Williamson, 'loyal, hardworking, persevering, phlegmatic, obstinate, unenthusiastic, courageous, always having his own opinion, never afraid to express it . . . . so clear-headed, and so honest, and kind-hearted to a fault, he was a most upright and valuable public servant', recalled a colleague.[3]

Williamson's right-hand man was 56-year-old Chief Inspector George Clarke, who had been a policeman since 1840. Williamson described Clarke as 'my most confidential and trusted assistant'.[4] The two were also close personal friends. Clarke's speciality was the investigation of betting frauds: he had been responsible for the exposure of many dubious operations and the arrest of seventy-one offenders, including Murray and Walters. Clarke had also for some years been employed by the Chief Commissioner of Police, Edmund Henderson, in 'business of a special and confidential character'[5] well beyond the scope of everyday police work.

Among the younger officers, 40-year-old Chief Inspector William Palmer was a reliable plodder who had joined the force in 1862; but the most promising man was the energetic Nathaniel Druscovich. London-born, of Moldavian extraction, he was just 32 years old and his intelligence, application and impressive record of success had ensured a rapid rise though the ranks. He had been promoted to sergeant when barely in his twenties, was an inspector before he was 30 and chief inspector by 1871. Skilled in languages, he specialised in investigating international crimes. Meiklejohn, his involvement with Kurr still unsuspected, had by then risen to the rank of inspector.

An inspector at this time received a salary of only £225 a year and a chief inspector £275. In addition to this they were entitled to reward money, usually £5 or £10 a time, for praiseworthy conduct. Druscovich had been the recipient of several such rewards. It was a long way from the high-rolling lifestyle of Kurr and Benson.

Anxious about the warrant hanging over his head, Kurr decided that the man he must target was Clarke, and that Benson should open negotiations. Unknown to either, Clarke already held the mysterious Mr Yonge under suspicion, as Mr Hall, a son-in-law of Mrs Avis, had noticed some odd comings and goings in Shanklin and had reported the matter to the police.

Benson sent an associate to tell Clarke that he had some information on the Walters and Murray case, and, in view of his disability, suggested Clarke meet him in Shanklin. The meeting took place on 12 April 1875. Clarke was welcomed with hospitable charm by Yonge, who explained that he knew Walters through carrying out a translation for him and changing a cheque, but had not initially been aware of his criminal activities. He was hoping, because of his difficulty in travelling, to avoid being called as a witness. The conversation, which had begun so pleasantly, now started to take a sinister turn. Yonge revealed that Walters, who had impressed him as a thoroughly bad type, had claimed that he had bribed Clarke and furthermore could prove it with an incriminating letter.

Clarke was momentarily shaken, but remained calm. He said that he recalled the letter, which he had written to Walters a year previously asking for a meeting. He had been investigating a burglary and had wanted to see Walters to obtain certain information. He denied any underhand intention and said that he had not received any money from Walters. Asked where the letter was, Benson said he did not know but that a man named Kurr, a poor dupe of Walters, did know. He then attempted to start Clarke on the slippery slope to criminality by offering him £100 if he (Yonge) could avoid the witness box. To soothe the policeman's guilt he added that other Scotland Yard detectives were also receiving bribes.

Clarke adamantly refused. He said that he would make a report of the meeting but that Yonge probably knew too little to be called as a witness in any case. The discussion was concluded, but next morning Benson suggested to Clarke that he might be able to get the compromising letter from Kurr. He left Clarke in no doubt that, if Kurr should be arrested, the letter would be made public. Before Clarke left, Yonge offered him twenty sovereigns, but he would not accept them. Clarke, now deeply concerned, returned to London, where he reported that in his opinion Yonge was a scoundrel but that he had no useful information about the betting fraud. Despite his calm denials of any wrongdoing, he was aware of how his letter to Walters could be misinterpreted.

Perhaps realising he had gone too far, Benson changed his tactics. Letters were exchanged in which Benson addressed Clarke as 'My dear Sir and Brother', an allusion to the fact that both men were Freemasons. Benson did not want Clarke to have a sample of his handwriting, so he asked Mrs Avis to make copies of his letters to send to Clarke. Mrs Avis was not a foolish woman. She was well able to pretend that she knew nothing of Benson's activities as long as he provided a pleasant home for her and paid for her son's schooling, but she must have suspected that Yonge was not what he seemed. Benson, for his part, saw her as a trusting domestic and made the mistake of underestimating her. Unknown to him, she retained the handwritten originals of his letters to Clarke. By June the two men were on friendlier terms, and Clarke made several more trips to Shanklin, of which he made no official report. The problem of Walters and Murray was by then temporarily solved. On being granted bail, both men had promptly absconded and sailed to America.

As the months went by, the vital letter was frequently alluded to and still dangled frustratingly just out of Clarke's reach. Clarke became increasingly anxious. Benson later claimed that he supplied money to Clarke on some of his visits, an allegation Clarke always denied. With the warrant still outstanding, Kurr had been lying low, but on Clarke's advice wrote to the Treasury to discover if he had any charges to meet: whether or not Clarke had anything to do with the decision is unknown, but ultimately the reply came that it had been decided not to proceed against Kurr. As for Clarke, although his letter was returned to him, he had been drawn into the web of Benson and Kurr.

The conspirators next turned their attention to Nathaniel Druscovich. This young star of the detective division must have appeared unapproachable, when he unwittingly delivered himself into their hands. Druscovich had recently guaranteed a bill for his brother, and had unexpectedly been called upon to pay £60, a sum quite beyond his means. Frantic with worry, he made the error of confiding his position to Meiklejohn, who did not hesitate to drag an honest man down. Claiming that he was unable to help Druscovich personally, he disclosed that he knew a man who could. The man was Bill Kurr.

Druscovich was tempted, but needed convincing that Kurr would keep quiet about the transaction. Meiklejohn assured him that Kurr was the soul of discretion, 'a perfect gentleman, an owner of racehorses'.[6] Shortly afterwards, Druscovich met Kurr and received £60, free of conditions. He must have known that Kurr, as a man of business, would not give something for nothing, but he cannot have known that he would pay for the small sum with his liberty, his career and, ultimately, his life.

The ease with which men suspected of betting frauds had recently been evading arrest had not escaped Superintendent Williamson, who, fearing that someone in his department was leaking information, began to make discreet inquiries. Realising that the younger recruits did not know enough to tip off the villains, he was forced to consider that a more senior man might be responsible. Only Meiklejohn had been active in all the cases under suspicion, but there was no proof of guilt. Williamson communicated his findings to the Commissioner of Police, and soon the Home Office set up an inquiry. While this proceeded, Williamson had the difficult task of behaving as if he knew nothing.

With senior detectives in his pay, Kurr was now ready to carry out a scheme of great audacity. He was tired of little businesses with small pickings, and shops that had to be closed after a few days of opening. He wanted to make big money. The new scheme was outlined at a dinner held on 4 August 1876 at which Meiklejohn and Charles Bale, an associate of Kurr's, were present. It required the intelligence and linguistic ability of Harry Benson and the organisational talents of Kurr to contrive a plan that was bold, lucrative and convincing. The previous swindles had been advertised through circulars and in the newspapers: this time they were going to operate a newspaper of their own, but not for the general public – this message was going to a very precisely targeted clientele.

Kurr arranged for Brydone, an Edinburgh printer, to publish *The Sport*, a racing journal. The paper claimed to have been printed in London, an anomaly which seemed not to worry Mr Brydone. Although numbered 1,713, to give the impression that it was well established, only one edition was issued and a few hundred copies printed: it did not go on general sale. Benson made a special study of French directories and was able to identify wealthy individuals who were ideal recipients of the publication. The contents were mainly copied wholesale from genuine sporting papers. The only original piece was a leading article written by Kurr and polished by Benson.

This article revealed that *The Sport* was the property of the fabulously wealthy Andrew Montgomery, who had amassed a fortune of £575,000 through intelligent application of his great knowledge of horse racing. So astute was the fictional Montgomery that the wagers he placed invariably won, which meant that the bookmakers, who had initially been so pleased to take his wagers, now refused to take any more of his bets; and that Montgomery was no longer able to take part in the sport he loved. *The Sport* railed with righteous indignation against mean-spirited bookmakers and declared that it would 'never cease to protest until we have compelled these vultures to discontinue such unfair conduct'.[7] Montgomery was not, however, the sort of man to take this lying down –

he was much too clever for that. The rules of the Jockey Club, he said, forbade the making of bets in an assumed name, but he could still employ agents to bet for him – for a suitable commission, of course. Once again, Kurr and Benson had come up with an ideal scheme. Their trademark was to offer a deal in which the participants, it seemed, could not lose. Montgomery was betting with his own funds, so if he lost he would be losing his own money, whereas if he won his agents would receive 5 per cent commission on the winnings.

The newspapers were packaged up to be sent to their targets abroad, with Benson's French translation folded inside. Initially they covered only one area of France, the Marne and the Gironde. Before the papers could be distributed, however, there was one little detail that needed attending to. Any continental development was bound to attract the attention of Nathaniel Druscovich. In anticipation of this, Meiklejohn sent Druscovich a letter saying that Kurr wanted to see him. To his surprise, Druscovich found that the meeting had nothing to do with the £60 he owed Kurr; instead, Kurr wanted to talk about his new business. He said he was going to open a betting office for customers living in France. Reassuring Druscovich that the business was quite legal, he said that all he wanted from the inspector was to be warned if he heard of any complaints about the operation, or if any warrants were issued, especially if they referred to someone called Montgomery. Although Druscovich was left with the worrying impression that the scheme was not all it should be, Kurr managed to convince him that it was not in itself criminal, but a means of sidestepping a technicality of the Betting Act. Kurr offered Druscovich £25 for his trouble, which the policeman refused, saying he was already £60 in Kurr's debt, but when Kurr thrust the money into the policeman's pocket, Druscovich made no further protest.

According to Kurr, he next saw Clarke and handed him £50 for a similar arrangement (which Clarke denied). He gave Clarke some envelopes on which he had written his address, saying that, should Clarke wish to see him, he should send one with a blank sheet of paper inside, to avoid any written correspondence between them.

The scheme was to involve large sums of money arriving from France. To avoid repetition of a scare the pair had encountered in an earlier swindle, when the French police had stopped their letters, Kurr approached Meiklejohn, who found him two Post Office employees, Jebb and Goodwin, who were happy, for a consideration, to give early warning of any investigation.

'Gambling in the Stocks' by George Cruickshank. From right to left are Lord Cochrane, Andrew Cochranc Johnstone, Richard Butt and Charles de Berenger. *(© The British Library)*

Below: Princess Caraboo's writing with Mary Baker's signature. *(The British Library)*

Right: Andrew Cochrane Johnstone MP, a contemporary portrait.

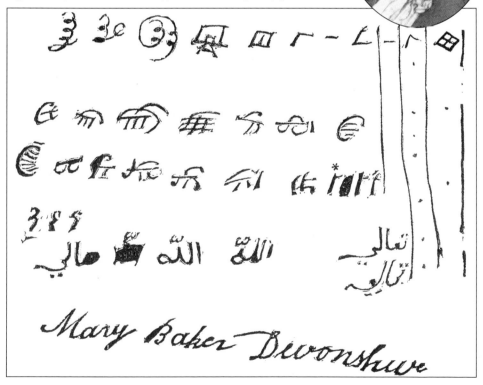

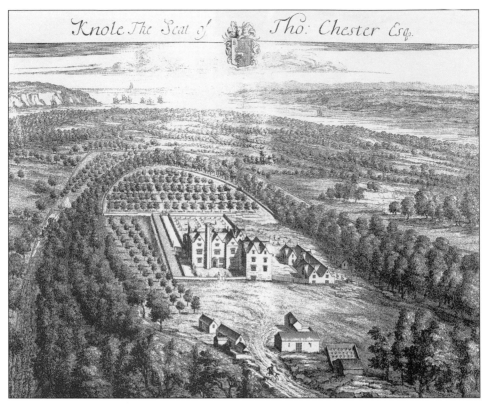

Knole Park, near Almondsbury, where Mary Baker masqueraded as Princess Caraboo. *(The British Library)*

Left: Princess Caraboo, a contemporary engraving, portrait by N. Branwhite. *(The British Library) Right:* Mademoiselle Lenorman, an 1821 engraving. *(Bibliothèque Nationale de France)*

Sections of the forged inscriptions on the back of Alexander Alexander's map of Canada. *(The British Library)*

Left: Jack Straw's Castle, Hampstead Heath, a nineteenth-century print. *Right:* John Sadleir MP, contemporary woodcut from a daguerreotype by William Edward Kilburn. *(Courtesy of the National Library of Ireland)*

Above: Meiklejohn, Druscovich and Palmer in the dock, a contemporary drawing.

Below left: Superintendent Williamson under cross-examination, a contemporary drawing.

Below centre: William Kurr, a contemporary drawing.

Below right: Harry Benson, a contemporary drawing.

Left: A Napoleon of Finance (a contemporary Hooley cartoon). *(The British Library)*

Above: A giant octopus drags a Malay pearl fisher below the waves. *(Wide World Magazine, illustration by Arthur Pearse)*

Left: Louis de Rougemont. *(Mary Evans Picture Library)*

Below: Ticket for Louis de Rougemont's talk at St James's Hall. *(The Sketch)*

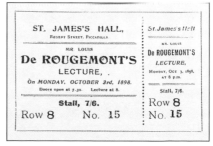

Whitaker Wright at a meeting of angry shareholders. *(Daily Mail)*

Whitaker Wright and his 'Palace' at Lea Park, with an artist's impression of his death. *(Illustrated Police News)*

Notes made by
Whitaker Wright
during his trial.
(Daily Mail)

Above: The
Marquess of
Dufferin and Ava
in 1898. *(The
Sketch)*

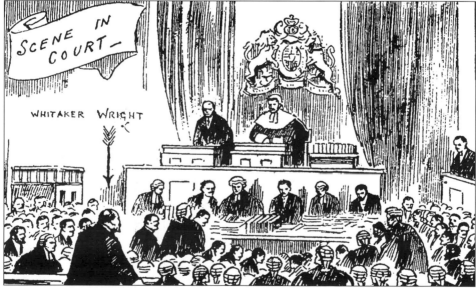

The scene in court during the trial of Whitaker Wright. *(Illustrated Police News)*

SOCIETY ON THE BENCH IN A POLICE COURT: THE FASHIONABLE AUDIENCE AT THE DRUCE CASE.

SKETCHES BY S. BEGG, OUR SPECIAL ARTIST AT MARYLEBONE POLICE COURT.

THE SCENE AT THE MARYLEBONE POLICE COURT DURING THE EXAMINATION OF MR. CALDWELL.

The Druce case. Scene at the Marylebone Police Court, November 1907. *(Illustrated London News)*

Left: Photograph produced in court as that of the 5th Duke of Portland. *Right:* Thomas Charles Druce, a photograph produced in court as that of the 5th Duke of Portland in the character of Druce.

Kurr now mobilised his gang, who opened branch offices in Fleet Street, Cleveland Row, Jermyn Street and Duke Street, which were all in the same postal district. The head office, which was rented from a Mr Flintoff, was at 8 Northumberland Street, not far from the back entrance of Scotland Yard. The plan was for all the incoming correspondence to be collected daily by Kurr and Benson's minions, usually Bale and Frederick Kurr, and brought to the plotters at head office. It had taken several weeks to plan the operation, but on 31 August 1876, 200 copies of *The Sport* were sent out, and Benson and Kurr waited for their wealthy dupes to respond.

The expected replies soon poured in, and each applicant received a personal letter from Mr Montgomery himself:

Your name has been favourably mentioned to me by the Franco-English Society of Publicity, and I consequently repose in you the most esteemed confidence. What I require of you is very simple indeed. I will send you for each race the amount which I desire you to put on the horse, which must, in my opinion, win. You will have to forward the money *in your name* but *on my account*, to the bookmaker, and thus will be able to get the real odds, which on account of my success and great knowledge are denied to me. The bookmaker will, on settling day, send you the amount added to the stake originally forwarded to him. This you will please remit to me, and on its receipt I will forthwith forward to you a commission of five percent.[8]

The dupes, flattered at having come to the notice of the non-existent Franco-English Society of Publicity and basking in the confidence of the equally fictitious great man, could see nothing in the letter that would entail risking their own money, and so readily agreed to the proposition.

The majority of those who were taken in by the scheme preferred to remain anonymous, but one lady who was unable to do so was the Comtesse Marie Cécile de Goncourt, a wealthy young widow residing at the Château de Goncourt in the Marne, whose trusting nature was the lure that would eventually draw the conspirators into the open. The Comtesse, now one of Montgomery's trusted agents, received a cheque for £200 and a letter with instructions that the money should be placed as a bet with a Mr Jackson, an English 'sworn bookmaker'.[9] The lady did not stop to wonder what a 'sworn bookmaker' was – it sounded impressive and she did after all have £200 of Montgomery's money. The bet was placed, the horse won, and in due course the Comtesse received a cheque with the winnings and the stake money. This she sent back to Montgomery.

The Comtesse was not to know that 'Mr Jackson' was one of Kurr's associates, that there was no such thing as a 'sworn bookmaker' and that the betting office was a front. Nor were the cheques genuine: they had been printed by the obliging Mr Brydone at the order of Kurr and Benson and appeared to be from the impressively named 'Royal Bank of London'.

Montgomery was pleased with the Comtesse – so pleased that his next cheque was for £1,000, which came with instructions to place the bet on a horse in the Great Northern Handicap with another 'sworn bookmaker', Mr Francis. This time it was hinted that the Comtesse might like to adventure some of her own money. This she did, and as evidence of her trust in her benefactor, she risked £1,000. Benson's skilful letters painted Montgomery as a man of the utmost respectability, a true philanthropist, deeply concerned with the welfare of the Comtesse, 'a woman without a protector' and her 'little children'.[10] He advised her that the 'sworn bookmaker' required a minimum of £2,000, and accordingly she happily sent the extra money. He then offered her the opportunity of insuring her bet against a loss, but this was only possible for a minimum bet of £4,000. She sent more money. Finally a change of venue increased the figure to £5,000. But the Comtesse's trust in her benefactor was rewarded with substantial winnings, which were paid over in the form of a cheque drawn on the Royal Bank of London. The Comtesse, delighted with her success, happily sent another £5,000, and won again. Her winnings now totalled between £80,000 and £90,000. Other dupes were making similar transactions, although not quite on the same scale. In just eighteen days the gang received a total of £15,000 (approximately £1 million today) and had written fake cheques for fictional winnings of £120,000.

The dupes were advised that, in order to comply with English law, they could not cash the cheques at once, but were obliged to hold onto them for three months. There was, of course, no such law, but the delay was essential to enable the gang to milk the scheme for as long as possible. It also meant that when the dupes wanted to place another bet they could not reinvest their winnings but had to send another personal cheque.

The plan was that in three months, when the dupes found that their cheques were worthless forgeries, the business would vanish, only to reappear in a new guise, targeted at another part of France, with a different fake newspaper and a different fake bank. There was, Benson believed, enough mileage in the scheme to keep them very busy for four years, by which time they would be multimillionaires.

In the meantime, Williamson, still suspicious of Meiklejohn, saw an opportunity at least to remove him from dealing with sensitive matters. The Midland Railway Company had asked for an experienced man to superintend their police, and so before long Meiklejohn was seconded and packed off to Derby, which did not discomfit him in the least since his senior position gave him more independence of action. While in Derby, he remained in constant contact with Kurr.

The racing fraud was prospering, and Scotland Yard was quite unaware of its existence when Benson made a classic error: he became greedy. Montgomery wrote to the Comtesse suggesting that she place a bet of £30,000 with another 'sworn bookmaker', called Ellerton. The lure was irresistible. Seven horses had been entered for a race at Ayr and of these six were to be withdrawn, leaving Montgomery's choice the inevitable winner. 'Never will you find a similar opportunity to win an immense fortune. If you have not the whole amount at hand see what you can stake and I myself will willingly advance the difference.'[11]

Benson's greed was only exceeded by that of the Comtesse, who was eager for another huge win. The only difficulty was that she had no more liquid funds. Anxious not to miss the opportunity, she went to her lawyer, Monsieur Chavance, for advice on how to raise the stake money. He at once suspected that she had been handing over her money to some clever villains and cabled Scotland Yard for advice. He received the reply from Williamson he had feared: 'The scheme is a fraud.'[12]

The London part of the investigation was entrusted to the Comtesse's perceptive and energetic solicitor, 52-year-old Michael Abrahams, who at once went to Scotland Yard and laid all the facts before Superintendent Williamson. Unable to trace any of the 'sworn bookmakers', he determined to obtain a warrant for their arrest. The superintendent decided to put his best man on to the investigation. Calling Nathaniel Druscovich into his office, he advised him that he had been told of a swindle that involved the sum of £10,000 coming in from Paris, and instructed him to call on Abrahams the following day.

When Meiklejohn got to hear about this, he at once advised Druscovich that Kurr ought to be told what was happening. On the afternoon of 25 September, Kurr was driving home from the office in his gig with Harry Street, when he happened to see Druscovich outside Scotland Yard and stopped to speak to him. Druscovich advised Kurr that he had been asked to look into a foreign swindle involving £10,000. He was not at the time aware that it was a betting scheme, and Kurr did not enlighten him.

Kurr did no more than advise him to keep matters in his own hands, but as he drove away he realised that it was time to shut up shop. When he got home there was an envelope waiting for him in his own handwriting. It contained a blank piece of blotting paper. He went at once to see Clarke, who said that he was both 'frightened and alarmed'.[13] He told Kurr that there was just time to change any banknotes, but that it would be dangerous for him to go near the spurious offices.

Aware that immediate action was needed, Kurr drove as fast as he could to Benson's lodging house. It was now almost midnight, and, unable to persuade Benson's valet to awaken his master, Kurr threw a stone at the window and broke it. Benson, who was feeling unwell, remained in bed, and eventually Kurr gave up trying to contact him. He sent a message to Druscovich asking him to meet him at Charing Cross the following morning; he then drove home.

Druscovich was both distressed and agitated when he met Kurr under the Charing Cross archway. The policeman had by now been told all the details of the fraud, and when Kurr calmly informed him that he was involved realised what kind of man had a hold over him. To the cool villain it seemed that Druscovich hardly knew what he was saying as the inspector had convinced himself he was being 'piped off' or watched. 'I have told you now, and you will have to look out for yourself,'[14] he said. Kurr asked if the notes were being stopped. 'I do not know what they are doing!' said Druscovich, who then turned and ran away.[15] Unknown to either of them, Abrahams was busy obtaining arrest warrants, but so far his investigation was hindered by not knowing the men's real names.

Kurr hurried to the Northumberland Street office, where the gang had assembled to wait for his instructions. He advised them to close the office and leave London at once. The French money had been changed into Bank of England notes, by a money-changer named Reinhardt, but Kurr felt they needed to cover their tracks further. He then made a fatal error of judgement, which was to be instrumental in the gang's downfall. English banks kept a record of the numbers of the notes they issued, but Scottish banks did not. He calculated that if the English notes were changed into Scottish notes they would not be traceable. Benson and two other gang members departed at once for Glasgow with £14,000 and began the process, obtaining some £10,000 in Clydesdale bank notes before their activities attracted attention.

Druscovich returned to Scotland Yard to declare that the gang had cleared out of their offices before he arrived. Williamson felt sure that the criminals had been warned, but this time it could not have been Meiklejohn, who had been in Derby for the last two weeks. It was almost unthinkable that another of his men was corrupt, yet there could hardly be another conclusion.

Abrahams had by now traced Reinhardt, who supplied him with the numbers of £12,000 worth of the English notes. Abrahams then passed on the information to Druscovich, which the officer had no alternative but to give to Williamson. Druscovich was now a very frightened man in a terrible dilemma, obliged to take action lest he excite suspicion, but afraid of doing too much in case his involvement should be revealed. He was able for a time to conceal his obstruction of the investigation under a guise of error, neglect and bad luck. Charged with the task of discovering the numbers of the remaining notes, he hesitated for as long as he was able before making them known.

Kurr was naturally anxious to find out exactly which notes had been stopped. Frustrated that Druscovich was supplying him with no further information, he had to rely on Clarke for news, and asked Meiklejohn to bring Druscovich to heel. Meiklejohn was confident that Williamson, whom he described as 'a calf', would 'never tumble to it in a thousand years'[16] and wired Druscovich to come to a meeting at the Midland Grand Hotel, St Pancras.

Druscovich arrived in a thoroughly agitated state. He told them of a meeting at which the police had studied the French documents, and remarked on the 'clever fellow' Bill had behind him. 'Talk about Victor Hugo, I never read such French in my life,' he exclaimed.[17] The Comtesse's brother, who had attended the meeting, was less impressed than appalled. Reading the Montgomery letters, all he could say, over and over again, was 'Mon Dieu!'[18]

Druscovich hinted that, in view of the warrants, it might be best for Kurr to go to America; but Kurr refused. 'I must arrest somebody over this job,' said Druscovich pleadingly. 'Arrest me if you like,' said Kurr. Intrigued by the audacity of this idea, Druscovich realised that, since Kurr had never been to any of the branches, no one would be able to identify him. 'I think I will,' he said.[19]

An appointment was made for the dramatic coup to take place at Kurr's house, but in the event Druscovich thought better of it. He was beginning to think that his best course of action was to have as little to do with Kurr as possible. When Kurr later asked Druscovich to supply him with the numbers of the stopped banknotes, the officer gave evasive replies, and it was Meiklejohn who ultimately provided the information, which was at once wired to Benson.

'How am I to get any information from Druscovich?' Kurr complained to Meiklejohn. 'He is frightened to come near me. Tell him to make all his business known at the office, and I am sure to know then from others.'[20] Still, Kurr believed he knew how to ensure Druscovich's loyalty. He sent him a cigar box containing £200 in gold.

On 3 October some of the notes Benson had been changing in Glasgow reached the Bank of England. Druscovich was at once informed of this, and his obvious course of action was to wire the Glasgow police, which could very well have led to Benson's arrest, while to do nothing would expose his involvement. As a compromise, he sent the information to Scotland by letter, providing a delay that allowed Benson to leave Glasgow the next day. Clarke, who had by now guessed that 'Mr Yonge' was involved, told Kurr he was a fool to have sent a man whose condition made him easily remembered and identified.

The day after Benson's return, he went with Kurr to Brighton. During this vist the *Police Gazette* published descriptions of the gang, the most distinctive of which was that of Benson under his various aliases: '5 feet 4 or 5 inches high, sallow complexion, black moustache, very thin round the waist . . . wears diamond studs and rings, pretends to be lame and carries two sticks, of Jewish appearance.'[21]

Two weeks later, no doubt refreshed from their holiday, Benson and Kurr were back in London. They had a meeting on 19 October with Inspector Meiklejohn, who had been thinking, as usual, of himself. He had come to the conclusion that he knew enough about Kurr and his business to demand a very substantial settlement, and so he asked for £2,000. After some wrangling, the sum of £500 was agreed, but the only cash available was in the form of £100 Clydesdale banknotes. While these were not numbered, they were sufficiently rarely seen in England to attract attention as soon as anyone presented one to a bank.

Meiklejohn, with careless self-confidence, began at once to change the notes, one in Manchester and one in Leeds, where he supplied his own name to the banks. The Leeds police wrote to Scotland Yard, but the letter went straight to Druscovich, who burnt it. Benson was furious with Meiklejohn, who claimed that he was a personal friend of the Chief Constable of Leeds and could get out of any trouble simply by writing to him.

The conspirators, now believing they were in the clear, started to plan the next stage of the swindle, and accordingly, early in November, moved their centre of operations to the Bridge of Allan in Scotland, where their Clydesdale notes would not be so noticeable. This was at the suggestion of Meiklejohn, who originated from the nearby village of Green Loaming and offered to introduce them to Mr Monteith, the bank manager there. Before they left they saw Druscovich, who warned that someone had mentioned Kurr's name to Abrahams. They pacified Druscovich with £100 and some jewellery for his wife.

Kurr (who was now calling himself Captain William Gifford), Benson (under his alias of G.H. Yonge) and Meiklejohn stayed at the Queen's Hotel, where they enjoyed convivial dinners and made plans. On Meiklejohn's recommendation, Monteith was happy to open accounts for Yonge and his associate, and accepted their Clydesdale notes. Kurr's new paper was called the *Racing News*. Soon, Brydone's presses were busy again.

In London, meanwhile, Abrahams was continuing his inquiries. Finding that the Scotland Yard officers were not pressing matters as fast as they should, he decided to engage private detectives, much to the alarm of Druscovich, who complained to Williamson that the latter were hampering his own inquiries. Abrahams decided to offer a reward of £1,000 for the apprehension of the fraudsters, still with the only names he was aware of, and on 8 November his advertisement appeared in newspapers and was circulated to banks and police stations. At last his efforts paid off. William Rayner, the Shanklin postmaster, saw the advertisement and recognised the description of the wanted man as Mr Yonge of Shanklin. On hearing this, Abrahams ordered that any letters arriving in Shanklin should be watched.

On 10 November Druscovich was ordered to go to the Isle of Wight, and on the same day an informant sent an urgent telegram to Kurr, warning him that if Benson was in Shanklin he should be told to leave at once. The telegram was followed up with a letter. Since Benson was in Scotland, Kurr was not worried. Before Druscovich could set out, however, further news arrived at Scotland Yard that necessitated a change of plan. A cheque from the Royal Bank of London had been cashed in Edinburgh and traced back to Brydone, who had, it seemed, helped himself to his own handiwork. When the police raided the print works, they found 1,000 copies of the *Racing News* and a pile of fake cheques. They promptly seized the material and the plates.

Meanwhile, Abrahams's watch of the Shanklin letters had intercepted correspondence between Benson's servant at the Bridge of Allan and a maid in Shanklin. Abrahams went to Scotland Yard with the news. Soon,

Williamson was reeling from another shock. The Edinburgh police had wired him to confirm the presence of Yonge and Gifford at the Queen's Hotel and revealed that Meiklejohn (who had booked in under his own name) had been with them. Druscovich, who had not yet set out for Shanklin, was ordered to go to Scotland instead. Both the initial and the altered plan had been revealed to as few officers as possible. At 7 p.m that evening Clarke and Palmer met at a Masonic dinner. At 8 p.m. an anonymous wire was sent to Benson and Kurr. 'D is coming down tonight, let Shanks [i.e. Benson] keep out of the way.'[22] A letter was also sent on a piece of blotting paper. It said: 'Keep the lame man out of the way at once.'[23] The writing was never identified, but Kurr later asserted that Clarke told him he had written it. The men packed their bags, Benson heading south. Kurr, who remained in Scotland, sent a telegram to Palmer's home asking for full details of Druscovich's movements, and received a reply that evening. The letters did not arrive at the hotel until the men had left and remained there for several days in the charge of the landlord.

Kurr wired Druscovich to meet him at Caledonian Station. 'Important. Come immediately on receipt of this.'[24] Druscovich arrived on 11 November and Kurr offered him £1,000 not to go to the Bridge of Allan, but the detective said he had no choice. 'He was more like a madman than anything else,' said Kurr later. 'He kept saying "Cannot I take him [Benson] and afterwards let him go?"'[25] Benson later observed that he had no intention of trusting himself to Druscovich.

Kurr went back to Derby while the talented and usually dynamic Druscovich continued the investigation, which – and this must have pained him deeply – he had to carry out as badly as possible. He dawdled for half a day and did not go to the Bridge of Allan until the afternoon, then sent a wire to Williamson saying that the men had left just before he got there. He had a watch kept on the printer's, knowing that the gang would not come near the place, and tried to convince the police at the Bridge of Allan that the meetings between Meiklejohn, Yonge and Gifford were of no importance, then sent them off on a false trail. Finally, when he returned to Edinburgh, without collecting the vital letters, he found two telegrams awaiting him from Abrahams, who was now deeply impatient with his lack of progress. Abrahams's investigations had established that Mr Yonge was the Harry Benson who had defrauded the Lord Mayor in 1871, and urged that his description should be circulated to all ports. 'You should get hold of their letters,' he instructed impatiently. 'What are you doing?'[26]

The gang next met in Derby. Kurr was anxious to retrieve the £3,500 deposited in the Scottish bank, but Meiklejohn was unwilling to go, so Murray (who had slipped back into England under an assumed name) was instructed to take his place. It was imperative that the easily identifiable Benson get out of the way, and so he sailed for Dublin.

In Scotland, a weary and ill Druscovich was obliged to collect the letters, which, he saw to his relief, did not implicate him. Returning to London on 17 November he handed them to Williamson. The superintendent was by now a very anxious man. His star officer was suspiciously lacking in drive and efficiency, and Meiklejohn had met the wanted men. When Williamson read the letters, he must have been thunderstruck. Not only did they describe the confidential orders given to Druscovich, but one letter was very obviously in the handwriting of an officer who so far he had not suspected at all, Inspector William Palmer, a solid hardworking man with twenty-two years in the force.

The letters were passed on to the Treasury Solicitor, and Williamson was asked to obtain formal reports from Meiklejohn and Druscovich, explaining their actions. Meiklejohn responded that he had gone to Scotland to inquire about a missing portmanteau, and met the fraudsters by chance. Believing the men to be respectable, he had introduced them to the banker, which he very much regretted. Druscovich's report stated only that the men escaped just before he arrived because they were elusive. Williamson, unable to take his own senior officers into his confidence, was obliged, while inquiries continued, personally to take on as much of the work of the department as he could. The only man he trusted was Clarke.

Benson, unwilling to go America as advised, sent his servant there, instructing him to send letters and cables when he arrived to give the impression that he, Benson, had gone, while in fact he returned to England and met Kurr. Kurr was a worried man, and to foil the ongoing investigations devised a new plan together with an associate, Henry Stenning, who was staying at his house. The two were of similar build, and exchanged clothes to make identification more difficult. On 28 November they learned that Murray's attempts to retrieve the money had led to his arrest, although he had been released on a technicality and was back in London. There he had managed to change two Clydesdale notes, but when he tried two more the next day the money-changers, knowing that the police had issued warnings about such notes, held on to them.

Kurr decided to employ a solicitor, Edward Froggatt, who was recommended not so much for his legal acumen as for his willingness to assist with fraudulent transactions. Froggatt, who soon realised that the money they were so anxious to change was not honestly come by, offered to get in touch with some friends who would look after it for a commission. Soon afterwards, Benson, Charles Bale and Frederick Kurr sailed for Rotterdam, where Benson booked into a hotel as George Washington Morton.

In London, Kurr felt that the 15 per cent commission demanded by Froggatt's friends was too steep, so Murray contacted another man, Savory, and a meeting was set up to arrange the transaction on 29 November. Unknown to Murray, Savory was an informant, and had invited others to the meeting: the police. Murray was arrested and Froggatt was sent to defend him. At their interview Froggatt pointed out dryly that Murray should have accepted the 15 per cent.

Soon afterwards, Kurr received very disturbing news. Benson, who must have been aware that, while a Clydesdale note was a rarity in England, it was virtually unknown in Rotterdam, had tried to change one at his hotel. On 3 December he and his companions were arrested. Kurr at once held an emergency meting with Meiklejohn and Froggatt, where they hatched a plan. A telegram was sent addressed to 'Chief of Police, Rotterdam, Holland':

Find Morton and the two men you have in custody are not those we want. Officer will not be sent over. Liberate them. Letter follows.
Williamson, Superintendent of Police, Scotland Yard[27]

Fortunately, the Dutch police decided to wait for the letter, which did not arrive. Instead, Druscovich was sent to Rotterdam with five other officers to apprehend Benson, and was obliged to wait there for the lengthy extradition proceedings to be completed. Before he departed he suggested that Kurr's house be watched. Kurr had been a suspect for some time, although he had kept so far in the background that it was hard to obtain evidence against him, and so Druscovich may well have felt safe in making that suggestion.

Froggatt also went to Rotterdam to try to bribe the Dutch authorities with £50. In this he was unsuccessful, but he learned that a French directory used by Benson to select victims and annotated in his writing had been left at an address in Hackney, and so he rushed back to England to try and get hold of it. He was too late: it was already in the possession of the police.

Kurr, who judged every man by his own dishonest standards, decided to see if Abrahams was willing to come to a compromise arrangement, and wrote him an anonymous letter, which the solicitor very wisely ignored. Kurr's eagerness to pay off Abrahams gave Froggatt a chance to make some money. He arranged for an accomplice called Sawyer to pose as Abrahams's agent, and arranged a meeting with Kurr for 31 December, when £3,000 was to be handed over, supposedly to square Abrahams and persuade the Comtesse to give up the prosecution.

The meeting did not take place. On 30 December Mr Flintoff told the police that he could identify the man who rented his offices at Northumberland Street. Consequently, a warrant was obtained for Kurr's arrest, which on the following day Williamson handed to 29-year-old Detective Sergeant (later Chief Inspector) John George Littlechild, warning him to keep the nature of the mission secret, even from his colleagues. Littlechild was puzzled, but did as advised, although he was sensible enough to take a trusted associate with him.

That evening, as three men, including Kurr and Stenning, emerged from Kurr's house, the watching detectives closed in on them and gave chase. Littlechild made after Kurr, but Stenning tried to trip him and then seized him around the body. Fortunately, Littlechild had armed himself with a stout blackthorn cudgel, and a blow on Stenning's head sent the man reeling. The detectives then darted off after their main quarry. Kurr suddenly turned, and Littlechild found himself looking down the barrel of a revolver. 'For Heaven's sake, don't make a fool of yourself,' he said. 'It means murder.' Kurr, suddenly realising what he had been about to do, replied 'I won't', and meekly allowed Littlechild to arrest him.[28] Languishing in his cell, he was alarmed to see Flintoff come in and confidently identify him. Sending for Froggatt, the two quickly cooked up a new plan to get Kurr off the hook. Stenning was sent to persuade Flintoff to change his evidence, but without success. As Flintoff came to court, Froggatt was waiting for him at the door. He told him that Kurr was 'a good fellow, a Freemason in distress',[29] and offered him £50 to declare that his identification was a mistake. But the only mistake was made by Froggatt: a Freemason's obligation to his brethren does not extend to helping them evade the law. Flintoff refused the bribe and identified Kurr in court. Froggatt and Kurr then had him prosecuted for perjury, a ploy that failed.

Littlechild was in court to hear the evidence, and spotted the familiar face of Stenning, who was promptly arrested. As he was seized, Stenning attempted to destroy a paper, which was taken from him. It was the details of an escape plan that he had been intending to pass to Kurr. Stenning was ultimately jailed for a year.

While all this was happening, Druscovich was waiting unhappily in Rotterdam for the extradition proceedings to be finalised. He received a letter there from Williamson. A Leeds police officer had visited the superintendent and mentioned the letter sent six weeks previously. Unable to find it, Williamson wanted to know if Druscovich had seen the letter. Druscovich replied that he knew nothing about it.

Druscovich was finally able to set sail for England with his charge. In a miserable private discussion with Benson he said he hoped the sides of the ship would open up and they would all go to the bottom. He knew that he was suspected, since in the twenty-five days he had been in Rotterdam no one had given him any information.

Back in England, Benson wrote a pathetic letter to his father begging for his assistance and expressing remorse for his crimes. At the same time he was writing coded messages to Kurr, hopeful that some arrangement might be made with the Comtesse to drop the case. In fact the Comtesse, who had recovered most of her money, did plead for the men to be dealt with mercifully; but at the trial that took place in April, William Kurr, his brother Frederick and Charles Bale were sentenced to ten years' imprisonment, Benson, who was regarded as the mastermind behind the plans, fifteen years, and Murray, as an accessory, eighteen months with hard labour.

While Meiklejohn and Druscovich remained under suspicion, the Home Office had not been able to prove anything against them, and it was eventually decided not to make any charges against the detectives. There the matter might have rested in an uncomfortable limbo, but Kurr and Benson still had a final card to play. Kurr had carefully retained every warning letter he had received, and in July 1877, hoping to get a reduction of his sentence, he exposed his police informants. The letters did not implicate Clarke, but Meiklejohn was soon in custody, while Clarke and Williamson personally arrested Palmer and Druscovich at Scotland Yard. Froggatt was arrested by Clarke at his own office. With all the suspects under arrest, Williamson must have thought he had no more shocks to bear, but in the magistrates' court he heard Kurr assert that Clarke had also been bribed. Williamson was obliged to arrest his old friend, and when Clarke joined his colleagues in the dock they wept. The trial attracted worldwide interest, and lasted a record twenty days. To the great mortification of the detectives, the chief witnesses against them were Benson and Kurr. Thanks largely to the clever counsel, Sir Edward Clarke, and a glowing testimonial from Chief Commissioner Edmund Henderson, Inspector Clarke was acquitted, but the others were found guilty and received sentences of two years with hard labour.

Soon afterwards Clarke retired on a pension. On their release, Meiklejohn and Druscovich became private detectives and Palmer a publican, but Druscovich, who probably never recovered either his mental or physical health, died of tuberculosis in 1881, aged 39. Froggatt was rearrested as he left prison and charged with embezzling money of which he was a trustee. He was imprisoned for seven years, and died in Lambeth Workhouse in 1889, aged 46. Williamson, his health affected by the stress of overwork, died in the same year, aged 58. Only Meiklejohn, who according to his own defence counsel 'would have corrupted a regiment',[30] was able to look the world in the eye. 'It is easy to blame a man for his shortcomings,' he claimed, 'but sometimes it is fairer to blame the circumstances behind the man.'[31] In his memoirs, which were published in 1912, he hinted that he might be able to reveal more about 'circumstances to which I can, and shall, if I am spared, give a very different colouring to that usually accepted',[32] but he never did so.

Both Benson, who gradually regained full use of his legs, and the Kurrs were eventually released and went back to their old lives of swindling, although this time in the United States, Belgium and Switzerland. On 14 January 1888 Benson was arrested in New York for a Mexico City scheme in which he had posed as the agent for opera singer Madame Patti, selling bogus tickets for a concert. In Ludlow Street Jail he awaited extradition to Mexico, which he dreaded, certain that it would mean 'extraordinary punishment'[33] and a cruel death. On 16 May 1888 he bolted away from his jail keeper and threw himself over a second floor railing. A few hours later he died of his injuries.

SEVEN

The Grappler

When Ernest Terah Hooley came to London, he was 'determined to make a million or go smash'.[1] He did both. In 1896 he was unknown; by 1897 his name was an international byword for conspicuous financial success; by 1898 he was bankrupt. There is a myth that Hooley was a commercial visionary who was able to spot those industries destined for future success, and that his only failing was his personal extravagance. In reality, Hooley had little understanding of high finance, and naïvely assumed that a boom that created rapid and illusory profits would last for ever. Many of his deals were, in his own words, 'warm [that is, dubious] to the point of sultriness',[2] though not actually illegal, but when bribery, fraud and slander were to his advantage he added these weapons to his armoury. His main talents were boundless audacity and the ability to lie copiously and without shame. His fleecing of the investing classes was something about which he remained cheerfully unrepentant to the end of his life.

Ernest Terah Hooley was born in Sneinton, Nottinghamshire, on 5 February 1859. His father, Terah, had a small lace-making business at Long Eaton. Young Ernest assisted his father and was eventually taken into partnership. The Hooleys regularly attended the Baptist chapel, where Ernest played the harmonium. He was a non-smoker and teetotaller, and was often to be heard lecturing others about the sins of alcohol, tobacco and evil speaking. The collection plate was carried by John Charles Cottam, Hooley's lifelong friend. For both men, the temptation of wealth soon overcame any moral scruples. The orphaned son of a railwayman, Cottam established himself as a company promoter. He used advertising to hike share prices to unreasonable heights, then quickly sold his holdings and walked away leaving the gullible public with worthless investments. Cottam's rash speculations resulted in his bankruptcy in 1894, but not before his early success had inspired Hooley to follow his example.

At the age of 30 Hooley told his father he was through with the lace trade. With capital of £20,000, he went to Nottingham, where he started dealing in houses, land and breweries. He had always wanted to be an old-fashioned country gentleman, and in 1888 acquired the historic house at Risley Hall and its surrounding farmlands for £5,000. Over the years he spent £100,000 on improving the property. By 1896, with £150,000 in his pocket, he found the Midlands too small for his ambition and, convinced that he had a magic touch with money, determined that from then on he would deal in millions.[3]

Together with Martin Diederich Rucker, manager of the London branch of bicycle manufacturers Humber and Co. Ltd, Hooley launched a number of subsidiaries. The mid-1890s was a time of massive speculation in the cycle trade. Cycling had become a craze, its popularity established on two crucial developments of the previous decade, the diamond-frame safety bicycle and the pneumatic tyre. Supply could not keep pace with demand. Dozens of new companies were being launched, manufacturing cycles, cycle parts and accessories, and the investing public was happy to snap up shares at a premium. In vain did the financial press utter words of caution. 'The public was in one of those rare moods when it could be swindled with impunity, and the shady promoter had a right royal time,' observed *Money* in retrospect.[4]

Rucker introduced Hooley to Alexander Meyrick Broadley, a barrister and writer, who ever since his defence of the Egyptian revolutionary Arabi Pasha in 1882 was known as Broadley Pasha. Broadley soon became Hooley's right-hand man and was able further to advance his career by introducing him into high society.

It did not take a business genius to spot that the youthful Pneumatic Tyre Company Limited (Pneumatic), which had been manufacturing the Dunlop tyre since 1889, was a good prospect. According to the anonymous author of *The Hooley Book*, it was Rucker who suggested that Hooley acquire the business. The asking price was £3 million. Hooley did not have that sum or anything approaching it, but that did not matter, because he had no intention of keeping the company. 'My great business was to buy something without the money to pay for it, sell it for as much as I could, and get out with the profit',[5] he revealed. 'I was never one to concern myself with what happened afterwards.'[6] 'Some people might say that by this method I robbed the public of millions of pounds, but nevertheless I did not do anything against the law,' claimed Hooley shortly after emerging from prison for the third time.[7]

He borrowed the money from 'colleagues of mine who, if they could not emulate me, could at least stand by in respectful admiration'.[8] The venture was planned in Ridler's, a rambling rabbit-warren of a hotel in Holborn, with dark, poky rooms where Hooley conferred with Martin Rucker, Broadley Pasha and Adolph Drucker MP, an ambitious young Dutchman with an inheritance that Hooley was happy to assist in spending. Hooley, 'alert in movement, quick of speech and impetuous in manner . . .',[9] was unable to sit still for long and dodged about jotting ideas down on scraps of paper. Artists, the financial press and advertising agents arrived, and articles and prospectuses were written and dispatched. Hooley took no chances, making large payments both in cash and shares to journalists to ensure their approval.

Many of the visitors to Ridler's were titled gentlemen, for Hooley liked to place 'ornamental directors' on the boards of companies he promoted and was willing to pay handsome inducements. These peers would later find they had been saddled with duties they had not anticipated and shares they could not sell, and that Hooley, once having disposed of the company, had no interest in either it or them. Chief among his noble 'front-sheet men' was the young Earl de la Warr, who, like many others, would learn to regret his involvement with Hooley.

Having bought Pneumatic for £3 million in a deal approved on 13 April and finalised on the 25th and added his 'names' to the Board, Hooley relaunched what was 'practically the same business'[10] as the Dunlop Pneumatic Tyre Company Limited (Dunlop) on 12 May for £5 million. It was a magnificent coup, and one that made his reputation. 'On the strength of the Dunlop "deal" Mr Hooley came to be regarded as the Napoleon of finance, at whose word capital could be created by the million and fortunes could be made as if by a magician's wand.'[11]

That the public was willing to pay such an inflated price was only partly because of the cycling craze, the massive advertising campaign and favourable articles in the financial press. Hooley also added extra value to the mix by making high publicity offers to buy out Dunlop's potential rivals, deals that he had no intention of honouring.

Pneumatic had granted licenses to the Beeston Pneumatic Tyre Company Limited (Beeston) and the Grappler Pneumatic Tyre Company Limited (Grappler) to manufacture Dunlop tyres. Neither of these companies had traded profitably. The licences were clearly worth something to Beeston and Grappler, but they were not transferable in the event of a takeover by another person. Exactly when Hooley saw the Beeston licence is unknown, but his solicitors had a copy of the Grappler licence by 6 May 1896 at the latest, six days before the Dunlop prospectus was to be published. He must therefore have known that, if he bought out these companies, he would not acquire the licences. Hooley's plan for both companies was to make a generous offer for their shares shortly before the Dunlop launch, and later to extricate himself from the deals with the excuse that the licences were not what he had supposed them to be, relying on the fact that the investing public would not have detailed information about the licences. Hooley also planned to make a personal profit, buying up Beeston and Grappler shares cheaply before making his offer, which he knew would increase their value, then quickly disposing of them before the deal collapsed. In neither case did this scheme go entirely to plan. Two years later the public exposure of Hooley's blatant share-rigging was to contribute to his eventual downfall.

On 10 April 1896 Mr Harry John Lawson, chairman and managing director of Beeston, was visiting the offices of the Humber Company when Hooley, whom he had never met, unexpectedly appeared and bought 20,000 unallocated Beeston £1 shares for £25,000. The company had traded at a loss in the preceding year but prospects were thought to be good. The next day the issued shares, which in the light of the cycle boom had been exchanging hands for £2, jumped to £4. But Hooley was far from finished with Beeston. He offered to buy out the company at an extraordinary £8 per share: 'cycle shares promise to become as inflated as the tyres', observed the *Financial Times* on 27 April as Beeston prices careered up to £6 10s. 'These same shares eighteen months ago could be procured at 3d apiece.'[12]

On 30 April the offer was discussed at an extraordinary general meeting of the shareholders. The mood of the meeting was to sell, but Lawson was against the move and spoke eloquently about the past history of the company, of the excellence of its tyre, which he claimed was better even than those made by Pneumatic, and the 'enormous' future prospects, predicting that in the following year either Beeston would buy out Dunlop or Dunlop would buy out Beeston – 'either way we will divide the trade between us'. He advised the shareholders against accepting the offer on the grounds that they would make much more in the long run: 'he thought the trade was boundless.'[13] Only a few months previously Beeston shares had been worth 1s, 'now, I may say, without being presumptuous, that if we are not doing it now, we soon shall be running neck and neck with the £5,000,000 company'.[14] A Dr Redmond responded that he had come to the meeting intending to vote to accept the offer, but Mr Lawson's speech had entirely altered his opinion. If it was worthwhile for Dunlop to offer £8, then it was worthwhile for Beeston to hold the shares. The meeting agreed and voted unanimously to reject the offer. A hearty vote of thanks for the chairman was carried with acclamation. Hooley must have been staggered at the result, but it played right into his hands, as he now had neither the trouble nor the expense of getting out of a deal he had never intended to complete.

Beeston shares continued to ride high, and Hooley further enhanced their value by backing a deal in which Beeston made a profit of £30,000 paid in shares. On 7 May, on the basis of this paper profit, Beeston declared a 100 per cent dividend of £30,000 and borrowed the necessary cash through Hooley. Meanwhile, the demand for Beeston shares had enabled Hooley to dispose of his holdings, and by 16 May he had sold all 20,000, making a personal profit of over £80,000.

The Irish-based Grappler Company had been formed in April 1893 with capital of £75,000 in £1 shares. By April 1896 a great deal of its capital had gone, it had never paid a dividend and was trading at a loss. The shares were then quoted at between 1s 9d and 4s. From that time on, however, and for no very obvious reason, the price began gradually to creep up and eventually reached the wholly unwarranted heights of 14s. Someone, it seemed, was quietly buying up Grappler shares. Although it was never proven, the buyer was almost certainly Hooley, who had arrived in Dublin with Rucker on 13 April 1896. How much Rucker knew of Hooley's real intentions regarding Grappler has never been established.

Hooley's plans appeared to be marching on without hindrance, but he reckoned without the persistent plain-speaking of Frederick Faber McCabe, editor of the *Irish Field and Gentleman's Gazette*, a weekly paper devoted to the manly pastimes of hunting, fishing, racing and cycling, with a regular financial column called 'City Notes'. McCabe focused a great deal of his attention on share dealings in the bicycle trade, and became alarmed at the Grappler developments. In March 1896, when the company tried to increase its capital by an appeal to the shareholders, the *Field* commented:

> with Irish shareholders the more unsuccessful a company has been the longer they stick to it, provided only that the directors hold out some hope, and *continue to ask* for more money. Such has been the history of the Grappler Pneumatic Tyre Company. . . . We have repeatedly told the shareholders to close their pockets to these appeals.[15]

This enraged Grappler's chairman, Joseph Tumulty. The *Field*'s city column was highly influential and its criticisms of the performance and prospects of Grappler were instrumental in slowing the rise in share prices. McCabe was at some pains to highlight those occasions where Tumulty had been sparing with the truth. While Tumulty had told the shareholders that the company was making profits, these, the *Field* pointed out, were only gross profits, that is, the difference between cost and sale price. The statement had not taken into account contingent liabilities, notably the expense of repairs carried out under guarantee.

In April rumours began to fly around Dublin, first that Mr Dunlop himself (who was long retired from the tyre business) had joined the Grappler board, then that the Grappler patents were to be bought by Pneumatic. On the basis of these rumours the shares shot up to 30s, but once the reports were found to be untrue, the price fell back to 10s. Quite who was spreading these stories was never discovered. It could have been either Hooley or Tumulty – although it was more Tumulty's style to omit unpalatable truths than to concoct lies. In any case, on 18 April the *Field* strongly advised investors to sell their Grappler shares.

On 30 April Hooley and Rucker, together with their Irish stockbroker Mr Daniel Bulger, went to the Dublin Stock Exchange, where Bulger bought up as many Grappler shares as he could. Rucker later denied that he had ever bought any such shares or even that he had understood what was going on. They then proceeded to the Grappler offices, where they met Russell Dowse, the managing director. Rucker, introducing Hooley as the man who had bought up Pneumatic, got straight to business, saying that it was no good beating about the bush but they had come to buy the company and asked that a board meeting be held. Hooley questioned Dowse about Grappler's capital and debentures, made some notes and offered to buy out the company at £4 a share, a price that caused Dowse to open his eyes wide in astonishment.

Hooley's intentions at that point may be judged from a telegram he sent on his return to London on 1 May to Mr William J. Watson, a Nottingham solicitor who had acted for him in a few small matters. 'Think you might buy yourself a few Grappler Tyre ordinaries for a sharp turn.'[16]

On the following day Hooley and Rucker met Dowse and Tumulty in the presence of Grappler's solicitor Mr Clay, at Rucker's office in Ely Place, Holborn, where Hooley repeated the offer. Four pounds was a ridiculous price, but Tumulty knew about the Beeston negotiations and thought he could get more. He was careful not to express any doubts about the licences. If Hooley thought they were valuable to him, Tumulty was not the man to argue. Eventually a price was agreed of £385,000 for all the shares and assets of the company. A deposit of £10,000 was payable, with a further £15,000 when the shareholders had confirmed the agreement.

An appointment was made for later that afternoon for Mr Hooley's solicitor to finalise the paperwork, but the solicitor did not arrive and another appointment was made for later the same day. Once again the closure of the deal foundered as Hooley wired that the solicitor could not come. Soon afterwards, Hooley sold all his Grappler shares.

The *Field* must have had good sources of information, for by 2 May its message to its readers had taken an unexpected direction. While the editor had not changed his opinions on the long-term future of Grappler, he suggested that investors who liked a gamble should buy Grappler shares for a 'short turn',[17] but understandably did not reveal his reasons. These became obvious when Hooley's solicitors, just in case no one had heard about the remarkable offer, published details in the Dublin newspapers. The share prices jumped again.

Tumulty waited for the deal to be concluded. He also waited for the deposit. An appointment was made for Hooley to go to Dublin, but he sent a telegram saying that his solicitor would be unable to attend. As time passed and nothing happened Tumulty showed himself to be more than equal to the dubious prevarications of Hooley. On 7 May, just five days before the Dunlop floatation, he wrote to Hooley through his solicitors saying that, unless the matter was settled on the following day, he would conclude that the offer was a bogus one and that it had never been the intention of Hooley and Rucker to buy the company. This he threatened to explain to the meeting of the shareholders on the following day.

Hooley called his bluff, but Tumulty was as good as his word, and the shareholders, many of whom had bought up Grappler shares for a 'short turn', heard that Hooley and Rucker were trying to get out of the bargain and had only made the offer in order to rig the market. Soon, allegations were published in the Dublin newspapers that warrants were out for Hooley's and Rucker's arrest. Telegrams flew back and forth between London and Dublin, and it became common knowledge that those people who had been induced to buy Grappler shares on the basis of the report that the company was to be sold had instituted a criminal prosecution in the event of the agreement not being signed.

Late in the evening of 11 May, Mr Clay went to see Hooley at the Midland Grand Hotel. Rucker was sent for, as was Mr du Cros, director of Pneumatic, and Hooley's solicitor. Reports of the encounter naturally vary depending on who told the story. Hooley later claimed that he and Rucker were threatened with arrest, but according to Clay he had said only that it would be a dishonourable thing for them to back out of the deal.

Clay agreed to wire Dublin on their behalf to find if there was any truth in the rumours that warrants had been issued. At first Hooley refused to sign the papers on the grounds that there was some doubt about the licences, but eventually, at 1 a.m., afraid that their arrest could ruin the Dunlop venture later that day, Hooley and Rucker signed the agreement and paid the £10,000 deposit. At 10 a.m. Clay received a wire confirming that the rumours about the warrants were untrue, but by then he had the signed agreement and the cheque.

Tumulty must have thought he had won, but the *Field* was blunt. The deal, it said, could never go through because Pneumatic did not grant transferable licences. This was the last thing either Hooley or Tumulty wanted to be made public, Hooley because this was his bargaining card for getting out of the deal at the right time, and Tumulty because he knew that the finalising of the deal would be threatened by the information. On the Stock Exchange, Grappler shares 'bounced up and down in the wildest manner',[18] rising to £4 then falling back to £1 5s.

On the morning of 12 May 1896, with a massive fanfare of advertising, the Dunlop Pneumatic Tyre Company Limited subscription list was open to the public. There was an immediate rush for shares, 4 million at £1 apiece and £1 million in debentures.

Meanwhile, Mr Tumulty was trying to finalise the Grappler sale. He was still at odds with the *Field*, which published an article on 16 May suggesting that the shareholders ought to appoint new directors, since the current ones did not understand the cycle trade. In vain did *The Economist* of the same date warn investors against companies whose shares had recently been worth a few shillings apiece and were now valued in pounds because of industriously circulated rumours.

On 27 May, by which time Grappler shares had risen to over 40s, Tumulty told a meeting of shareholders that there was no reason to believe the agreement would not be carried out, which must have been a relief, as many of them had bought in recently at high prices. The *Field*, he said, was 'a relatively unknown publication . . . either praise or censure from such a quarter is not worth noticing',[19] and promised that in a very short time the market value of the shares would be much greater. He revealed that the company had made a gross profit of £4,000 in the last four months. A voice from the floor cried out 'What are the net profits?'[20] 'I am dealing with gross only,' he responded. 'I think that is sufficient for the present purposes.' He advised the shareholders to 'hold onto your shares hard and fast'.[21] The meeting voted unanimously to ratify the agreement with Hooley and Rucker. Again, the *Field* insisted that the deal would not go through. 'Messers Rucker and Hooley are shrewd men of business, but they must have been led into error in some incomprehensible way.'[22]

At another meeting, held on 11 June to discuss the liquidation of the company in preparation for the sale, shareholders were again told to take no notice of rumours. By 20 June the second instalment of the deposit had been paid, and Tumulty was claiming that the Grappler shares were worth even more than the offer price, but there followed a long delay, and the remaining £360,000 did not appear.

On 18 July the *Field*, which had had its ear to the ground to pick up all the rumours, reported that Hooley and Rucker, claiming that the directors of Grappler had misled them as to the nature of the licence, were pulling out of the deal and taking legal action for the return of the £25,000. On reading this report, many of the shareholders sold their Grappler shares. Tumulty was furious, and on Monday 20 July he was in court obtaining permission to bring a libel action against the newspaper, which he said had written a false and malicious article with the sole intention of depreciating the shares. The case was heard on Thursday 23rd, and the *Field*, which had no supporting evidence for its allegations, was obliged to make a contrite apology, withdraw the article and pay the costs. Tumulty was triumphant, but only briefly. On 24 July Hooley's solicitors wrote to Tumulty saying that the deal would not be completed on the grounds that the nature of the licence had been misrepresented. On the 25th, the same day the *Field* published an account of its defeat in court, Tumulty was obliged to send a circular to all the shareholders advising them of the letter. The circular and the letter were published in the *Field* of 1 August entirely without comment. Grappler shares fell to 20s. The reaction of the shareholders is unrecorded. Many may have believed that they would prosper even without Hooley, and continued to ride the cycling boom as if it would never end.

Hooley's £25,000 deposit was never returned. Whether or not he made money from selling his Grappler shares at the top of the market – and it was never proven that he was behind the initial rise in share prices – his interest in the company had undoubtedly raised the value of Dunlop. As was his usual practice, he sought only to make a cash profit from the Dunlop venture and retained no personal investment in the company.

For a time the investing public was enthralled by the romance of Hooley's success. 'The daring manner in which he treated millions dazzled them,' observed the *Pall Mall Gazette*, 'and they were ready to believe that he would extend to them, by means of some strange power that they did not altogether understand, the same capacity for amassing wealth that he undoubtedly showed in his own case.'[23] It was not only the public who regarded Hooley in this light: 'the millions I had made before I was forty had turned my head,' he later admitted. 'I fondly imagined there was nothing I could not do.'[24]

Hooley now took a suite at the Midland Grand Hotel, which he established as his London centre of operations. The rooms were in a constant bustle. Everyone wanted to see Mr Hooley. He would breakfast usually with several visitors, then hurry off to examine the post. Printer's devils brought in proofs of prospectuses, lawyers arrived for consultations, wires went to and fro, transfers were effected and cheques written, with Hooley darting back and forth between the different rooms. Coordinating all this scurrying about was Broadley Pasha.

Many callers simply wanted to borrow money, others had business ideas they wanted to discuss. An American put forward a proposal to market petrol to drive the internal combustion engine, but Hooley did not think the idea had a future and turned him down. Large numbers of visitors were invited to stay to lunch, and there were sometimes several groups eating at the same time, all at Hooley's expense. At breakfast the tables were laden with fruit, eggs, fish, cutlets, kidneys and bacon. This was repeated, with the addition of expensive wines, for lunch and dinner, with snacks in between. Less welcome to Hooley was the assembly of anxious nobility in the corridor, who sent 'imploring messages asking to see him, but he treats them with contempt. Once he has got from them all he wants they are of no further use, let them . . . "go off the board" . . . if they are dissatisfied, there are others to take their places.'[25]

Most of his 1896 flotations were cycle companies, including Singer in June, but in August he was offered the chance of acquiring Bovril. The company, while recognising its international possibilities, had concentrated its efforts on developing the home market. J. Lawson Johnston, the industrious Scotsman credited with the invention of Bovril, and who was certainly the man responsible for its success, must have been seriously misled by someone when he put before the shareholders Hooley's offer to buy the company for £2 million. 'The new ship will of course embody, in an enhanced degree, all the advantages of the old one, *plus* Mr Hooley's well-known financing facilities and singular capacity for exploiting subsidiary companies the world over . . . We are not financiers: Mr Hooley is; and we must conclude that the business, *plus* Mr Hooley will be capable of much greater things than it could possibly be without him.'[26] Hooley's business acumen was, as would be seen, illusory, and even if it had been genuine he certainly did not intend to use it for the benefit of Bovril. The resolution to sell was carried unanimously on 13 October, and six weeks later Bovril (British Foreign and Colonial) (Limited) was offered at £2,500,000. *The Times*, concerned about the glowing estimates of future profits, commented:

> A short while ago the business of the old Bovril Company was sold to Mr ET Hooley for £2,000,000, and it is now offered to the public, and incidentally to the old shareholders, for £2,500,000. We must assume, we suppose, that something has happened to add 25 per cent to the value of the concern since the beginning of October, though it is not easy to imagine what it can be.[27]

In May 1897 Hooley added another famous name to his portfolio: Schweppes. He was then at the height of his success and was determined to live up to it. He had already bought a yacht, the *Verena*, for £5,000, not because he was interested in yachting but because it was the thing to do. He now found that the splendid Risley Hall had become 'too small to satisfy my ambitious tastes',[28] and so he bought Papworth Hall Estate in Cambridgeshire for £70,000. As the farms were in poor condition, he bought out the farmers, ejected them and farmed the land himself. Naturally he had to have the best of everything. He spent £250,000 in renovations, £40,000 in furniture and paintings, and £14,500 stocking the cellars with fine wines and cigars for his visitors. 'The lavish manner in which I spent my money made me the most popular man in England,' he claimed.[29] 'The public fairly hungered for news of my latest extravagance.'[30]

A great believer in the flamboyant gesture, he once bought 200 tons of linseed cake and sent the same number of carts to St Ives to bring it back, the horses decorated with red, white and blue ribbons. 'I was the greatest advertiser the world has ever known,' he declared; 'the more they talked about me the more they bought shares when I floated a company.'[31] One or two farms were not enough, however, and ultimately he owned about twenty. He later estimated that he was living at the rate of £100,000 per year, of which £10,000 was losses on farming.

Soon after moving in to Papworth he met the under-sheriff of Cambridgeshire and Huntingdonshire, which gave him the idea of becoming sheriff himself. Enquiries were made, strings were pulled, and no doubt money changed hands. Within three months of his arrival Hooley was high sheriff and deputy lieutenant of the two counties, and a magistrate. He was also able to acquire the position of lieutenant of the City of London, a nominal post that required him on public occasions to wear a uniform consisting of a scarlet tunic, blue trousers, a tricorn hat with a white plume and a sword. Some of his titled acquaintances thought he should have a London residence, so he rented 33 Hill Street, Mayfair, for £2,000 per annum, where he entertained all-comers. 'I made millions and I spent them as though my wealth was inexhaustible,' he said later.[32]

This reckless extravagance also informed his business life. He often entered into contracts only to back out of them, and was therefore obliged to pay compensation. He was not the only man to pay newspapers to 'puff' his promotions, but the sums he offered were foolishly large. Later he claimed that he had been blackmailed. Other people preferred to see it as bribery.

Whether or not a financial genius, Hooley was now well enough known to feature as such in music hall and pantomime songs:

> He walks into the Stock Exchange, and everybody there
> Cries 'Look out! Here comes Hooley, the famous millionaire!'
> He can buy a share for twopence, and sell it for a pound,
> When he's bought St Paul's Cathedral, he'll buy the Underground.

> It's Hooley this, and Hooley that, and Hooley everywhere,
> And it's 'here comes Mr Hooley, the famous millionaire!'[33]

His reputation for being able to conjure up money had spread abroad. Early in 1897 he was approached by an American visitor representing a syndicate who wanted to raise a loan to purchase Cuba, the amount being between $150,000,000 and $200,000,000 (about £30 to £40 million today): 'the Americans had read so much about [Hooley] in the papers they must have thought him capable of anything'.[34] Even Hooley knew that the Cuba loan was too big for him, but in August 1897 he was tempted by an approach from the Chinese government asking if he could provide a loan of £16,000,000. A possible £1 million was payable in commission. Excited by the vista that opened before him, Hooley sent agents to China to open negotiations. For two months it looked as though the deal was as good as settled, when quite suddenly it fell through: the arch-bluffer had been bluffed. The Chinese had probably always intended to borrow from the

Hong Kong and Shanghai Bank and had sought an advantage by playing off one negotiator against another.

Hooley's ultimate ambition was to enter parliament and become Minister of Agriculture. In March 1897 he was adopted as Conservative candidate for Ilkeston, and a handsome donation to party funds ensured his admission to the Carlton Club. He was also hoping for a baronetcy in the Queen's Diamond Jubilee honours list. Since he did not think it would come to him for nothing, he decided to purchase it with good works. He made a donation of a solid gold communion set, profusely decorated with cherubs, to St Paul's Cathedral (later restoration considerably simplified the design, which had made it impossible to clean) and made a great splash with newspaper interviews about setting up a Jubilee charity fund. He claimed to have set aside £400,000, the annual income of which, amounting to £15,000, would be devoted to the relief of the poor in his district. In fact he did not set aside the money, since 'fortunately for me nobody felt inclined to come forward and demand the payment of the full amount forthwith', he admitted. 'Everybody believed me in those days, which was just as well.'[35]

Shortly before the Jubilee he promised to give £10,000 to the Nottingham General Hospital Victoria Fund provided that a corresponding sum was subscribed in Nottingham. Hooley had provided £2,000, and, as the collection approached its target, the committee asked for the remainder. The Jubilee over, and no baronetcy in sight, Hooley did not see why he should part with any more money and tried to claim that he had only promised to match funds subscribed by working men. After prolonged and acrimonious negotiations, in December 1897 Hooley was eventually obliged to provide a further £5,220. It must have been a wrench, for by then his account with Lloyds Bank was overdrawn. Careless extravagance in both his personal and business life had finally taken its toll.

Hooley's reputation was safe as long as the businesses he promoted did well and people were willing to pay inflated prices, but by May 1897 the cycle boom was ending. Foreign imports and overproduction meant that supply began to exceed demand. Even if Hooley took no interest in a company after he had floated it, city analysts were beginning to take a critical look at his record. In July *The Economist* was reporting that the market in cycle shares had been at a low ebb for some time and many of the companies that had been floated at the height of the boom were unsaleable. Not only had Dunlop shares declined in value, but other industries had suffered – the £1 Bovril shares stood at 17s and Schweppes also saw its premiums shrinking. 'In the past, no doubt, the mere fact that Mr Hooley was known to be interesting himself in any joint-stock undertaking acted as a powerful lever in the movements of prices. . . . But this personal influence is distinctly on the wane.'[36] *The Economist* was less surprised at the shrinkages as 'that there should ever have been any premiums upon capital which were obviously greatly inflated at the outset'.[37] By August it was reporting that 'people here have learned to look askance upon Mr Hooley's peculiar method of regenerating home industrial undertakings by loading them with heavy additions to their capital accounts that represent nothing but the intermediary profits of himself and his financial associates'.[38]

The Beeston Tyre Company did not survive the downturn and went into liquidation in the following year. Grappler survived a little longer and was eventually reconstructed as New Grappler, with Mr Tumulty still in the chair.

As 1898 opened, Hooley was still riding high in public opinion. A supplement called 'Men of Millions' published by the *Financial Times* in February described him as 'a young man who has come upon the City during the last two or three years like a whirlwind, and literally carried all before him'.[39] His close associates had by now realised that his day was almost done, and the early months of 1898 were unhappy ones in which he did very little business and saw court cases erode his reputation. Many of the visitors to the Midland Grand were creditors, and so Hooley stayed away, preferring to hold business meetings at the Hotel Victoria.

On 12 February, despite knowing that he was on the brink of bankruptcy, Hooley was at Wolferton stud farm near Sandringham with the Prince and Princess of Wales, the Duke of York and an array of earls, lords and ladies, where he bought a brood mare for 360 guineas and was narrowly outbid on his offer of 1,100 guineas for the popular filly Sea Breeze. His outward good humour was a mask for anxiety about a pressing load of litigation, but for a time his reputation was enough to ensure that, when charged with fraud, he would be given the benefit of any reasonable doubt.

On 27 March Thomas Bayley MP brought an action against Hooley for false representation. He had bought some shares in a Hooley promotion, Fairbanks Wood Rim, on the strength of a draft prospectus which had portrayed a substantial factory premises. The final prospectus as issued to the public showed that the company occupied only a small part of that impressive building. The shares had been purchased from a Mr Thomas

Lambert, who denied that he was acting as an agent for Hooley, and as a result the case was dismissed.

In Dublin on 8 May a Mr J.H. Naylor, licensed vintner, brought an action for conspiracy to defraud against a group of alleged co-conspirators – Hooley, Harvey du Cros, the managing director of Dunlop, Hooley's stockbroker, Bulger, and Frederick McCabe of the *Field*. The action was to recover damages for fraudulent misrepresentation on the formation and floating of the Component Tube Company. This was a small concern that Hooley had bought and then dismissed from his memory; subsequently, in November 1896, Bulger and McCabe had taken over the promotion from Hooley. It was alleged that three of the contracts mentioned in the prospectus were fictitious, and the claim that the company was prosperous was false. Hooley, although served with a subpoena, failed to attend court and later protested that he had nothing to do with the wording of the prospectus. The court found for the defendants.

Adolph Drucker MP, whose lack of business acumen and fondness for alcohol had led Hooley to regard him as a fool who could be milked of his money, finally saw the light and on 10 May sued Hooley for fraudulent misrepresentation. Hooley had offered to relieve Drucker of some 'practically worthless'[40] shares in return for others he claimed were worth £8,000. Drucker later found that Hooley had been selling the supposedly worthless shares at a profit, while those he had received in exchange were unsaleable. Drucker had gone to see Hooley to demand his shares back. Hooley refused, but suggested that if Drucker would call upon him the next day he would 'fix things up'.[41] Drucker later received a telegram from Hooley saying that he could do nothing for him. The court took the view that, while Drucker had made a bad business deal, there was no evidence of fraud.

If Hooley had forgotten all about the unfortunate shareholders in Grappler, they had certainly not forgotten about him. On 17 May Mr Robert C. Reid, a Belfast merchant, brought an action again Hooley and Rucker, claiming damages for 'fraudulent conspiracy' and 'fraudulent misrepresentations' aimed at inducing him to buy shares in Grappler.[42] In 1896 Reid had read in the newspapers about Hooley's offer for Grappler and had bought 100 shares at prices ranging between 37 and 50s. In May 1898 Grappler shares were being quoted at 6s.

Counsel for the plaintiff was Sir Edward Clarke QC. When he revealed Hooley's and Rucker's offer to buy Grappler shares at £4, a burst of laughter was heard in court. There could be only two explanations, said Clarke.

'Either they wanted, having got hold of a lot of shares, to create a market, so that they could get rid of them at a profit, or secondly, that they had got hold of some secret information regarding the prospects of the company and were anxious to secure a good thing.' Sir Edward suggested that the former was the true explanation.[43]

Crucial to the defence was whether Tumulty had misled Hooley and Rucker into believing that Grappler's licence was transferable had Hooley bought the company. Cross-examined by Hooley's counsel, Mr Stanger, Tumulty admitted that at the time of the meeting in early May 1896 he had known about Hooley's Dunlop venture and was well aware of the importance of establishing a monopoly over licences to produce Dunlop tyres. Asked if he had told Hooley and Rucker that the Grappler licence was unconditional, he replied evasively: 'I cannot say that I put it that way.'[44]

Clarke was also careful to question Hooley about the Beeston Tyre offer. Either of the cases examined in isolation might have been looked at leniently, but together there was evidence of a systematic campaign to rig the market, and the court cannot have been unaware of the other cases against Hooley, both those in which he had been given the benefit of the doubt and those still pending.

In his summing-up the Lord Chief Justice made the point that the case was of far greater importance to the defendants than to the plaintiff, in that, if the verdict went against Hooley and Rucker, 'they would not be entitled hereafter to the reputation and character of honourable men'.[45] The most important question the jury had to consider was whether the agreement to purchase was *bona fide*. The one thing that 'passed his comprehension' was how the agreement 'could have been come to with the assent of any legal mind. . . . there had, in fact been no real investigation as to whether there was a licence at all or not.'[46]

On the third day of the trial, the jury, who must have felt their responsibilities weighing upon them heavily, retired shortly before 5 p.m. At 5.10 p.m. they sent out a note: they were unable to agree. The Lord Chief Justice asked if counsel would take a majority verdict, but Stanger said he did not think so and the foreman thought there was no possibility of an agreement after further discussion. The jury was discharged. It was a victory for Hooley, but a brief and bitter one. More than any other case, the Grappler dispute, which was reported in detail, exposed the unpalatable foundations of his dealings: 'the case has thrown such a strong light upon the financial methods of Mr Hooley and his associates that it has naturally attracted a large amount of public attention,' commented *The Economist*.[47]

Although Hooley was victorious over Naylor, the Component Tubes case gathered momentum as increasing numbers of shareholders sought compensation. In mid-May it was reported that nine new actions had commenced and another seventy were pending. By 2 June there were 150, and the numbers were still growing.

On 27 May the *Pall Mall Gazette* published a devastating analysis of the performance of Hooley promotions. 'Do the public realise what they have lost by reposing confidence in Mr Hooley?' it asked,[48] providing a tabulated list of seventeen companies floated by Hooley that showed a loss in value of £4,300,000 on a total capital of £8,500,000, while shares in other Hooley-promoted companies were unsaleable. The fault was not entirely a result of the downturn in the cycle trade. 'Over-capitalisation has been the bane of nearly every concern touched by this particular promoter.'[49] The public had already come to the same conclusion. None of Hooley's 1898 promotions was successful. In two cases, the take-up of shares was so poor that the subscriptions had to be repaid.

By the end of May Hooley had been warned not to draw from his account at Lloyds Bank, but he took no notice and a number of small cheques were returned. He was asked for an immediate settlement of £3,000 for work done to one of his estates. The man who had once dealt in millions was unable to pay. The Component Tubes writs were piling up – there were eventually to be over 300 – and there was only one way to cock a snook at his creditors: on 8 June Ernest Terah Hooley filed for bankruptcy. To those in the know, the only surprise was that it had happened earlier than expected.

The Economist commented:

Mr Hooley, on his own showing, was very far from being a financial genius. He had a certain boldness of conception, but he was entirely lacking in organising and directing power, and although he obtained millions of profits out of his flotations, at the expense of the public, he became a mere channel through which those profits found their way into the pockets of much cleverer people than himself. Whatever the investigation does, it has undoubtedly shattered the idea that Mr Hooley was a serious financier.[50]

There was initially some public sympathy for Hooley. At the Palace Theatre Miss Julie Macey sang:

Terah–rah Hool–ey–ay!
Terah–rah Hool–ey–ay!
Tear not your wool–I–ay!
Don't fret and mope–I–ay!
But live and hope–I–ay!
You may yet rule–I–ay!
Terah–rah Hool–ey–ay! [51]

There were suggestions that the St Paul's communion set should be handed back to help pay off Hooley's creditors, but Canon Scott-Holland wrote:

Hooley represented a more genial and rowdy type of daylight gambling; popular, loud, open-handed, showing his hand, sharing his spoils, working hard for his money, with a strange perverted British–Philistine belief in the rightness of his cause. There is nothing sinister or crafty about the man. . . . He simply uses, with blunt force, all the advantages which a loose money-market allows him . . . [52]

Hooley's explanation for his plight was that he had been too generous to others, had paid away huge sums in blackmail, and had been 'surrounded by incompetent men'.[53] He remained confident that he would win over the public again, although when a *Telegraph* reporter asked about the man who bought shares on the strength of his name, 'Well, he was a fool,' said Mr Hooley, curtly. 'That's the truth.'[54] Unsurprisingly, his legal representatives warned him to give no more interviews.

Mr Brougham, the Official Receiver, soon found he had some difficulties. Hooley's books of account were 'imperfect and incomplete'.[55] There was no proper cash book, no ledger showing the dealings with his creditors, no account of his personal expenses and drawings, neither had he 'prepared a profit and loss account or balance sheet at any time'.[56] 'I suppose I might as well admit', Hooley confessed in his 1924 memoirs, 'that I never made the slightest attempt to keep any proper books.'[57] The claims against him, most of which he repudiated, exceeded the value of his estate by about £1 million.

When Hooley appeared at his public examination before Mr Registrar Hood, it was with a cheerful determination that, if he had been ruined, then he was going to take everyone else with him. Declaring that the chief cause of his failure was the withdrawal of capital by Rucker, he claimed to have paid substantial amounts to his associates in inducements, inflated commissions and bribes, and he was happy to stand in court and name names. On the Dunlop promotion alone, he said he had paid away £50,000 to Earl de la Warr, of which half was for distribution to other directors. His solicitors had received £20,000 each, and he had spent £63,000 on supplying newspaper representatives with options to buy shares at par. Some of these claims were probably true – the counterfoil of a cheque for £1,250 bore the legend 'quieting papers generally on the pneumatic'.[58] He also claimed to have paid the *Financial Post* £1,000 for the privilege of writing his own article, which the editor immediately denied, and indeed the correspondence pages of *The Times* were, for a period, filled with letters from solicitors, nobility, the press and many others who had had dealings or acquaintance with Hooley, angrily denying either that they had been paid anything at all, or stating that money received had been for demonstrable *bona fide* business purposes. J. Lawson Johnson announced that, so far from receiving money from Hooley as alleged, he and his co-director had advanced Hooley funds of £130,000. Earl de la Warr was especially aggrieved. He had taken his duties as a director seriously and had had to chair meetings of angry shareholders in cycle companies Hooley had promoted. He said that he had not received anything like the sums Hooley said he had paid, and those he had received he considered he had earned.

Hooley's accusations were so numerous that Hood departed from the usual practice in bankruptcy hearings and permitted those men who had been named to appear in court and make their denials. This happened on 10 August, when Mr Hooley was absent on grounds of ill health. Mr Mackworth Praed of Lloyds Bank commented that on one occasion when Hooley came to the bank for an advance he had said: 'You know, Mr Praed, that I have lied to everybody, but have always told you the truth.'[59]

On 28 July Rucker went to see Hooley at the Brunswick Hotel, in response to a telegram requesting him to do so. Hooley, representing that his wife and children were in danger of starving, said that unless the Humber directors helped him he would 'make it very hot for them'[60] on his next examination. A payment of £1,500 was ultimately agreed, but four days later Hooley claimed in open court that he had been approached by Earl de la Warr, Rucker, Broadley and Bradshaw, a broker and creditor, on behalf of the Humber directors, who offered him a bribe to commit perjury. He also accused Broadley of having diverted company money to his own use. All four gentlemen were subject to an order to commit them to prison for contempt of court.

Mr Justice Wright commented on Hooley:

so far as I have had an opportunity of observing him in the box on this and other occasions . . . he is not a witness on whose evidence it would be safe to rely. He is rash, reckless and inaccurate, and sometimes seems to be under illusions which he treats in his evidence as if they were real. So much that is unfounded is mixed up with what is true in his statements that it is hopeless to attempt to disentangle what is true from what is not.[61]

The case against Bradshaw was dismissed for lack of evidence, and Broadley and de la Warr were simply asked to pay costs. Rucker had undoubtedly agreed to pay Hooley money, though Wright, accepting Rucker's explanation, was obliged to wonder if an offer of money to induce someone to tell the truth was indeed a contempt of court. Rucker was fined £200.

On 1 March 1899 Mr Brougham submitted a report revealing that ledger number 1, which recorded Hooley's dealings with 'certain persons' and last seen in his possession in February 1898, was missing, and books 2 and 3 had been clumsily renumbered to conceal its absence. Ledger 2 – now renumbered 1 – which contained details of the Beeston deal, had been removed from the London office by Hooley in April 1898 and was nowhere to be found. A cash book had been recopied omitting all reference to the missing ledgers, the new pages rebound in the old covers. A petty cashbook and a diary for 1898 both seemed to have been destroyed, and the counterfoils for some cheques had been cut out. Hooley, he said, had 'concealed, destroyed mutilated or falsified . . . certain books or documents' and he recommended that 'an order should be made to prosecute the bankrupt accordingly'.[62] Ultimately, however, for reasons that were never made clear, the Treasury took no action against Hooley. Perhaps there were too many titled gentlemen who did not want their names mentioned in court. The estate was not realised until May 1903, when, after expenses were paid and mortgages redeemed, the 355 unsecured creditors eventually got a payout of 4s 4d in the £1.

Hooley was able to retain both Risley and Papworth, which he claimed had been transferred to his wife as presents by some friends, and lived the comfortable life of a country gentleman, although he often complained that all his aristocratic friends had deserted him, for reasons he seemed unable to comprehend. He bought and sold estates in the names of nominees, and had resolved to have no more to do with company promotions, but in 1900 the lure of millions proved too strong and he bought out a number of companies which he claimed would win him back everything he had lost.

In 1903 an investment unexpectedly matured. Adolph Drucker, who had been made bankrupt in 1901, had declined into alcoholism. Some years earlier his associates had used a crooked agent to insure his life for £100,000, but they soon found the premiums too expensive. Just as the policy was about to expire, Hooley had agreed to take it on, and thought no more about it. In December 1903 Drucker collapsed in a New York street, and died shortly afterward in hospital. Allegations that he had been murdered were later believed to be unfounded. Hooley described the incident as 'the best bit of luck I've had in years'.[63] The luck was short-lived. His new businesses failed, and in 1904, after selling shares in a worthless gold mine, he was tried for conspiracy to defraud, but was acquitted.

Hooley had agreed to provide the trustee of his estate, Duncan Basden, with regular financial statements, but by 1911 Basden realised that these would never be forthcoming and he had Hooley committed to Brixton Prison for five weeks for contempt of court. Hooley was obliged to sell Papworth Hall. In 1912 he was in court again on a charge of obtaining a £2,000 advance on a land deal with a fraudulent statement. Extraordinarily, given his long career, this was the first time he was found guilty of fraud, and he was sent to Wormwood Scrubs, where he served nine months. He observed: 'though I knew that a sentence of imprisonment practically meant the end of my career, I was philosophical enough to realise in my heart of hearts that I was more sinned against than sinning.'[64] There were then claims against him of £250,000 for property deals he had been unable to complete. 'I had no money to pay any of my creditors, and, furthermore, I hadn't the slightest intention of finding any,' he wrote.[65] Hooley became bankrupt again, and was obliged to sell the Risley estate.

Despite these setbacks, in 1919 he was once again entertaining in style at the Midland Grand Hotel. This time it was the boom in cotton that had attracted his attention, and he floated Jubilee Cotton Mills Ltd, a company whose failure landed him in court once again in 1922 on charges of conspiracy to defraud. He was sentenced to three years in prison and became bankrupt for the third time.

Martin Rucker's career had also declined. The large sums he had received during his association with Hooley were squandered in unwise speculations, and he became a commission agent selling patents from an office in Fenchurch Street. In 1905 he filed for bankruptcy. He died in 1922, aged 67.

When Hooley came out of Parkhurst in 1924 he declared that if he had his time over again he would live the same life. He saw himself as a great public benefactor: 'if I had done a certain amount of harm to my fellow-beings, at any rate I had also done a very considerable amount of good.'[66] 'I am the man who put cycling all over the world,' he claimed,[67] and by setting the fashion of appointing ornamental directors, 'I saved many a noble family from ruin.'[68] Even in prison he had obtained some consolation from the thought that 'I had left my mark on the history of the world. . . . I boomed the pneumatic tyre, I had a great deal to do with the coming into being of the motor car. . . . it was I who established Bovril as a world-wide food.'[69]

Hooley's actual impact on society, stated the editor of *Money*, was that 'thousands of investors are now saddled with shares bought at a high price which are now either unsaleable or only realisable at alarming discounts'. He continued:

The common type of the genus promoter is a plausibly clever person, of small education, and a large amount of self-conceit. He deals in but one commodity – money – the very lowest form of industry. His plan of operations is to buy something – it does not matter what – at a very low price, and to sell it for a high one. He may pose as the heaven sent friend of the inventor or as the man who lays the foundation of a new industry. In reality he adds nothing to the world's wealth, nor one iota to its productiveness. . . . His one mistake is that he never knows when to stop.[70]

Hooley continued dealing in a small way almost to the end of his life, although his final years saw him in very reduced circumstances. No longer the owner of a landed estate, he had returned to his roots and was living at 197 College Street, Long Eaton. His fourth and final examination for bankruptcy took place shortly after his eightieth birthday, when he cut a somewhat pathetic figure. Reminded of his glory days, he commented: 'I have descended in the financial world since then.'[71] He was still running a small property-dealing business five years later. He died in 1947, aged 88.

Whether the public learned caution from Hooley and his like is doubtful. The editor of *Money* further commented: 'When the Hooley fiasco has been forgotten the next big promoter will be able to do the same thing, and to do it with impunity. A new generation of investors will have arisen who knew not Hooley, and the same game will be played out with another set of puppets.'[72]

EIGHT

The Greatest Liar on Earth

In the spring of 1898 a thin, shabbily dressed middle-aged man visited the Southampton Street offices of the *Wide World Magazine*. With him he had a letter of introduction from Australian-born John (later Sir John) Henniker Heaton MP, which he presented to the editor, William Fitzgerald. His name, declared the visitor, was Louis de Rougemont. Timidly, he said he understood that the magazine published true stories of adventure and wondered if his was of any interest. He thought not, as unfortunately he had nothing in writing. The stranger was sunburnt, with piercing eyes set in a rugged, heavily lined face, and Fitzgerald, sensing that the man might have a story worth hearing, invited him to stay. He was not disappointed. Once launched into his tale, de Rougemont had a dramatic and eloquent manner of speaking which at once commanded attention. He spoke of the mysterious silent spaces of uncharted Australia, dangerous exploits by land and sea, and almost thirty years spent in the wilderness living with tribes of cannibals. Surviving shipwreck, battles, thirst and disease, he had become a great chief, taken an aboriginal wife, rescued two white girls from the doom of a horrible slavery, discovered a lost explorer and wandered the most inhospitable wastes known to man.

Exciting as this was, Fitzgerald did not at once rush into print. The *Wide World Magazine*, an 'illustrated monthly of true narrative, adventure, customs and sport', had commenced publication in April, with the motto 'Truth is Stranger than Fiction' and the promise 'There will be no fiction in the magazine, but yet it will contain stories of weird adventure, more thrilling than any conceived by the novelist in his wildest flights'.[1] The first edition contained such articles as 'The Romance of Seal Hunting' and 'Queer Sights in China'. The founder, Sir George Newnes, had made his name with *Tit-Bits* in 1881, an instant popular success, and had followed this with the *Review of Reviews* and *Strand Magazine*. He had an instinctive appreciation of what the general reader would enjoy: it was he who had recognised the potential of the Sherlock Holmes stories and bought up every one for the *Strand*. He was sent so many articles about foreign adventure that he realised that there was enough interest and material for another periodical; and so the *Wide World Magazine* was born.

Questioned at length in the Southampton Street offices, de Rougemont remained consistent and convincing, but before publication it was essential to test the truth of his story. Fitzgerald, with no expert knowledge of his own, now made his first serious error. He called in Dr John Scott Keltie and Dr Hugh R. Mill, respectively the secretary and librarian of the Royal Geographical Society, to interview de Rougemont and verify his tale. Unfortunately, neither of these eminent men had visited Australia or had expertise in Australian geography or anthropology. They met de Rougemont several times, conversing with him for about two hours on each occasion, and finally expressed their opinion that he could have acquired his knowledge of the region and its people only through personal experience.

Over a period of weeks, de Rougemont made regular visits to the offices of *Wide World Magazine*, recounting his story, which was recorded in shorthand and subsequently became a series of ten articles. While it was never divulged how much he was paid for his memoirs, from that time on de Rougemont no longer looked shabby and was able to dine in style.

The first instalment appeared in issue number five, dated August 1898, which went on sale in the third week of July. 'The Adventures of Louis de Rougemont' was given the status of a leading article, which the editor introduced as

the most amazing story a man ever lived to tell. . . . it will be obvious that after his thirty years' experience as a cannibal chief in the wilds of unexplored Australia, his contributions to science will be simply above all price. He has already appeared before such eminent geographical experts as Dr J. Scott-Keltie [*sic*] and Dr Hugh R. Mill, who have heard his story and checked it by means of their unrivalled collection of latest reports, charts and works of travel. These well-known experts are quite satisfied that not only is M de Rougemont's narrative perfectly accurate, but that it is of the very highest scientific value. . . . we have absolutely satisfied ourselves as to M de Rougemont's accuracy in every minute particular.[2]

Keltie and Mill were a little alarmed to see their names used in this way, since neither of them had vouched for the accuracy of every detail of de Rougemont's story as suggested by the overenthusiastic editor; nevertheless, they saw no reason to doubt the astonishing tale that was unfolding.

De Rougemont claimed to have been born in Paris in 1844, where his father was 'a prosperous man of business'.[3] He stated that he had later moved to Switzerland, where he learned English from English schoolboys. At the age of 19 he left home to travel in search of adventure. In Singapore he joined the pearl-fishing expedition of the Dutchman Peter Jensen, in a 40-ton schooner, the *Veielland*, with forty Malay divers who worked from small 'cockleshell' boats, and a dog called Bruno. After a busy season they had amassed pearls to the value of £50,000 and 30 tons of oyster shells. The greatest enemy of the divers was the 'dreaded octopus'.[4] One man, pursued in the water by an immense black specimen, scrambled back into his boat, when 'to the horror of the onlookers it extended its great flexible tentacles, enveloped the entire boat, man and all, and then dragged the whole down into the crystal sea'.[5] The illustrator Alfred Pearse, guided by de Rougemont's description, obliged the reader with a dramatic picture of a man in the grip of an octopus very much larger than himself. Calling at New Guinea to replenish stores, Jensen offended the tribesmen, and soon the schooner was under attack from twenty fully equipped war canoes, the men armed with bows and arrows. Battle ensued, but the guns and grapeshot of the pearlers drove the natives away. One fateful morning in July 1864 de Rougemont had been left on the schooner with only Bruno for company while Jensen and the Malays fished for pearls, when a hurricane swept away his companions and carried off the sails and much of the deck structures of the ship, including the wheel. Left 'alone on a disabled ship in the limitless ocean'[6] with little experience of seamanship, de Rougemont was nevertheless able to make repairs and sail the craft single-handed for two weeks. Drawn close to some rocks, he feared he would be wrecked, but he was able to push the 40-ton boat with its 30 tons of oyster shells away from the rocks with a single oar. He survived another native attack, this time with boomerangs, but the ship finally foundered on a reef, and, swimming for a sand-spit, the adventurer was saved by the indefatigable and faithful Bruno, who first pulled him along by his hair and then allowed his master to grasp the end of his tail in his teeth and tugged him along, a feat that did not in any way impede his ability to swim. The desolate sand-spit, 100yd long by 10yd wide, was to be their home for the next two and a half years. De Rougemont built a small boat, but he would not entrust it to the open sea. Recovering stores from the ship, he was able to build a house from oyster shells, plant corn in a turtle shell containing sand moistened with turtle blood, eat fish caught for him by obliging pelicans and condense an adequate supply of fresh drinking water from a single kettle.

I also played the part of Neptune in a very extraordinary way. I used to wade out to where the turtles were, and on catching a big six hundred pounder, I would calmly sit astride on his back. Away would swim the startled creature, mostly a foot or so below the surface. When he dived deeper I simply sat far back on the shell, and then he was forced to come up. I steered my queer steeds in a curious way. When I wanted my turtle to turn to the left, I simply thrust my foot into his right eye, and *vice-versâ* for the contrary direction. My two big toes placed simultaneously over both his optics caused a halt so abrupt as almost to unseat me.[7]

This first thrilling instalment ended with the arrival on the sand-spit of a catamaran carrying unconscious human figures. The editor inserted an additional notice saying that 'The Adventures' were 'a serial of unique importance and interest, which will run for several months. You would therefore do well to order subsequent copies in advance.'[8]

There was no doubt that *Wide World Magazine* had struck gold with 'The Adventures of Louis de Rougemont'. The sensational stories, written in a bold confident and eminently readable style, appealed to readers of all ages and all walks of life. It was as if a genuine Robinson Crusoe had returned to civilisation with thrilling tales made all the more compelling by being true, and, better still, the man himself was actually living in their very midst. The magazine was soon deluged with enquiries from people wanting to see the adventurer in the flesh. Anyone who could pack a lecture hall was assured of a good income, and Fitzgerald could also see that the popularity of his new discovery would boost sales of the magazine. Carried away on a roller-coaster of enthusiasm, neither he, de Rougemont or Newnes stopped to consider the wisdom of leaping from the world of popular consumer science into the more stringent realms of academia. If de Rougemont's tales had remained as articles, all might have gone well; had he ventured only into the public lecture halls, his career would have been rather longer than it in fact turned out to be. Fitzgerald's error was to offer two de Rougemont talks to the annual conference of the British Association for the Advancement of Science, which was to take place in September in Bristol; and the Association's error was to accept them.

At the end of August a second instalment of 'The Adventures' was printed, even more fascinating than the first. Once de Rougemont had restored the natives on the catamaran to health (a woman called Yamba, her husband and two boys), the home-made boat was got into trim, and, leaving the pearls buried in the sand-spit, they were able to return to the mainland, where de Rougemont's life with the tribe was to commence. A huge feast was prepared in his honour, and he was offered a native wife, a young girl, but it was Yamba whose intelligence and resourcefulness had impressed him and he offered his new wife to her husband in exchange:

Ah! Noble and devoted creature! The bare mention of her name stirs every fibre of my being with love and wonder. Greater love than hers no creature ever knew, and not once but a thousand times did she save my wretched life at the risk of her own.[9]

Curiously, though his native language was French, he chose to teach Yamba English. Food was plentiful; he dined on kangaroo, emu, snakes, rats, fish and a kind of worm, which he ate grilled. Having already astonished the natives with his clothing, his boat and mirror, he felt it was important that he should excel in everything he did. Using a tomahawk and a harpoon that he had salvaged from the ship and whose cold metal fascinated the natives, he took up hunting dugong (a large sea-mammal) and dried the flesh to use in later expeditions. Readers interested in tribal customs must have thrilled to read about the nightly corroborees, when, decorating their bodies with paint and feathers, the tribesmen danced or chanted songs, and the hunting parties, when they stalked kangaroos, speared fish or trapped emus, and which were followed by great gorging feasts.

By now, de Rougemont's claims were coming under the close scrutiny of Australians living in Great Britain. In September one of these, calling himself 'an Australian', wrote to the *Daily Chronicle*. This first serious published criticism asked if Drs Keltie and Mill were absolutely satisfied of the truth of the story, for 'the pearl-sheller, the Australian explorer, and the man acquainted with the Australian blacks will not be so convinced'.[10] The £50,000 worth of pearls was, he said, an unheard of amount, and added that he had never seen an octopus weighting more than 15lb in the shallow waters where pearlers work. As for the turtle riding, a feature that had captured the popular imagination and was to become one of the most controversial aspects of de Rougemont's story, 'I have caught and handled some thousands of turtles, both afloat and ashore, and I never yet saw one which when afloat and touched anywhere on its body, did not sink almost vertically. Furthermore, if a turtle's eye is touched, even when he is on land, he contracts his neck and turns his head downwards and won't go for a spin even if you use spurs.' On hearing of the as yet unpublished story of the two rescued white girls, 'Australian' asked: 'who are they, where are they now, why has no-one in Australia heard of them?'[11]

De Rougemont's talks were awaited in Bristol with great anticipation. On 9 September the demand for seats for his address to the anthropology section was so great that the venue was moved from the Catholic Schoolroom in Park Place to the 2,100-seat Prince's Theatre, where the stalls, pit and two tiers of the gallery were packed with a keenly attentive audience. The press criticisms had provoked considerable comment, but de Rougemont, who had looked nervous and unwell, nevertheless made a favourable impression, with his excellent command of English: 'it suited the temper of the meeting to enthrone for the moment a traveller whose singular experiences in Central Australia promised the possibility of sensation,'[12] reported the *Daily Chronicle*. Towards the end of the lecture, Edward Tylor, the first professor of anthropology at Oxford University, asked for the local names of a number of words such as man, woman, sun, moon, fire, water and common objects, so that he could identify the tribes. De Rougemont obliged him with some words, but to Tylor's disappointment they sounded unfamiliar, and he sat down 'as one on whom the spirit of enquiry had set its imprint'.[13]

On 12 September de Rougemont's talk to the geographical section was also given to a packed house. Here he revealed that in the Australian desert he had encountered four white men whom he later realised were members of the Giles expedition of 1874. He rushed up to them excitedly, not recalling that his tanned skin coated in the traditional aboriginal dress of black greasy clay made him look like a native. They fired upon him, and he despaired of making himself known. (William Tietkins, the only surviving member of that expedition, was later to deny this account with some heat, saying that they never fired on unarmed men.) Shortly afterwards he discovered a lost explorer wandering in a state of imbecility, who lived with him for two years before expiring, only to reveal in a moment of deathbed lucidity that his name was Gibson. (Alfred Gibson had been lost in the desert in April 1874. His body was never found and the Gibson Desert was named in his memory.) De Rougemont had also found a tree marked 'Forrest', presumably inscribed by John Forrest, another noted explorer. His fluency in English was explained by the fact that he had returned to civilisation three years earlier, arriving in Melbourne in 1895.

At the end of the talk, Dr Keltie gave a vote of thanks to the speaker, whose information 'was of considerable value'.[14] Six months ago, he told the meeting, he and Dr Mill had had two or three interviews at which they had questioned him and 'were thoroughly convinced of the *bona fides* of M de Rougemont'.[15] Dr Mill concurred. While there were many at the lecture who wholeheartedly believed in de Rougemont, some were left with a few minor quibbles they wanted to clarify, others felt that the claims were an exaggeration of the truth, and others still, while believing in the good faith of the speaker, had doubts about the sensational treatment of the story in print. It was left to the *Chronicle* to point out the 'singular coincidence'[16] of finding traces of two expeditions in the mighty deserts, and indeed de Rougemont, never afraid to egg the pudding a little more, later claimed to have found traces of the lost German explorer Ludwig Leichhardt.

This was Louis de Rougemont's finest hour, and he returned to London to the acclaim of his believers. *The Times* commented that de Rougemont's appearance had been 'the most striking event of the meeting . . . The general impression is that M de Rougemont is telling the simple truth; that he has come to the Bristol meeting somewhat reluctantly; that some of this ethnographical information is of considerable scientific value; and that he is hardly to blame for the sensational style in which his adventures have been served up to the public.'[17] In the *Home News* de Rougemont was the 'lion' of the meeting 'with his wondrous story. . . . in dramatic interest there can be no doubt that his narrative wholly eclipses that of Selkirk [the real-life castaway whose adventures were to inspire the novel *Robinson Crusoe*]. It is probably the most remarkable story ever told of personal experience.'[18]

Even the normally cynical *Times* gushed 'we claim the privilege of endeavouring to believe him', enchanted by the notion that all the best virtues of human nature were 'actually existing and in full working order among tribes whose refinement has not yet arrived at the use of clothing', nor could any heroine of fact or fiction have 'displayed more of the tenderness and self-devotion of her sex than the native wife'.[19] A *Daily Chronicle* reporter was less susceptible and found the atmosphere of the stories reminiscent of *Boy's Own Magazine*, in which everyone was full of noble sentiments. All was 'vague ideal and emotionally effective'.[20]

The new sensation soon acquired an agent, Monsieur André, who booked public lectures at St James Hall, Piccadilly and St George's Hall, Langham Place, to commence in October, with tickets ranging between

2s 6d and 7s 6d apiece. As overseas cablegrams poured into the offices of the *Wide World Magazine* enquiring about translation rights, George Newnes Ltd took full-page advertisements in the newspapers claiming that Louis de Rougemont was 'The Lion of the British Association Meeting'.[21] The Marquess of Dufferin and Ava had, it was claimed, 'greeted the Cannibal King as a fellow-ruler of the Empire' and 'startling and sensational developments' were promised 'which will assuredly bring conviction to millions' and were 'considered by scientists to be unparalleled in the history of the world'.[22]

Others were not so convinced. The letter from 'an Australian' had sparked off intense interest at the *Daily Chronicle* offices, unmatched by any other newspaper. On 12 September the paper published two critical letters, one from a correspondent who thought that 'The Adventures' sounded very similar to publications by previous writers, while an experienced yachtsman, commenting that 'to pretend that a man could keep a vessel of 40 tons and carrying 30 tons of oyster-shells, off rocks in a tide race with an oar is really too *outré*', concluded that the single-handed voyage, 'far from convincing the nautical reader, tempts him into doubt at every turn'.[23] On the same day the paper also published a long and passionately partisan letter from William Fitzgerald, who proposed that a committee of experts should be appointed to examine his protégé. He claimed that de Rougemont was organising an expedition to verify the truth of his adventures, and offered £500 of his own money, which he said he could ill afford, to anyone who could prove that he was an impostor who had faked the whole story. Fitzgerald's enthusiasm may have had something to do with an element of the story alluded to in the talk to the British Association, yet to be published. De Rougemont's experiences were of more than just scientific value. During his wanderings he had, he claimed, discovered a fortune in gold, rubies, opals and tin, just waiting to be picked up. Fitzgerald answered one of the searching questions already posed – the two girls de Rougemont had rescued were called Gladys and Blanche Rogers, and he believed they came from Sunderland, having sailed from there with their father in 1869, 1870 or 1871 and were never heard of again. Reporters, none of whom commented on the similarity between the names 'Rogers' and 'Rougemont', were at once dispatched to Sunderland, where weeks of enquiries found no trace of the supposed voyage.

Naturalist Professor Henry Forbes wrote to the *Daily Chronicle* with eighteen detailed queries about the speeches to the British Association, which he said were only a few of the points that had puzzled him, and the explorer and writer Arnold Henry Savage Landor wrote to *The Times* to state that, when he had heard that Louis de Rougemont was going to address the Association, he had withdrawn his name and declined to appear.

As criticisms multiplied, so de Rougemont's champions hurried to his defence, pointing out that he had never claimed to have any scientific training or special knowledge of the geography or wildlife of the areas he had explored, that he had been thrown into the adventures against his will, had existed for years without any means to check or record facts and had told his stories entirely from memory. If errors and embellishments had been thrown into the mix, this was the fault of his editor and need not necessarily detract from the underlying truth. The artist Alfred Pearse declared: 'No-one who is in daily contact with him can doubt the truth of his thrilling narrative.'[24] Admiral John Moresby wrote to support fully the account of riding a turtle, and an Australian named M.P. Cosgrove wrote to say he had met a Captain Peter Jensen in New Guinea in 1897, who had spoken of losing some valuable pearls in a wreck some thirty years before. Cosgrove said he had met and spoken to de Rougemont and was 'convinced of his absolute honesty and truthfulness'.[25]

While the *Chronicle* declared its attitude to be that of the 'open minded sceptic',[26] there was no doubt that the editor had thoroughly taken up the cudgels. A correspondent of the paper met the famous man in an Italian restaurant, finding his face more furrowed and his hair coarser than in his photographs. A lady was heard to remark 'no wonder the cannibals did not eat him'.[27] The reporter looked at de Rougemont's hands, expecting to see some sign of the hard physical life he claimed to have led, but saw instead long clean nails, delicate tapering fingers and soft white skin. His long thin face, emphasised by a short beard, was, said the reporter, that of 'a man who has been misunderstood, who has met severe mental disappointments; of a man who has dreamt dreams, never to be realised, who has never been able to march in step with his fellows, who has throughout life been his own enemy'.[28] His manner of speaking was

> not without certain impressiveness . . . . when justifying himself, his tones become singularly persuasive – one might almost say sweet. Strangely enough he speaks like a man who has been accustomed to holding forth to great or small audiences. . . . He gives every word its full meaning. He uses too considerable variety of tone, and even at times throws out a sentence in that humorously exaggerated colloquial manner which the best French comedians employ with such admirable effect.[29]

The reporter observed de Rougemont's 'extraordinary powers of, possibly unconscious, assimilation. This shows itself at once in the way he takes suggestions.'[30] De Rougemont, sipping a glass of lager and daintily touching a cigarette to his lips, was relaxed in the company of his questioners, and seemed unaware he was being tested. He was asked if the soles of his feet had become thickened in the years he had gone without shoes. It appeared that this idea had not struck him before, but he agreed that his soles had changed. Someone remarked that the sole would swell and form a thick soft pad like India rubber, and he readily agreed that this was what had happened to his feet. Another person suggested that the sole might become covered with a horny growth like a corn. De Rougemont, seeing nothing incompatible with these two concepts, agreed that the soles of his feet were like an enormous corn. De Rougemont spoke of the effects he meant to produce on his audiences. He intended to tell them that his wife had killed and eaten their first child. She had done it to save her husband's life, as he had been ill at the time and she was giving him suck. He thought that would make a certain sensation. Asked what disease he had been suffering from, he hesitated. Fever was suggested, and he agreed.

Articles and letters began to appear in the *Chronicle* daily, and as a result it was arranged that de Rougemont would present himself for interview by the editor, H.W. Massingham, at the *Chronicle* offices on 14 September, accompanied by Fitzgerald. Edward Clodd, author and ex-president of the Folklore Society, also attended. Massingham found de Rougemont's English surprisingly refined for a man who claimed to have spent so little time in an English-speaking country. De Rougemont stated that he had been born in Paris on 9 November 1844, where his father, Samuel Emanuel de Rougemont, had a place of business on the Boulevard Haussmann. He had learned English before he left home, but had never before been to England. Following his return to civilisation he had worked as a canvasser selling properties for a James Murphy of Sydney, and had done many other odd jobs. In Brisbane he had worked for a tea-merchant whose name he could not remember. Asked about the language of the tribe, he refused to supply any more details, saying that a syndicate had been formed by himself and Mr Murphy, who was now in England, to go to Australia to mine the gold deposits he had found there – 'if you had the words of the language you would have the tribe, and if you had the tribe, you would have the location,' he declared.[31]

De Rougemont agreed to a meeting at the *Chronicle* offices two days later with 'an Australian', now revealed to be the traveller and writer Louis Becke.

Becke undoubtedly came off worst in the confrontation, since he was obliged to admit he had never ridden a turtle afloat. De Rougemont offered to show him how it was done, but Becke declined, saying he was 'not so venturesome'.[32] He then launched into a series of detailed questions about the single-handed voyage, all of which de Rougemont was able to answer to his own satisfaction. There was just one last question from the editor. He asked if he could see de Rougemont's bare arm. The reason, according to the editor, was that a man who had spent thirty years living almost naked in the outback would be as tanned on the arms as he was on the face; but there was also another unstated reason. Rumours had been abounding that de Rougemont had been a convict, in which case his arms might show the marks of shackles or branding. De Rougemont said he found the question impertinent, and the editor withdrew it.

The *Chronicle* continued to be deluged with letters, some in favour of de Rougemont, others that critically examined his story in great detail. Professor Forbes believed that statements regarding birdlife 'present insuperable difficulties to the acceptance of his story',[33] whereas C.J. Whelan, who provided tales of mariners attacked by giant cuttlefish, wrote: 'I think the public will now be inclined to "pass" the octopus.'[34] De Rougemont eagerly seized upon the supportive letters of Whelan and Moresby and wrote of Becke: 'I am sorry to have to humiliate him, but he has gone out of his way to look for it.'[35]

The October issue of *Wide World Magazine*, published in the third week of September, revealed that:

> it is very probable M de Rougemont may shortly be induced to lecture in the principal towns and cities of the United Kingdom. Moreover, he is at present giving sittings to that well-known artist, Mr John Tussaud, who is preparing a portrait model of this marvellous man, which will shortly be on view at the world-renowned galleries in the Marylebone road. It is impossible for us to reply individually to even a tithe of our 'De Rougemont' correspondents. And M de Rougemont himself is busy working up his scientific material for the learned societies, tracing his relatives in Lausanne and Paris, etc etc.[36]

The 'marvellous man' had indeed disappeared abroad, although it is unlikely that he told his publisher exactly where he was going.

Part three of 'The Adventures' brought a fresh storm of criticism and ridicule. De Rougemont claimed that, within a month of his arrival on the mainland, he witnessed a battle with a nearby tribe, which was followed by a cannibal feast, the bodies being roasted on hot stones buried in the sand. 'I saw mothers with a leg or an arm surrounded by plaintive children, who were crying for their portion of the toothsome dainty.'[37] Out hunting in his boat, he succeeded in harpooning a whale calf when the boat was destroyed by its angry mother. Both whales were later washed up on shore and he was accorded enormous prestige as the natives thought he had killed both single-handed. The ever-resourceful Yamba soon replaced the boat by making a canoe: 'One day I decided to go and explore one of the islands, in search of wombats, whose skins I wanted to make into sandals for myself. I knew that wombats haunted the islands in countless thousands, because I had seen them rising in clouds every evening at sunset.'[38] Even the adulation of the natives began to pall. He found tribal life monotonous, and decided to try to reach the coast and find a ship. Yamba accompanied him wherever he went. 'Her dog-like fidelity to me never wavered, and I know she would have laid down her life for me at any time.'[39]

While experts argued about the size of octopi or whether it was possible to ride a turtle, and others just wanted to recover the buried pearls, the *Chronicle* took a commendably practical view on the mystery and sent its Paris correspondent to check the registers of baptisms. On 19 September it announced to its readers that no trace had been found of the birth or baptism of Louis de Rougemont in Paris between 1840 and 1849. Moreover, the Boulevard Haussmann, where he was supposed to have been brought up, had not existed when de Rougemont was a child. Senior members of the de Rougemont family had been asked if they could identify the traveller from his published portraits, but denied any knowledge of him. It looked increasingly probable that the mysterious adventurer had lied about his name. Criticism in the newspapers was hardening. Becke, having established that, apart from any minor errors that might have crept into the manuscript, it was published essentially as related, now cast considerable doubts on de Rougemont's ability to handle the schooner as claimed, while David Carnegie, an Australian explorer and prospector who had substantial experience of portable condensers, could not see how a simple kettle could produce enough pure water to keep alive a man and a dog and later the four aboriginals as well. Another letter pointed out that, as the wombat is a burrowing marsupial, it could hardly rise in clouds. 'How could his editor allow such an absurd statement to appear?'[40]

Keltie and Mill, backtracking with remarkable rapidity, wrote to the *Chronicle* saying that they had questioned de Rougemont solely on the nature of the land and the habits of the people, and found his replies 'in the main accordant with published statements of reputable travellers'.[41] In view, however, of the sensational manner in which the story was presented, they had contacted the publisher and asked for their names to be withdrawn.

Wide World Magazine easily weathered the criticism, presumably taking the view of many of de Rougemont's supporters that, since his experiences were apparently unique, there was no one sufficiently qualified to contradict him. That October, in the introduction to the November instalment, the editor promised 'some truly amazing developments of the story . . . Arrangements are already being made for its translation into every European language from Spain to Sweden. M de Rougemont begs his hundreds of thousands of friends not to think him discourteous if he is at present obliged, though pressure of work, to decline all social engagements, lecture arrangements, etc etc.'[42]

Although the editor was later reluctant to reveal how the published 'Adventures' had affected sales, an advertising circular issued that month claimed that 'No magazine which has been published during the past quarter of a century can claim such a *startling increase* of circulation as has followed the appearance of this periodical. In less than seven months we are able to announce a solid sale of 400,000 copies per issue.'[43]

Meanwhile, issues of the magazine had been eagerly bought in Australia, where there was considerable excitement over de Rougemont's claim to have discovered Gibson. A sketch of the author appeared in the *Sydney Daily Telegraph*, which resulted in a number of people visiting the newspaper offices to say that they recognised the subject. All gave the same name, Henri Louis Grien, sometimes spelled Grein or even anglicised to Green. He had lived in Sydney, and had gone from there to New Zealand the previous year, leaving behind him a wife and family. Grien, it was said, had a wonderful gift for spinning yarns and often spoke of his pearl fishing adventures and time spent among the savages. The *Sydney Evening News* located Mrs Grien, a fair-complexioned lady in her early thirties who, shown a picture of Louis de Rougemont, readily identified him as her husband, from whom she had been separated for about two years. The newspapers also located Grien's lodgings in Sydney, and were told that, after his departure, letters had arrived there from his brother, Pastor François Grin of Suchy in Switzerland. The final pieces of the puzzle began to fall into place. Soon, cables were passing back and forth between Australian newspapers and the London *Daily Chronicle*, which was rapidly accumulating information that would finally expose the truth about Louis de Rougemont.

Louis de Rougemont's first public lecture took place at St James' Hall, Piccadilly, on 3 October 1898. Newnes Ltd advertised the event, stating that the speaker would 'answer a number of the important questions which have been lately put in the newspapers'.[44] Fitzgerald had told a visiting reporter that he was sure de Rougemont could clear up all the queries. He admitted that his protégé had used the name Green in Australia. Forgetting that de Rougemont had claimed only two weeks earlier not to be able to recall the name of the tea firm he had worked for, he said that the firm was called Green and that de Rougemont had used the name while in their employ.

On the platform at the distinguished occasion were Sir George Newnes, Mr Henniker Heaton and Mr Atherley-Jones QC MP. At first, the talk was, to many, a disappointment. Much of the material had already been covered in the pages of *Wide World Magazine*, and the speaker was reluctant to anticipate anything that had yet to be published. Queried by the more critical elements in the audience, he excused the size of the octopus as a boyish exaggeration. On the absence of his birth from the Paris registers he could say only that this was where he had believed he had been born. To those who questioned the details of his wanderings he pleaded ignorance of the geography of the area. As the audience filed out, a man rose and asked if de Rougemont would show his arms, a suggestion that caused immediate uproar. The speaker hesitated. 'If the request had been made in any place but this', he began, but the rest of his sentence was drowned by cries of derision. 'But as it is made here, I will show it!' he went on.[45] He then removed his coat and pulled back the sleeves of his shirt to show tanned arms with no sign of any convict markings. What had been a disappointing evening turned into a personal triumph as he received three hearty cheers. Despite his triumph, the 'marvellous man' developed cold feet about presenting himself for public questioning a second time, and abruptly cancelled the remainder of his appearances, to the annoyance of André, who instructed his solicitors to take legal proceedings. On 7 October Madame Tussauds waxworks advertised its latest sensation: 'The Modern Robinson Crusoe, taken from life, M. Louis de Rougemont'.[46]

It was not only in Australia that people had recognised Louis de Rougemont's portrait in *Wide World Magazine*. In London several readers recalled a shabbily dressed man who in the spring of 1898 had approached them asking for financial assistance to develop an invention. On 5 October William May, a noted Australian salvage diver, walked into the *Chronicle* offices. He was visiting friends in London and had heard about a city firm being approached about a diving apparatus. The story had a familiar ring. He was shown the August issue of *Wide World Magazine* with de Rougemont's portrait, a tactical error on the *Chronicle*'s part, since May, in common with so many others, was at once so amused and diverted by the story that there was great difficulty in bringing his attention back to the subject in hand. He confirmed that the portrait was of a Mr Green he had known in Sydney for three or four years. Green, he said, was a member of a firm called McQuillan (spelt McQuellan in the Australian newspapers) and Green, which had been trying, with some success, to get interested parties to invest in a new design of diving apparatus. Made of copper, it consisted of a frame with holes through which the diver passed his arms, and on to the apparatus was screwed an ordinary diving helmet. It had, said May, one defect: 'It gave the diver about four and a half pounds of air to live upon when he wanted about thirty. One day, about two years ago, I was asked to inspect the invention. I did so; and I said to the firm that in my opinion they had discovered a highly successful murdering machine.'[47] The apparatus had been tested in January 1897, when a Dane, Christien Madsen, dived from a steamer off Dawes Point. Fifteen minutes later he was brought to the surface dead. It was 'Green' who had been holding the end of the exhaust pipe. An inquest later found that Madsen's death was the result of a collapsed spine resulting from an old injury.

May said that when he had first met 'Green' in Sydney in 1895 he had seemed to be a settled inhabitant and did not appear to have just returned from a long sojourn in the wilderness. The *Chronicle* sent a telegram to the *Sydney Daily Telegraph* asking how long Grien had lived in Sydney and the age of his eldest child. The reply was short but revealing: 'Seventeen years. Frequently away. Eldest child fourteen.'[48] As the *Chronicle* succinctly put it: 'the names he had given in the *Wide World Magazine* do not fit, the dates do not fit, the story does not fit'.[49] The claim to have spent thirty years in the wilderness was clearly unrealistic.

On 7 October the *Chronicle* finally identified Louis de Rougemont to its readership. His real name was Henri Louis Grin, and he had been born in Gressy, Switzerland, in November 1847, later going to live in Yverdon. Over the next few days the paper published more of the history of Henri Louis Grin, eventually compiling the story into a book, illustrated by *Punch* artist Phil May. Grin's father, far from being a wealthy merchant, was a notorious drunkard who had hanged himself in prison in 1885. From his earliest years, Louis, as he was usually known, loved stories of adventure and told yarns to anyone who would listen. Leaving home at the age of 17, he obtained a post as travel courier to the actress Fanny Kemble, who was often in Switzerland and was then undertaking reading tours. By 1870 he was in England, where he spent some time in service with the de Miévilles, an Yverdon family with a house in London, and accompanied his master on his travels. While he was diligent and useful, he was unpopular, having 'overbearing and superior ways'.[50] He was particularly insolent towards hotel servants and customs officials, and was once caught trying to smuggle watches in his master's luggage. It is not known when he left the de Miévilles, but the 1871 London census finds Louis Grin, aged 24, as a house servant with the family of retired merchant John Alexander at 49 Porchester Terrace, Paddington. Early in 1875 he was on the move again, having obtained a place in the household of the Governor of Western Australia, Sir W.C.F. Robinson. While in service at Perth, he waited on tables at elegant dinners where the governor entertained well-known explorers and heard their tales of adventure. In a year he had lost his place, but had accumulated savings with which he might himself taste the adventurous life. At least one part of his adventure stories was possibly true. Captain Jensen did exist and Louis Grien, as he was now calling himself, may have been a pearl fisherman. Their vessel was wrecked in approximately 1877; from then until 1880, Louis's family had no knowledge of him. During that interval, as the *Chronicle* admitted, it was possible that Grin had actually lived with an aboriginal tribe and taken a native wife.

He arrived in Sydney around 1880 and was obliged to live off his wits. 'Our friend is, in fact, well-known in the Antipodes for inventing marvellous projects and floating wild-cat schemes,' the *Chronicle* revealed. 'He has, as we learn from the "Sydney Telegraph", formed various mining syndicates at different times, which have uniformly failed.'[51] In Sydney he was employed by businessman James Murphy as a tout to sell small plots of land on the Holt-Sutherland Estate. In 1881 he met a Miss Ravenscourt, then only 15 years old, whose parents kept a fancy goods shop. He courted her, and they were married in 1883. Seven children were born, of whom three died in infancy. The couple later separated.

Henri Louis Grin arrived in England in March 1898 on the SS *Waikato*, with 'no more luggage than would fill a matchbox',[52] having worked his passage as a stoker from Wellington, New Zealand. He had whiled away spare moments on the voyage by telling adventure yarns and conducting spiritualistic séances. He was later to claim that spirits had warned him not to travel on the SS *Mataura*, which was wrecked in the Straits of Magellan in January – with all hands, according to Grin, but in actuality with no loss of life. He had family in London, a married sister and a maternal aunt. Presumably they were unable to assist him, since he took modest lodgings at 5 Frith Street and considered how he might make a living.

He first tried to raise money to develop the diving suit he had previously worked on in Australia, which he registered at the Patent Office in April. Using the name de Rougemont, he called on Swiss businessmen and families, carrying with him letters of recommendation purporting to come from a Bishop called either Grien or Grin. As he had no model or even drawings of the apparatus, and his description was unconvincing, he was unsuccessful. The firm of Heinke and Co., marine engineers, dismissed him as a crank and thought no more of his visit until recognising his portrait in *Wide World Magazine*. De Rougemont had claimed that the apparatus had been lost in the wreck of the SS *Mataura*, but according to William May it was still in a machinery shop in Sydney. Although Australian newspapers attributed the invention of the apparatus to McQuellan, May believed that 'Green' was the inventor and that McQuellan had provided the finance. Either way, de Rougemont's rights to exploit the invention may have been as illusory as his flying wombats.

The second string to his bow was photography, in which he had some skill, but he was unable to find much work in that line. His claim to be an artist was equally fruitless – his art was no more than making drawings from photographs. He was commissioned to make a portrait of the head of a Swiss firm, with the assumption that he would produce an original drawing, but his avoidance of appointments for a sitting and repeated requests for a photograph aroused suspicion, and this too came to nothing. His third idea was to write a book. He sought the advice of his brother, who had published a number of books, but he wisely advised him that authorship was not an easy way to make his fortune.

It was at this low ebb that he at last had a stroke of luck. He chanced to bump into James Murphy, who had come to England to exploit the Western Australian financial boom, and told him about his attempts to make money. Whether it was the ties of friendship or something about Grin that Murphy saw could be exploited is unclear, but Grin left his shabby lodgings to share Murphy's apartments at 13 Bloomsbury Street. As the idea of the book took shape, it must have been apparent that it would be better and probably easier to publish as true memoirs rather than as fiction. Grin obtained a reader's pass for the British Museum under his real name, and soon his slight gaunt figure and heavily seamed face became well known in the reading room, where he devoured books of travel and adventure.

Before meeting Mr Henniker Heaton, he had taken his story to a number of potential patrons, including a Mr Townend, a well-known Australian journalist, who asked the very pointed question 'whether M de Rougemont's statement was in effect that he had for twenty or thirty years been trying to get back to civilisation and had failed'.[53] On being told it was, he declined to accept the story.

Throughout the publication of these revelations, de Rougemont, according to an English acquaintance who preferred to remain anonymous, maintained his good spirits, making light of the *Chronicle's* attacks. 'He had a patronising manner when he chose, and I fancy it has carried him a good bit in the world.'[54] On 7 October de Rougemont and Murphy called upon the acquaintance, who commented 'it's getting pretty hot, isn't it?'[55] 'Oh,' said Mr Murphy, 'we have a complete answer – a complete answer', a sentiment echoed by de Rougemont. 'You had better get it out, for the thing is a long distance past an advertisement for you,' replied the acquaintance emphatically. As the two men left, de Rougemont turned back and exclaimed: '*You understand: all engagements cancelled!*'[56] They left and never returned.

The *Chronicle* was blunt: 'Sir George Newnes can do nothing else but stop this egregious imposture, and leave this strange creature, who has gulled even the British Association, to the derision of the public.'[57] It denounced the syndicate as a myth, and demanded Fitzgerald's £500, which it proposed should be invested for the benefit of the abandoned wife and family in Sydney. Sir George Newnes, however, maintaining that the groundwork of the story was true and that the public wanted to read it, relentlessly went ahead and published the remaining instalments. The November number had already been printed, and Newnes was naturally unwilling to sustain the loss of withdrawing the entire issue. A Norwegian paper was less accommodating. It had bought the copyright of the story, and in mid-October ceased to publish it.

Further information arrived. On 11 October a colonial gentleman called at the *Chronicle's* offices to say that he had known Louis Grien in Sydney in 1879. He and an old seafaring man called Jensen owned a small sloop, and it was believed that the two were engaged in 'black-birding', the kidnapping of men from the South Pacific islands to labour in Australian sugar-cane plantations. The *Chronicle* commented that Grin's 'available leisure as a "cannibal chief" is growing very narrow indeed',[58] and the paper later decided to 'withdraw its admission that he lived for any notable time out of touch with civilized men'.[59]

There was one last attempt to prove that the *Chronicle's* conclusions were untrue. On 12 October an undated letter signed 'H.L. Grin' with no address was received by the editor, the writer claiming that he was a private person who had never called himself de Rougemont or lived with savage people, and that it was the details of his life and not that of the author of the 'Adventures' that the *Chronicle* had been publishing. 'We do not suppose anyone will be deceived by this silly trick,' commented the editor.[60] The writer of the letter was invited to attend the offices of the *Chronicle*, which stated: 'We shall publish anything he has to say.'[61] The writer did not appear. On 13 October Henri Louis Grin left his Bloomsbury lodgings without any luggage other than a rug, and bought a ticket to Lausanne.

William Fitzgerald had been sent to Switzerland, where presumably he was able to establish for himself how thoroughly he had been duped. Despite this he felt able to hold on to his £500 until such time as 'you [the *Chronicle*] disprove de Rougemont's residence among the blacks'.[62]

By now, Newnes himself was under attack. *The London Morning* commented: 'Sir George Newnes' reputation for a high-minded straightforwardness, which until now no man has had a right to call into question, is in danger of being tarnished . . . everybody will be glad to see him shake himself free from the coils of a deception to which he could never for one instant have been a consciously assenting party.'[63] Newnes Ltd was obliged to insert a printed slip into the November magazine, stating: 'Since this magazine went to press, certain evidence has come to light which causes us to publicly state that we do not vouch for the truth of this story, although portions of it are admittedly based upon real experiences.'[64]

As more information about Grin accumulated, so some mysteries were explained. The reason for his absence from England in the summer of 1898 was not an attempt to trace his family – he knew exactly where they were to be found and had used some of his new wealth to visit them and an old sweetheart in Switzerland, where he boasted of his prosperity, which he claimed had come not from writing, but from inventions, one of which he said was a diving apparatus. The *Chronicle* also discovered the origins of his assumed name. One of Grin's youthful friends in Yverdon had been a poor man who nevertheless bore the distinguished name of de Rougemont. No doubt this appealed to Louis a great deal more than his real name: one of his sons in Sydney bore the name Cecil de Rougemont Grien. The picture was complete with the discovery that two of his daughters there were called Blanche and Gladys.

The introduction to the December issue was more apologetic.

Wide World is a magazine started with the avowed intention of publishing true stories of actual experiences and avoiding fiction. 'The Adventures of Louis de Rougemont' were commenced under the belief that they were the true account of the life of the author. It now turns out that it is not possible for him to have been thirty years among the savages as stated. . . . after what has transpired, we wish it to be distinctly understood that we do not publish it as a true narrative, but only as it is given to us by the author, leaving it to the members of the public to believe as much or as little as they please. . . . We may conclude, in the witty lines of the *World*: 'Truth is stranger than fiction.' But de Rougemont is stranger than both.[65]

Wide World Magazine continued to prosper. Sir George Newnes announced at the Annual General Meeting in July 1899 that sales were still increasing and the de Rougemont affair had not injured the magazine. De Rougemont 'wrote an interesting story which the public liked to read, and if the writer had only said at the outset that it was founded on fact, instead of claiming that every line was absolutely true, nobody would have had any ground for complaint'.[66] The words seem to contain a note of irritation, and indeed the whole episode had caused no little annoyance, yet Newnes's biographer, Hulda Friederichs, believed that Newnes 'always retained a sort of unwilling admiration for the man'.[67] In the following month Newnes, eager to wring the last penny out of the fiasco, published *The Adventures of Louis de Rougemont* in book form, priced at 6s. A comparison with the original articles reveals that a bolder editorial pen was used for the book. The 'toothsome' cannibalistic 'dainty' had become a 'fearsome dainty'[68] and the flying wombats are no more – the suggestion of one of de Rougemont's supporters that they might have been 'bats or flying foxes'[69] was accepted verbatim.

Hugh Mill felt that the affair had 'brought undeserved aspersions on the Association and its officers';[70] indeed, *The Sketch* had commented that 'it is now generally understood among men of science that this is the beginning of the end with the British Association. Henceforth it will only be recognised as a third-rate picnic.'[71] The Association did recover its reputation, but from time to time Mill and Keltie would be distressed by unfounded claims that they had somehow been in collaboration with de Rougemont. Mill, writing in his autobiography many years later, stated that he and Keltie had been asked only to test the truth of de Rougemont's statement that he had been to Australia. He also claimed that he had opposed the British Association's acceptance of the talks, but the decision to go ahead was carried by a majority.

Louis de Rougemont (Grin never resumed his true name) continued to capitalise on his adventure stories for the rest of his life. On 12 April 1899 *The Times* advertised that he would give two lectures at the Crystal Palace on Monday next at 3 p.m. and 8 p.m. on his life and adventures among the cannibal blacks of Australia, illustrated by lantern slides. Seats were available for as little as 6*d*. It is not known how he was received, but perhaps it did not go well, since he soon declined from serious lecturer to vaudeville act.

On 16 March 1901 he appeared at the Bijou Theatre, Melbourne. The performance was not a success. 'M de Rougemont . . . has probably never had a less enjoyable five minutes than he spent on the stage on Saturday evening,'[72] commented the Melbourne *Argus*. 'The audience was intolerant from the outset. . . . De Rougemont was billed to tell no fewer than 25 wonderful stories, but he told none. The audience did not want them. The prospect of sitting still while 25 stories were told, even by de Rougemont, was too much.'[73] The audience was so vocal that he was hardly audible. 'The gallery was boisterous and rude, and kept up a running fire of comment. . . The storm grew and howled around him. From above, a pitiless hail of rude interjections smote and stung him, while the thunder of stamping feet pealed ominously.'[74] Finally, someone in the wings suggested he leave the stage, which he did.

The following week he appeared at the Tivoli Theatre, Sydney, which advertised:

> Come and hear the greatest liar on earth.
> The world famous
> Louis de Rougemont[75]

The *Sydney Morning Herald* observed that 'the theatre was not by any means crowded', but he was 'received with good-natured tolerance'[76] by an audience determined to treat him as a joke.

In the next few years de Rougemont's movements are unknown, but in July 1906 he was back in England, appearing at the Hippodrome for one week only, billed as 'The Modern Robinson Crusoe'[77] and demonstrating turtle riding in a large tank of water, to prove that what he had always claimed was possible.

Writer and traveller The Hon. Sir John Kirwan saw one such performance. A turtle was placed in a huge rubber tank filled with water, which was placed in the arena. When de Rougemont appeared he presented a comic spectacle. He was partly bald, what hair he had was grey, and he wore a rug or blanket over his shoulders. He was in a bathing suit, which revealed his thin legs. Most of those present laughed, and some hissed, but he maintained his dignity. The remarkable piercing blue eyes slowly surveyed the audience, then in a calm and clear voice that could be heard distinctly throughout the building he said quietly and impressively, 'Ladies and gentlemen, I am an old man.'[78] There was a sudden and complete silence. Those who had mocked him began to feel ashamed, and they listened respectfully. After a pause he added:

More than threescore of years have passed over my head. [He was actually 59.] Throughout my long life I have met with many misfortunes, but the greatest of all my misfortunes was when I ventured to write down the experiences and adventures that befell me. They were strange – so much stranger than fiction – that those who could not judge said they were untrue. I said that when living on an island I amused myself by riding turtles in the water. They jeered and said it could not be done. I am old, and my strength is not what it was, my limbs have lost the suppleness of youth, but still I am prepared to show you that I can do it.[79]

He slipped in the water, took hold of the turtle and then

there was a fearful splashing, a struggle went on, but whether de Rougemont was riding the turtle or the turtle de Rougemont was not quite clear. One second the bald crown of the man's head was on top, but a second later it was below the water and the turtle's head showed up. And so it went on. Judged by points I should say the turtle won, though occasionally de Rougemont had the best of the contest.[80]

In June 1921, aged 74, Louis de Rougemont was admitted to Kensington Infirmary under the name Louis Redman. He died on 9 June, and was buried five days later in Kensal Green Roman Catholic Cemetery.

NINE

The Juggler with Millions

On 17 December 1900 the shareholders of the London and Globe Finance Corporation (Globe) assembled at Winchester House for their fourth annual general meeting. They were in restive mood. The company's financial year had ended on 30 September, yet the meeting that should have been held soon afterwards had been unaccountably delayed, and one shareholder demanded to know if the present assembly was legal, since he had received the directors' report only that morning. Globe's main business was speculating in mining properties, especially those of Western Australia, which, since a rich seam of gold had been discovered in Kalgoorlie in 1895, was a hugely popular investment in Britain. It was nevertheless a volatile market. Investors were at the mercy of inflated and sometimes falsified reports of output and rumours of mismanagement or difficulties in extraction, which caused the price of shares to rise or fall dramatically. In June 1899 *The Economist* had commented that until it was possible to get more reliable information from the mines the market 'would remain a medium for gambling rather than for investment'.[1]

By December 1900 confidence in mining shares was on the wane, while the heavy expense of war in South Africa had depreciated the stock market. Globe had an additional problem. In 1897 it had signed a contract with the Baker Street and Waterloo Railway. Incorporated in 1873, the company had been formed to build a new line linking north and south London, but had since remained virtually dormant from lack of funding. Globe appointed a builder, and work started in August 1898. In two years it had incurred expenditure of £750,000, which it could ill afford. The delayed meeting had only hardened suspicions that the company was in difficulties. Nevertheless, one glance at the members of the Board of Directors must have inspired confidence. In the chair was the highly respected Marquess of Dufferin and Ava. Born in 1826, he had devoted himself to a life of public service: he was a past Governor General of Canada, Viceroy of India and had served as Ambassador in St Petersburg, Constantinople, Rome and Paris. Although he had retired in 1896, he could not bear to be idle. In the following year, despite failing eyesight and hearing, he had accepted the chairmanship of Globe. The other eminent men on the board were Lieutenant-General the Hon. Somerset J. Gough-Calthorpe and Lord Edward Pelham-Clinton, son of the Duke of Newcastle. All these gentlemen had three things in common. Their impeccable reputations inspired enormous public confidence in the company, they knew very little about high finance, and they could be relied upon to rubber stamp decisions made by the managing director, Whitaker Wright, without asking any awkward questions. They were what was known in the financial parlance of the day as 'guinea pigs'. The real power in the company was, however, no less inspiring. Whitaker Wright was a self-made millionaire. He had gone to America, dirtied his hands and risked his life in the goldfields of the Wild West and used his experience to make a fortune. Now aged 54, he looked every inch the man of money. There is no picture of him in his youth, but if he had ever been slender, then good living had swelled him to unattractively corpulent proportions. His body was round and fleshy, his head overlarge even for that huge frame, with small eyes peering though gold-rimmed pince-nez spectacles, and thick rolls of fat around his neck that bulged over his starched collar. This was a man who enjoyed the good things of life in abundance.

The chairman's opening remarks were made, according to *The Times*, 'during the prevalence of some disorder in the body of the hall',[2] but his experience as an orator, his 'scholarly, elegant and persuasive'[3] style, ensured that the mood soon settled. Unknown to his listeners, Dufferin's speech was composed entirely from notes made by Whitaker Wright. The company, he said, had not been able to escape the 'severe financial depression, in consequence of the war in South Africa',[4] but the efforts of the board once again to place the company on a prosperous footing had enabled it to present a balance sheet showing a substantial profit. The shares held in mining companies stood at £2,332, 632 even after writing off a large amount for loss and depreciation. The building and equipping of the railway had absorbed a great deal of funds, and the balance at the bank was only £113,671, not enough to recommend the payment of a dividend. The company was negotiating with a syndicate that wanted to buy out the investment. The mines, however, were showing good returns, with every sign that profitable production was on the increase. By now, Dufferin had the meeting on his side, and when he said that, while it was unpleasant to pay no dividend, sometimes it was necessary, and that 'it was the only honest course to follow',[5] he was greeted with shouts of 'hear hear' from the floor. He raised a laugh by adding that the directors would suffer also, since when there were no dividends there were no fees. By the time he had finished there was no doubt that the meeting would unanimously re-elect him as chairman.

Whitaker Wright then rose to answer questions, the hint of northern burr in his deep voice overlaid with an American accent. Immediately he received vociferous complaints about the lateness of the balance sheet, and one shareholder demanded that the meeting be adjourned to 7 January. Although seconded, this motion was overlooked when the final vote was taken. Wright declared that the investments had been written down as low as possible, and if the railway could be disposed of it would not be long before the company could resume paying dividends. This announcement was greeted with cheers from the floor. The meeting formally adopted the report and ended on a note of optimism, with a vote of thanks to the chairman and directors. The failure to pay a dividend wiped £800,000 off the market value of the company's most prized shareholding, Lake View Consols, but on 19 December the *Financial Times* advised its readers that, in view of favourable reports on the mine's performance, they should hold on to their shares and await developments. Only nine days later, however, it was announced that the company had been unable to meet its liabilities on the Stock Exchange and was going into liquidation. Over the next few months the whole precarious structure that was the Whitaker Wright group of companies collapsed in ruin.

Whitaker Wright's father, James, was born in Macclesfield. As a Methodist minister he was required to serve in a succession of ministries, so the family moved about the country, and each of his five children was born in a different county. The oldest son was James Whittaker Wright ('Whittaker' being his mother Matilda's maiden surname), who was born on 9 February 1846 in Stafford.[6] He rarely used his first name and later lost one 't' from 'Whittaker'. It is not surprising that many years later Whitaker Wright was unable to recall where he had been born, and believed that he was, like his parents, a native of Cheshire.

At the time of the 1861 census the Wright family was living in Ripon, and 16-year-old James was a printer. He is the main source of information about his early life, and in view of his later reputation for exaggeration, evasion of truth and downright lies, his account should be viewed with some caution. Young men of ambition saw America as a land rich in opportunities, and after the death of his father, James sailed there in 1867, armed with little more than £100 and an interest in inorganic chemistry.

Gold was the magnet that drew him to the West, where he set up in business as an assayer and used his profits to speculate in mining properties. It was a time when fortunes could be made and lost with spectacular rapidity, but the life of a miner in the American West could be rough and dangerous. Years later James told the story of how, when prospecting in Idaho, he had given a plug of tobacco to the wife of an Indian camping near his hut. Later, when a party of Indians threatened to kill him, the woman persuaded them to go. Whether or not this was true, Whitaker Wright was looking for a less precarious existence, and moved to Philadelphia.

Finding company promotion more to his taste than mining, he launched the Sierra Grande Silver Mine Company and the Colorado Coal and Iron Company. At first these ventures were successful, and he boasted that he was a millionaire at the age of 31, President of the Philadelphia Mining Exchange and a member of the Consolidated Stock Exchange of New York, but after the profits shrank and turned into losses and one of his companies failed, he sensed that it was time to move on. He returned to England in 1889 with his American wife, 27-year-old Anna Edith, and their three children.

Opening a small office in Copthall Avenue, he launched a number of small mining companies. These ventures did not work the mines but used shareholders' capital to acquire the companies that did, the object being to sell the investments at a profit. Depreciation in American securities saw his fortunes disappear, but then came the Australian boom. In 1894 he launched West Australian Exploration and Finance Corporation and in the following year London and Globe Finance Corporation, with a modest share capital of £200,000 each. By then the craze for mining speculation was in full swing, and there were eager buyers for the shares. Twenty mines he promoted proved ultimately to be worthless, but in 1896 he floated Lake View Consols, and when the mine struck a rich seam of ore and the company started to pay handsome dividends, he rapidly acquired a reputation as a financial genius. His next venture, the Ivanhoe mine, also gave rich returns, and investors were eager to participate in anything bearing the name of Whitaker Wright. The journalist Raymond Radclyffe, who travelled the goldfields of Western Australia and wrote about them in 1898, described the huge reserves of gold to be found at the Lake View and Ivanhoe mines, each of which he estimated could yield almost £1,000,000 worth of gold a year: 'they are a standing tribute to the acumen and ability of Mr Whitaker Wright.'[7] Of Wright, he stated that 'no man in the City of

London has a higher reputation for financial ability and business integrity. . . . [he] is something more than a mere financier and is no "juggler with millions". His practical mining experience on the goldfields . . . has been of the highest value to himself and those associated with him in his ventures.'[8]

In 1897 Wright formed the new London and Globe to absorb all his previous holdings, with a capital of £2,000,000, and filled the board with the names of men who would inspire confidence. Many shareholders in the company were later to state that they invested 'secure in the easy conviction that all must go well in a concern with which so distinguished and honoured a name as that of Lord Dufferin was connected'.[9] Lord Dufferin's biographer commented that it was strange that the personnel of a board of directors was more material to investors than the inherent soundness of the enterprise, but that 'the easy process of glancing at the names of the directorate, and making *that* the main criterion, seems to exercise the greater fascination'.[10] Before accepting the chairmanship, Dufferin had taken the precaution of making enquiries about the duties of such a role and was reassured that the financial interests of the company would continue to remain in the hands of the managing director. To show his confidence in the company, he bought 5,000 shares at 30s each.

In December 1897 Wright formed the British America Company (Brit-Am) with the same directors as Globe, which acquired mining properties in British Columbia, and in 1898 he formed the Standard Exploration Company (Standard) with share capital of £1,500,000, whose directors were Lord Donoughmore, a former member of the Council of the Royal Geographic Society, the Australian-born solicitor Howard Spensley, and a Cape Town merchant, Sinclair Macleay. This company acquired Wright's earlier unsuccessful ventures in return for a million £1 shares. A further 213,848 £1 shares were purchased by Globe, and, when the rest were offered on the stock market, another £286,152 poured into the company coffers. No doubt the public believed that the £500,000 in cash now in Standard's bank would be expended on developing its impressive-looking list of assets, but this was not the case. In the years since the youthful Whitaker Wright had prospected in the Wild West he had lost interest in the development of mines. The properties on Standard's balance sheet were in a state of neglect, and there were no plans to spend any more on them than was strictly necessary. Wright's object was to utilise the companies as window-dressing, to enhance the image of Standard and to bring in investors' money for the occupation that was by now his passion – speculation on the Stock Exchange.

Globe, Standard and Brit-Am all had their offices at the same address, Whitaker Wright's large new premises at 43 Lothbury, and were managed by the same team of clerks. Wright kept a careful watch on the markets and in particular dealings in shares in his companies. When Globe made an issue of shares in a mine called Le Roi No. 2, it was initially unsuccessful. Out of 600,000 shares only 50,000 were sold, and Globe and Brit-Am bought up the rest. Wright – and as later became apparent, all activities of this nature were carried out by Wright with little or no input from the other directors – now indulged in what he later described as a 'usual policy . . . of . . . "supporting the market"',[11] and bought up every share in Le Roi No. 2 that was offered for sale. The poor initial take-up of the shares had created a 'bear' market – speculators were entering into contracts to sell shares they did not yet own, anticipating a drop in price before they needed to buy to fulfil their commitments, so that when the settling date came round they could pocket the difference. Wright made use of this situation by contracting to purchase more shares than actually existed. When the accounting date arrived, he had cornered the market and the bears discovered that they were unable to deliver what they had agreed to sell. They were obliged to bid among themselves for shares to deliver, and when the price of the £1 shares rocketed to £25, Globe sold part of its holdings, realising a profit of £124,000. Wright made a personal profit of £50,000.

Wright, now lauded as a Midas among men, established a private life to match. He bought an elegantly furnished home in Park Lane and two yachts, the *Sybarita* and *White Wings*. In 1896 he purchased Lea Park near Godalming, together with an adjoining farm. The 2,000-acre estate, now called Witley Park, cost £250,000, but over the next three years he spent more than £1 million creating a palatial retreat. The natural beauty of the landscape did not appeal to him, and so he drafted in hundreds of workmen to bend nature to his design. Hills were removed and new ones created; artificial lakes were stocked with trout; terraces, rare trees, fountains, pagodas and costly marble statues – which were his especial passion – abounded. On the largest lake a boat would take visitors into a grotto resembling something out of an Eastern fairy tale, with rich and exotic decoration. Underneath the lake was a conservatory with a glass roof, where the owner could cool his great bulk in the heat of summer. The house was naturally fitted with every modern comfort and also boasted a ballroom, a private theatre, an observatory and elegant oriental furniture. Even the stables, large enough for fifty horses, were adorned with decorative mouldings depicting hunting scenes. Wright, who lavishly entertained both aristocracy and royalty, must have believed it was only a matter of time before he added a title to his name.

By the autumn of 1899 Wright was looking for another coup. The manager of the Lake View mine had reported a handsome monthly output of 30,000 ounces of gold, which he thought could be kept up indefinitely, and Wright decided to acquire all the shares he could. Unfortunately, most of Globe's available cash had been spent on railway development. Wright took a gamble, borrowing money from Standard to buy Lake Views, but the output rapidly dropped to 10,000 ounces a month and the value of the shares fell. Whitaker Wright had learned nothing from his American business failure. His companies were launched on a tide of optimism, leaving no room for recession. They were asset-rich, but those assets were shares in other speculative ventures. When he got into difficulties, there was no legitimate way to ride out hard times. Globe was obliged to sell at a loss just to stay in business. Globe and Standard lost over £1 million between them.

This disaster could not have happened at a worse time. Settling day on the Stock Exchange was 29 September, and the very next day was Globe's accounting date. There was no time for the ailing company to recoup its losses before it needed to report to the shareholders. Wright dared not reveal the truth and decided to delude the shareholders into thinking that the company was prospering, to give him enough time to stage a recovery. He desperately needed to boost Globe's bank balance to a level that would pay a dividend and in such a way that the money appeared to have come from trading profits. The man who had remoulded nature on his estate now fashioned a new financial reality. In just a few days, £359,000 was milked from Standard in a series of transactions that went largely unrecorded in its books and were reversed soon after the balance-sheet date. Loans of £84,000 were repaid to Globe, and Standard provided another £275,000 in share deals, the largest of which was its purchase of 6,888 Lake View shares. The market value of Lake View was then £8 a share, but Standard bought them at £23. Not that Globe had 6,888 shares to sell. It was obliged to borrow almost 3,000 from Whitaker Wright to make up the amount. This was only part of the fraud. Standard, as Wright well knew, did not have £359,000 to pay to Globe. It was forced to borrow £113,000 from Brit-Am, £140,000 from brokers and £40,000 from Wright to make up the total.

In October 1899 Globe presented its accounts for the year ended 30 September. Lord Dufferin, who as usual was reading a speech written by

Whitaker Wright, told the shareholders that 'the corporation was never in a sounder condition than it is at present'.[12] The accounts showed profits for the year of £483,000 and £534,455 in cash at the bank, 'one of the best witnesses we can point to in support of the success of our operations'.[13] On this basis, said Dufferin, it would have been possible to declare a dividend of 25 per cent, but the company's financial policy dictated a more prudent 10 per cent. Wright assured the shareholders that the Lake View mine 'is just as good as ever it was', adding 'you hold shares in a corporation about which you can feel perfectly easy in your minds'.[14] Everyone went away well satisfied, and many shareholders, on the strength of the report, went straight to their brokers and increased their holdings.

Lord Dufferin was beginning to find his chairmanship of London and Globe more arduous than expected. The strain and anxiety brought about by the realisation that he was bound to a company whose scale and complexity he could not begin to understand, coupled with his gradually failing health, meant that by 1899 he was hoping to be relieved of his post. He had stayed on only because of the resignation from the board of the ailing Lord Loch, aware that the departure of two directors at once could have been misinterpreted. He had asked his solicitor, Mr Leman, to sit in on board meetings to advise him, and Leman became a director on Loch's retirement, but Leman shared the confidence of his fellow directors in Whitaker Wright.

In November 1899 Wright was told by his accountant that he must lend the corporation £400,000 of his own money or close it down. He provided the funds, later claiming it was money he was about to settle on his children. It was now necessary for Wright to shore up Brit-Am, which was preparing its accounts up to 28 November and was in danger of showing a loss. Options valued at £250,000, Brit-Am's share of a joint venture with Globe, had been retained on the Globe balance sheet. They were returned to Brit-Am in time for them to appear on its balance sheet. The reversal of other transactions completed the restoration of Brit-Am's accounts to an outwardly healthy appearance, and the company was able to pay a dividend. On 27 February 1900, at the Brit-Am shareholders' meeting, Wright declared that the securities owned by Brit-Am were being quoted at 100 to 150 per cent over their balance-sheet value, a statement that Leman later described as 'a mistake'.[15]

Wright's hoped-for revival did not come. The magic was gone. In November 1900, in an article entitled 'Why Westralians are Weak', the *Financial Times* stated that 'share rigging has been the bane of the

181

Westralian market',[16] also citing poor management and insufficient expenditure on development. Wright had been guilty of all three. Early in October 1900 Mr Worters, the then company accountant, brought a balance sheet to Whitaker Wright. In the previous twelve months the company had made a loss of £1,645,748, mostly in Stock Exchange speculations, and was insolvent. The correct thing for Whitaker Wright to have done was to present the bad news to the investors and wind up the company, but he was too used to a luxurious life, elegant social circles, the adulation of the City and the admiration of the public. He was not about to let this go, and so he planned instead to reverse Globe's fortunes by a massive financial coup beside which Le Roi No. 2 was insignificant. Even if he was to be successful, however, he would need time, and time was not on his side. The company accounts had by law to be presented before a shareholders' meeting within three months of the accounting date. To buy time he put off the balance-sheet date to 5 December and manipulated the figures to make it look as if the company was solvent.

Among Globe's many investments was a block of 200,000 shares in West Le Roi Company and another of 150,000 in Columbia Kootenay, two of Wright's Canadian companies. These companies had sold almost all their property to another company but had made no distribution out of the proceeds. Wright introduced a non-existent distribution, crediting Globe with the receipt of £213,000 from West Le Roi and £103,000 from Columbia Kootenay, making the necessary adjustments in the accounts of all three companies. He then sold the now worthless shares to Brit-Am for £350,000. Globe owed Brit-Am £250,000: Wright ensured this debt did not appear on the balance sheet by surrendering it to Brit-Am on 16 November. He then returned it to Globe on 13 December. Globe also had 75,000 £1 shares on its books in the virtually dormant Victorian Gold Estates, while Brit-Am had another 125,000. Wright quickly floated some new companies, which bought the Victorian Gold Estates properties at a hugely inflated price, and Brit-Am passed its shares, now valued at £500,000, to Globe at par. On 22 November an agreement was signed to sell some mining shares to Brit-Am 'ex div', which meant that Globe retained the right to the next dividend. Wright later claimed that this was an error and they should have been sold 'cum div' (with the dividend rights). Whatever the reason, the 'error' increased the amount of Globe's assets by £250,000. Other liabilities for share purchases of £150,000 were simply omitted from the balance sheet. With these and a host of other manipulations, the balance sheet was in the black and the accounts now showed an adjusted loss on the year's operations of only £36,327. A sweep of the pen amalgamated this with a £500,000 depreciation reserve, creating an apparent profit of £463,673. The main element lacking on the Globe balance sheet was cash. Early in December £75,000 was transferred from Victorian Gold Estates and a further £25,000 was hired from a broker for two days at a cost of £500. By now, Wright's efforts to make a killing in Lake View shares was in full swing, with agreements in place to purchase 105,000 shares at a cost of over £1,400,000, and large numbers of other speculative transactions were open. Naturally, he did not want these desperate gambles to appear on the balance sheet, and on 29 November a directors' meeting attended only by Wright and Macleay passed a resolution transferring the bulk of the speculations to Brit-Am and Standard without informing any of the brokers involved.

The auditor, Mr Ford, had only a few days to provide accounts in time for the meeting, and at 2 a.m. on Sunday 15 December he was hard at work in the Globe offices. Henry Malcolm, who had succeeded Worters as company accountant, urged him to sign the balance sheet, but Ford refused to do so, as he had not been shown the brokers' written consents for the transfer of the open speculations. Malcolm assured him that he had all the consents and would supply them in the morning, and eventually, on that verbal assurance, Ford was persuaded to sign. Later that day he enquired after Malcolm and found that he had left London. He did not see Malcolm again until after the meeting of 16 December, when he discovered that the consents had neither been obtained nor requested. None of the massive speculations appeared in Globe's balance sheet at 5 December, and the transfers were reversed a few days later.

The buying-up of huge blocks of Lake View shares was putting a strain on Globe, and Wright was eventually obliged to shore up the company with a loan of £500,000, which he borrowed from a group of stockbrokers he later referred to as 'the syndicate'. The security for the loan was a block of Lake View shares, which the group acquired at £11 per share, with, according to Wright, an agreement that they would not sell until the share price rose to £17. Unfortunately for Wright, the stipulation was not included in the written contract for the loan, but is hard to imagine that he would have entered into such a compact without knowing that the syndicate had agreed not to flood the market with Lake View shares until the moment it suited him. Wright continued, as he had done for Le Roi No. 2, to buy up all available shares in Lake View, yet it seemed to him that, despite his efforts to corner the market, there were always plenty of shares available, and the price did not rise as he would have hoped. He eventually discovered that the syndicate was selling its holdings and that he had been buying back his own shares all the time. He must have known before the crash came that he was bound for disaster, yet he was already laying plans to soften the blow with other people's money. At the end of December 1900 Globe was subject to claims on the Stock Exchange of £968,000 on the Lake View speculation, which it was unable to meet. No more cover-ups were possible. The crash hit the stock market like a thunderbolt. Twenty firms of stockbrokers were unable to meet their obligations because of non-payment of their accounts, and were declared defaulters. Many of these firms were ruined, and even those that survived only did so after suffering enormous losses. It was later estimated that hundreds of small investors were bankrupted by the collapse of Whitaker Wright's companies, and thousands more saw their savings disappear. Individuals who had been managers or accountants in the Globe empire, and knew nothing of Wright's manipulations, found their future careers blighted by the cloud of suspicion and distrust that naturally attached itself to their financial dealings.

The year 1900 had been an unhappy one for Lord Dufferin. His eldest son had been killed at Ladysmith in January, and the following April the trusted secretary who had been with him for twenty years also died. With the decline in Globe's value in 1900 Dufferin decided to stay on as chairman and not shirk the responsibilities that fell to him. He was to pay a heavy price. Soon after the shareholders' meeting in December, Dufferin learned that his third son had been wounded in South Africa. Here at least was a reason to give up the chairmanship that everybody could understand. Resigning all his City interests, he booked a passage to South Africa. A few days later came the news of Globe's failure, which he later described as 'an indescribable calamity which will cast a cloud over the remainder of my life'.[17] He cancelled both his resignation and his voyage, and, duty-bound to a fault, agreed to chair the public meeting, fully expecting to be verbally torn to pieces.

On 9 January 1901 an extraordinary general meeting of London and Globe was held at the Cannon Street Hotel. Although fixed to start at noon, the shareholders began to arrive shortly after 10 a.m., and the great hall and galleries were soon crowded. It was estimated that some 2,000 people were present. Wright had already tried to defuse criticism by issuing a statement claiming that the assets of the company were sufficient to pay more than 20s in the £1. Shares of Globe, which in 1897 had been changing hands for 45*s*, were being bid for on the stock market at 7*s* in anticipation of an eventual payout. As the directors entered the room, they were greeted with cheers and a few hisses. When Dufferin rose to speak, however, it was clear that his personal popularity was undented, especially as he was a substantial shareholder. If there had been errors of judgement, he said, the policy of the board had been honest and within the powers granted by the company's constitution. He urged the shareholders not to permit Whitaker Wright to assume full responsibility for what had happened, since he 'had never met anyone more devoted to the service of those with whose interests he was charged'.[18] Finally, he expressed his gratitude to the shareholders for the patience and generosity with which they had listened to his observations. It was an emotional speech and it was greeted with loud cheers.

Whitaker Wright's address to the meeting was probably one of the most important speeches of his life. Unable for once to rely for popularity on the promise of golden prospects, he set out to win the day with pure force of personality. He started with some good news. The directors 'had practically arrived at an arrangement with the creditors of the company . . . and . . . "with a long pull, a strong pull, and a pull all together" their good ship would soon be off the rocks and sailing once more in smooth water'.[19] Wright, who liked to take full personal credit for success, generously offered to take responsibility for failure, and then proceeded to blame it on everyone else. He blamed the mine engineers for an inaccurate report, he blamed the war for lack of confidence, and most of all he blamed the syndicate. He proposed to adjourn the meeting until 14 January, by which time all the company's debts would be settled and he would be able to announce a scheme of voluntary liquidation followed by reconstruction to ensure future prosperity, pledging 'his health, his strength, his life, and as far as might be his private fortune, to carry the enterprise to a successful issue'.[20] There were rousing cheers from the floor, although not everyone was convinced. A Mr Seal suggested appointing an independent committee to look at the company's affairs, but was shouted down by Wright's supporters. Seal, who realised that any reconstruction scheme would require the shareholders to advance still more funds, commented: 'If . . . they were prepared to throw their money broadcast into the sea, let them do so – nothing in the world perhaps would stop them until they had further adversity and further distress.'[21] Wright was defiant, and his lies were bold: 'We are not afraid of investigation. We have not a single transaction to cover up – everything is open to the light of day.'[22]

He himself, he claimed, had at first suggested the appointment of the official receiver, but the creditors and shareholders had implored him not to do it because (and here he raised a terrifying spectre) if that course was taken the shareholders would get nothing. The meeting voted for adjournment and closed with three cheers for Lord Dufferin.

The press was less sanguine about Globe's prospects. The *Pall Mall Gazette* summed up the meeting: 'there were generalities on assets, much skilful handling of an audience, various vague promises as to the future and that was all.'[23] The *Daily Mail* was blunter still: 'The directors' attempt to have a voluntary winding-up is a little too transparent, and is the usual device of directors of companies when there is something to hide.'[24]

In May, with Globe shareholders still waiting for the proposed reconstruction scheme to be announced, Brit-Am suspended operations owing to 'complications . . . in which liability is claimed against the corporation for the same shares in several directions',[25] and the financial papers demanded that all three companies of which Wright was the guiding spirit should be compulsorily wound up. At the end of May it was announced that Brit-Am was unable to meet its obligations, and on 3 June Sinclair Macleay, as chairman of Brit-Am, presided over a stormy meeting where it was explained that the company's failure was a result not of its own mismanagement but claims made against it following the Globe crash and 'complications' on the Stock Exchange. He proposed voluntary liquidation to be followed by reconstruction. This proposal was seconded by Whitaker Wright, whose contribution was greeted by hisses. One shareholder, a Mr Stavacre, said he regarded the conduct of the company as 'a disgrace to the commercial world',[26] but a Mr Atkinson urged the meeting not to be 'led away by any spiteful feeling toward the directors' and said that a compulsory liquidation would 'wipe his shares off at once'. A cynic from the floor cried out: 'They are wiped off already.'[27]

Whitaker Wright addressed the meeting, attributing the Globe crash to 'the treachery and default of members of the Stock Exchange',[28] a comment that caused an angry outcry from the floor. Proposals for the reconstruction of the Globe business would be announced later in the month, and the company had 'practically sold the Baker Street and Waterloo Railway for £500,000'.[29] He advised shareholders not to 'cut their own throats and rush hastily to a decision which they might regret afterwards'. The new company would, however, have to do without him. 'Nothing under the sun would ever induce him to be a director again in any company in the city of London.'[30] Once again, and to the regret and astonishment of the financial press, Wright carried the day, and the meeting voted for a voluntary liquidation to be carried out by a committee. When on 13 June dissenting shareholders petitioned for the compulsory winding-up of Brit-Am, it was revealed that the company had substantial creditors and only £157 in the bank. Soon afterwards Standard, too, went into liquidation.

On 30 July the first meeting of the creditors of Standard was held under the chairmanship of Mr Barnes, the Senior Official Receiver, and for the first time the cloak of obscurity thrown over the dealings of the Whitaker Wright companies was pulled aside and the public were able to see what lay beneath. It was not an attractive sight. The directors had lodged a statement showing assets of £1,160,000 and liabilities of £362,000. As far as the assets were concerned, the figure was based on estimates made by the directors, 'and he was afraid that they were quite impossible estimates'.[31] Fourteen mines valued on the balance sheet at £767,000 were not earning any income. Many of them had had no money spent on them, and several should be regarded as having no value at all. He also revealed, to the astonishment of the investors, that none of the properties supposedly owned by Standard had ever been transferred to the company, all of them still remaining in the names of their original companies or those companies' liquidator. The investments in shares were valued at £61,860, but most were being held as security by the liquidator of Globe. Most of the shareholders' money had been lost in Stock Exchange speculation. More shocking still, while these vast speculations were going on, no record of purchases and sales could be found in the company's books. As if this was not enough, Barnes now told his listeners that he had to refer to another matter he regarded as 'extremely serious',[32] the transfer of Globe's open speculations in 1900 to Standard and the writing-back of the transaction on 13 December. To date he had not received a satisfactory explanation of these activities.

Finally, he advised the shareholders to 'consider among themselves whether there was any property worth saving, and whether it was worth while to put more money into the concern. . . . calmly and dispassionately'.[33] No one was feeling either calm or dispassionate. Strong words were used in the ensuing discussion, and at one point several shareholders rose to their feet and, addressing those directors who were present (Whitaker Wright was wisely absent), 'referred in vehement language to the conduct of the company's business'.[34] There were to be no more compromises. The meeting voted to retain the Official Receiver as liquidator.

Wright was still director of Le Roi Mining Company Limited, whose directors, on reading the revelations, politely asked him to resign. He refused, and they were obliged to hold a special meeting to remove him. Fresh petitions were now presented for the compulsory winding-up of Globe, which Wright tried to avoid by sending out proposals for reconstruction, but no one now believed him, and the winding-up order was made. At a meeting on 16 December 1901, Barnes revealed that Globe had unsecured creditors of £1,142,000. Assets were estimated at £424,000, but unfortunately these were partly made up of claims against Brit-Am and Standard totalling £210,000, which could never be realised, and shares valued at £121,000, which were worth rather less.

Barnes described how Globe's funds had been dissipated in speculations, and exposed the complex cross-dealings that had taken place between the Whitaker Wright companies to make Globe appear solvent. There was virtually no mention of these enormous movements of debts and assets in the minutes, and he was satisfied that none of the other directors knew what Wright was doing. The meeting closed with the feeling that, shocking as the revelations were, the truth was beginning to emerge, and there was something the angry creditors had to look forward to: the courts had ordered that Whitaker Wright should submit to a public examination.

Lord Dufferin's sense of personal responsibility for the Globe crash led him, despite his own losses, to offer compensation to some of the shareholders. Touched by their unexpectedly friendly spirit, he remained grieved at the effect of the crash on his wife, and that her 'life should be thus suddenly overshadowed, just as we thought to enjoy the evening sunshine of our days in our happy home'.[35] Early in 1902, his energies exhausted, Lord Dufferin was compelled on the advice of his doctor to take to his bed. From there he continued to follow the inquiries, and on 22 January, now realising that he had been duped by a rogue, wrote to the Official Receiver stating that the Lake View speculations 'were entered upon without my knowledge and consent. . . . I should have considered myself highly criminal if I had knowingly consented to the shareholders' money being gambled away in such a manner'.[36] He promised that, should he recover, he would offer himself for examination. Soon afterwards he suffered a relapse, and on 12 February he died.

The purely nominal position of the company directors was fully exposed at the public examination, which commenced in January 1902. Asked what the directors did at board meetings, Macleay replied: 'We confirmed past transactions of the managing director,' and Worters, asked if the directors ever saw the company books, said: 'Not to my knowledge. They may have seen the outsides.'[37]

Gough-Calthorpe, director of both Globe and Standard, and present when on 16 November 1899 £250,000 had been transferred from Globe to Brit-Am, had supposed 'that the Globe was so rich it could afford to do anything'.[38] The reasons for the transfer had not been explained to him, but he did not think he would have understood if it had been, 'as it was a matter of City finance'.

'May I ask what were the duties of the directors?' asked Mr Barnes.

'As far as I could ascertain my only duty was to sign my name many thousands of times to the share certificates,' replied Gough-Calthorpe.

'You did not guide the policy of the company in any way?'

'Oh dear no!' said Gough-Calthorpe.[39]

When the companies were finally wound up, it was apparent from the report of the Official Receiver that assets worth £5 million had been irretrievably lost in just two years. Total debts were close on £3 million, with payments to creditors ranging from a few pence to a few shillings in the £1. The shareholders had lost everything.

Whitaker Wright took the stance that he maintained to the end – he was innocent of any wrongdoing, and his actions were simply standard business practice. Errors had been made by the accountants, for which he was not responsible. He had more difficulty in explaining away payments made to financial journalists. These were disguised as share deals, the shares having being sold at a discount and repurchased by the company. Wright denied all accusations, but Barnes proved him a liar by producing the contract notes. Wright simply shrugged these off – journalists, he said, would not take an interest in a company unless they owned some shares. Barnes pointed out that in the case of one contract the repurchase had taken place on the following day. When the inquiry closed at the end of February, it was clear that the failure of the companies had been the responsibility entirely of Whitaker Wright, and, although failure was not in itself a crime, attention now focused on the false balance sheets, and both press and public felt that there was ample material here for a criminal charge. The difficulty was that in 1899 and 1900 it was not a criminal offence to issue a false balance sheet.

Wright stood firm, pinning his hopes on legal proceedings to recover damages of £1,000,000 from the syndicate, but in June 1902 the final decision went against him. Wright must have known that, in England at least, he was finished. Quite what he did over the next few months is unknown, but by the end of 1902 the outward trappings of substantial wealth had disappeared. The yachts were sold, and his estate, by now heavily mortgaged, was vacated. The family relocated to nearby Tigbourne Court.

Meanwhile, efforts were made by the shareholders and creditors of Globe to persuade the Attorney General, Robert Bannatyne Finlay, to authorise legal proceedings. On 20 December 1902 stockbroker John Flower, a leading campaigner for the prosecution of Whitaker Wright, received a letter from the Treasury stating that papers he had transmitted to the Attorney General 'contain nothing to alter his conclusion that this case is not one which should be taken up by the Director of Public Prosecutions'.[40] The decision was deplored by the financial press, and questions were asked in the House of Commons, but Prime Minister Balfour merely regretted that company law was inadequate to deal with the matter, an anomaly he promised to rectify. Flower was persistent, however, and he organised meetings of interested parties to raise funds for a prosecution under the Larceny Act of 1861, under which it was an offence to make a false statement with intent to deceive or defraud. Early in 1903 Flower was able to apply for a direction to prosecute before Mr Justice Buckley. Wright became increasingly concerned. The hearing on 17 February was adjourned, and on 19 February the case was discussed again in the House of Commons. On the following day Wright drew a cheque for £500, and on 21 February he sailed for France, reaching Paris four days later. His wife kept him informed by telegram of the progress of the proceedings. On 5 March she cabled: 'Case to prosecute settled today: everything looks bad.'[41] Wright quickly packed his bags and cabled back. 'Give Florence five hundred pounds she sails tomorrow Friday evening will meet her Havre forward no more letters.'[42] He was on the run. 'Florence' was Florence Browne, Whitaker Wright's American-born niece, who was to be the go-between in her uncle's flight from justice.

In the event Buckley's decision was not made until 10 March, when he directed the Official Receiver to institute a prosecution against Whitaker Wright. A summons was quickly obtained, but when an official was sent to Tigbourne Court he found only Mrs Wright, who declared with gracious dignity that her husband was an honourable man and had gone to Egypt for the sake of his health. Soon afterwards banknotes known to have been in Wright's possession were found in Paris, and he and Florence were traced to Le Havre, where it was found that on 7 March they had booked a suite under assumed names on a liner, *La Lorraine*, bound for New York.

Wright's distinctive description was cabled to the New York police, who boarded the liner on its arrival. Wright submitted quietly to arrest, and, charged with being a fugitive from justice, was taken to Ludlow Street Jail. Florence, left standing on the pier with the luggage, eventually took a cab to a hotel. Questioned by the police, she maintained that, of the money (£710) found on Wright's person, £100 was hers and £500 had been provided to her by Mrs Wright. Eventually, £600 was returned to her and she was released. What she did thereafter is unknown.

After several months of fighting extradition proceedings, Wright agreed to return to England voluntarily. Arriving on the *Oceanic* at Liverpool on 5 August, he was placed on an express train and faced the London magistrates that same afternoon. His defence counsel, Richard Muir, who later achieved considerable distinction as Senior Counsel to the Treasury, was a man who, having taken up the cause of a client, would always believe the best of him. Muir deplored the suggestion 'promulgated by the baser class of newspaper'[43] that his client had confessed his guilt by absconding. Wright, he said, had simply decided to start a new business life in America. His eloquent pleading was successful, and Wright was granted bail of £50,000.

Early on, Muir decided that it would be in the best interests of his client to have the case heard not at the Old Bailey but at the civil court in the Strand, before a special jury who would be more likely to understand the financial intricacies. It was a decision that would have momentous and unexpected consequences. The trial opened on 11 January 1904. Wright arrived dressed in the flowing frock coat of a City man, a little thinner and greyer than the public remembered him, and sporting a small pointed beard known as an imperial. Since it was a civil court, he was permitted to sit in the well of the court among his legal advisers. For a time, it seemed that he was the calmest person there.

The prosecution team was formidable. Rufus Isaacs (later First Marquess of Reading) was experienced in complex financial cases, with a mind that was able to follow a multitude of separate threads while keeping the overall picture clear. His approach would be essential in steering the jury through the maze that was Whitaker Wright's financial dealings. He was quiet, courteous and unruffled. 'His tactics', wrote his son, 'were never to bludgeon his man, but to lead him gently and politely to destruction.'[44] The crown witnesses were to be examined by Horace Avory (later Mr Justice Avory), who was also adept at handling the complexities of such a case.

Justice Bigham (later Lord Mersey), who was to hear the case, was for Wright an unfortunate choice. It became obvious in the early stages of the trial that he was hostile to the defendant, and made frequent interruptions, usually to clarify dubious transactions for the jury's benefit, though he could not resist the occasional stab of dry humour. When Isaacs showed how the 200,000 £1 Victorian Gold shares were manipulated to a value of £800,000, giving a paper profit of £600,000, Bigham's comment was: 'I observe that they did not propose to pay any of it in dividend.'[45] Isaacs's opening statement was a masterpiece, detailing exactly what manipulations had taken place. The jury, even if unable to commit the torrent of figures to memory or make notes in the time available, were still left convinced that there had been a series of complex transactions in which every cheque had been signed by Whitaker Wright. Expert witnesses were now produced – Mr Waterlow, who had printed the accounts and spotted amendments in Wright's handwriting, cashiers, who testified as to the cheques drawn by Wright, and Globe's secretary, who took minutes at Wright's dictation of a directors' meeting that had never happened. Arthur Russell, the senior examiner to the Official Receiver, was a particularly devastating witness as he laid bare the maze of transactions unrecorded in the company books, all with the unmistakeable touch of Whitaker Wright. The assets of Globe, said to be worth £2,332,632 in the company's 1900 accounts, had, he told the court, been found to have a value of nearer £1 million. Lawson Walton, who led Muir for the defence, did his best. When Bigham commented that many of the companies promoted by Wright were 'only shadows', Walton protested that there were boards and shareholders in each case. Bigham retorted that 'if there were real boards he would like to see the minute-books'.[46]

Henry Malcolm was questioned about losses on sales of shares that had been treated as depreciation, thus giving the false impression that the shares were still the company's property. He was an uncooperative witness, and it was with some difficulty that Avory extracted from him the admission that the entries in the books had been made on Wright's instructions. With the prosecution case complete, Walton called his one and only witness for the defence: Whitaker Wright. Before he did so he asked Mr Justice Bigham to agree that the cash in Globe's bank of £534,000 at 5 December 1900 was genuinely the property of Globe. 'There are two ways in which these things may be regarded,' observed Mr Justice Bigham, making his own opinion very plain. 'It may be what you may call justifiable window dressing, though I do not like it. Or it may be a scheme to throw dust in the eyes of the shareholders.'[47]

When Wright entered the witness box he declined a seat, preferring instead to stand and lean forward with his arms on the box. He answered

Lawson Walton confidently, boasting of the early success of his companies, and insisting that nothing was ever done without the unanimous agreement of the directors. Bigham interrupted frequently.

'Why did you as a director of the Globe sell to the Standard? Why should you roll the profits of one company into the lap of another?'

To which Wright's weak reply was: 'Lord Loch wanted us to have as many liquid assets as possible.'[48] (Lord Loch had died in June 1900.)

Wright's attitude, as it had been during the public examination, was that all his activities were standard procedure and anything untoward was someone else's fault. The system of valuing mining shares was 'not his invention',[49] and it was not he but the accountant who was responsible for errors on the balance sheet. The real guilty people were the mine engineers, who had, he claimed, been in collusion with people in London and given false information.

When Rufus Isaacs began his cross-examination, Wright, determined to appear unconcerned, leaned casually back on the rail behind him and adopted the same brazenly confident air as before, claiming that it was 'a mere coincidence' that he had gone to America after receiving the telegram from his wife. When Isaacs demanded to know why he had been at such great pains to bring cash into Globe's 1899 balance sheet, Wright declared: 'You will never get me to the crack of doom to admit that there is anything the matter with the 1899 balance sheet.'[50] Isaacs suggested the shareholders would be more impressed with the company's aims to pay a regular 10 per cent dividend if they saw the cash on the balance sheet, to which Wright said: 'I am not responsible for the inferences the shareholders may draw.' Isaacs eventually got Wright to admit that market value had very little to do with his balance sheets, and then confronted him with his own statement at the 1899 meeting that shares were written down to the lower of market value or cost. His reply – 'It is the sort of statement that 99 chairmen out of a 100 would make at a shareholder's meeting' – was greeted with laughter.[51] Questioned further, he stated that this was 'a slip of the tongue',[52] his usual explanation when caught out in a lie. Piqued at Isaacs exposing the failure to record transactions in the minutes, Wright declared that he was not responsible for the minutes. 'Would counsel like him to be chairman and secretary and everything?'

'No,' replied Isaacs. 'I think you were quite enough.'[53]

As Isaacs ruthlessly picked apart the complex network of lies and manipulation, Wright's confidence withered, his lips twitched nervously, his eyes appeared sunken and his great bulk seemed to shrink and sag.

More and more questions were answered simply with 'I don't know'. Eventually he subsided onto the chair placed for his use 'and remained a huddled heap of weariness for the rest of the afternoon'.[54] Denials of wrongdoing and attempts to shift the blame onto others became less and less convincing.

On 21 January, as the trial moved into its ninth day, Mr Justice Bigham told the court that there had been attempts to interfere with the course of justice. He supplied no details, but the court was left with the impression that efforts had been made to bribe the jury. He issued a stern warning to the offenders, and Wright once again went into the witness box, where Isaacs savaged him about the claim made at the 1900 meeting that the shares appeared in the balance sheet after £1 million had been written off for depreciation.

'Have you any doubt that this statement is untrue?' demanded Isaacs.

'In its connexion it is true,' said Wright. 'But I ought to have said "loss and depreciation". It was an extempore utterance.'

'That is, as it stands, the statement is untrue?'

Wright was unable to reply, and shortly afterwards Isaacs goaded him: 'Would you like to say it was a slip of the tongue?' He pointed out that it appeared in a report edited by Wright and had not been corrected. Wright was reduced to claiming that 'his time was absorbed. The manager or secretary ought to have looked at it. In this company he had to do everybody's work.'[55]

Isaacs let the pathetic evasion stand without comment.

After the evidence had been taken, with even the judge commenting that 'some parts of this case passed the wit of man to understand',[56] it was decided that, for simplicity's sake, only two counts should go to the jury, whether or not the 1899 and 1900 balance sheets were false and fraudulent.

During the summing-up, Wright became pale and agitated. He doodled on a notepad, the word 'INTENT' written in bold capitals, his own initials metamorphosing into the Roman numeral VII repeated over and over again, suggesting he fully expected to get seven years in gaol. It took the jury less than an hour of deliberation to find him guilty.

When Wright stood to receive sentence he was outwardly calm and did not flinch when Bigham sent him to prison for seven years. He was taken by the tipstaff to the consulting room below the court, which had been reserved for his use. There he was joined by his friend John Eyre, who had stood surety for him, Worters, and assistant court superintendent Arthur Smith. He asked to go to the lavatory and Smith conducted him there, waiting outside the door while he was inside. Back in the consulting room, Wright, who seemed the calmest person in the room, was enjoying a drink and a cigar when he was joined by his solicitor, George Lewis, with whom he discussed plans to apply for a new trial. He then took his watch and chain from his pocket and gave them to Eyre, saying he would have no use for them where he was going. Shortly afterwards Wright slumped into an armchair and asked for another cigar. He was about to light it when Lewis saw that his client was breathing very heavily and looked ill. A doctor was sent for, but a few minutes later Wright was dead.

At first it was thought he had died of natural causes, but the post-mortem showed the unmistakable effects of poison. It was believed he had put a prussic acid tablet in his mouth when in the lavatory and then swallowed it down with the drink. Because Wright had been tried in a civil and not a criminal court, it had been no one's duty to search him. Another tablet was found among his effects, and, in a hip pocket, a six-chambered revolver, fully loaded and cocked. The body was taken by train to Witley, where a large number of people had gathered at the station, then by road to the now empty Lea Park, where it lay, watched over by faithful servants. He was buried at Witley Church, Godalming, on the following day. Hundreds of villagers came to pay homage, and the funeral was attended by family friends and City gentlemen as well as representatives of the charities to which he had made generous donations. When his affairs were settled, the former man of millions left £148,200.

Taking stock of Wright's career, the *Telegraph* observed that from 1889 he had launched thirteen companies, with capital of £11,225,00, and of these only Lake View and Ivanhoe, worth £3,325,000, had been successful. Investors had lost far more than the difference of almost £8 million, as many shares had been sold at a premium from the start.

The failure of the Whitaker Wright companies marked the end of the stock-market boom in West Australian gold, and a change in emphasis from gambling on new and unproven properties to enhancing existing ones. The mansion at Lea Park was burned down in 1952. Today the estate is a conference centre, and nothing remains of the days of Whitaker Wright. If he has any monument to his enterprise, it is the Baker Street and Waterloo Railway, which was completed by a syndicate and opened in 1906. Nowadays it is called the Bakerloo Line.

TEN

The Double Duke

In December 1907 workmen were constructing a large wooden shed around a tomb in Highgate Cemetery. To prevent investigation by inquisitive eyes, the shed had no windows and a single door, the interior illuminated through skylights placed in the roof. There was nothing remarkable to be seen, yet the work drew huge crowds of onlookers. Inside the shed, a stone monument weighing several tons was removed to expose the entrance to a vault. By 30 December the work was almost complete. Sleet and a cold biting wind did not deter the public as they gathered outside the gates of the cemetery, which was closed to all except those with special permits. Large numbers of policemen were there to prevent any disorder, but the crowds were quiet. At 5 a.m. electricians arrived to complete the installation of artificial lighting, followed two hours later by workmen who removed the flagstones covering the vault and carefully hoisted a coffin to the surface. As the morning progressed, there were more arrivals, Mr Augustus Joseph Pepper, surgeon, and pathologist Sir Thomas Stevenson, representing the Home Office, while Chief Inspector Dew and Assistant Commissioner Sir Melville Macnaghten represented the police. It could not have been more sombre or impressive if a case of murder was to be resolved. It was, in fact, the culmination of twelve years of court actions and public controversy that would decide the ownership of a fortune of more than £16 million.

The name plate on the coffin was inscribed 'Thomas Charles Druce, Esqre. Died 28th Decr., 1864, In his 71st year'. Photographs were taken, the lid was unscrewed and an inner lead coffin revealed. Carefully, a workman cut the lead around the outer edge, and as the lid was lifted it brought away with it the top of the inner wooden shell. The onlookers peered into the coffin. Either the contents would prove to be the body of Thomas Charles Druce, or, as had been alleged, his funeral had been a hoax and they would find only lead weights. Either way, the ramifications would be extremely serious, and criminal charges were already in preparation, the only question being who would become rich and who would go to prison?

In June 1895 Mrs Anna Maria Druce, 'a tall slim pale and rather sallow aquiline featured woman . . . with just a suspicion of faded gentility about her',[1] applied to the Bow Street Magistrates Court for a summons against persons she believed were depriving her son Sidney George Druce of his rightful inheritance. Born Anna Maria Butler in Ireland around 1848, the daughter of a land steward, she had been employed in 1872 as governess to Bertha Druce, youngest daughter of Thomas Charles Druce and his wife Annie (née Annie May). In December that year, much to the family's distress, Anna Maria Butler, then 24, married the Druces' youngest son, 20-year-old Walter. Five children were born to the couple before Walter died of typhoid in 1880, aged 28. Their eldest son, Sidney George, was born in 1875 and joined the Navy, but by 1898 he was farming in Australia. He seems to have played no part in his mother's actions on his behalf.

Thomas Charles Druce had, to all outward appearances, been a prosperous furniture salesman and occupied substantial premises at 68 and 69 Baker Street known as the Baker Street Bazaar, also the original home of the Tussaud waxworks. According to Anna Maria, however, Thomas Druce had never existed. He was merely the assumed *alter ego* of William John Cavendish Bentinck-Scott (usually known as John), the eccentric 5th Duke of Portland, who had died unmarried in 1879. The Duke's estates, which were inherited by his cousin, provided an annual income of £300,000. There was ample evidence that Thomas Charles Druce had died at his home, Holcombe House, Mill Hill, in 1864, but according to Anna Maria the death and the funeral were a sham, and she demanded that the coffin be opened to prove her point. Delusional she may have been, but Mrs Druce was also persistent and single-minded. When she was rejected by the magistrates' court, her next similarly unsuccessful appeals were to the Home Secretary and the House of Lords, demanding that the present incumbent of the dukedom should be ejected and Sidney George put in his place.

Had the 5th Duke been a gregarious man with a large social circle, it would have been easier to contest her claims, but his preference for seclusion, although not apparent in his youth, amounted in later life to an obsession, and he was rarely seen in public. Even during his lifetime he had been considered rather odd. Widespread rumours that there was a man's body in a coffin on the roof of one of his London houses were only dispelled by a visit from the sanitary inspectors, who found nothing suspicious. He was born in 1800, and his early careers – neither of which appealed to him – were the Army from 1818 to 1824 and politics from 1824 to 1826. He had inherited the dukedom in 1854. The family seat was

Welbeck Abbey, near Worksop, and he commenced a programme of improvements and additions, which was to occupy him for the rest of his life. Hundreds of workmen were employed landscaping the estate, constructing kitchen gardens and building underground tunnels, one leading to a magnificent riding hall, and another as a carriage ride to Worksop station. He dressed in a curious old-fashioned style, with a high top hat, frilled shirt and loose heavy coat, sometimes with another underneath and an extra coat carried over his arm. He constantly complained of ill health, so the coats may just have been a precaution against the cold, wet and mud as he inspected the building work. This may also explain why he always carried a large umbrella and why his trousers were fastened under the knees with straps. His London residence was Harcourt House, Cavendish Square, where he had an iron and glass screen built at the back for privacy. He would travel there in a special carriage in which he was protected from prying eyes by heavy curtains. That such a man might have led a secret double life was not thought to be impossible.

The origin of Anna Maria's obsession was financial jealousy. On attaining his majority (then 21 years), her husband Walter had come into possession of his inheritance, just over £18,600. He took up farming in Staffordshire, but the couple squandered the money through bad management and extravagance, returning to London with only £500 and some furniture. The oldest Druce son, Herbert, had been a partner in Druce and Co. since 1867 and gave Walter a job as a clerk on condition he put all his money into the business. When Walter died, his estate was valued at £1,500, of which the company gave Anna Maria only the original stake. The rest was tied up in a Chancery suit, which meant that she was obliged to rely on her mother-in-law for support, while the industrious Herbert was a prosperous man. Anna Maria, however, had a powerful weapon that she was not afraid to use, a piece of information then known only to one other person, Thomas Druce's widow. Thomas Druce and Annie May had not married until 1851. Before the marriage they had cohabited, and thus their three eldest children were illegitimate: Walter was their oldest legitimate son. As Anna Maria commenced legal proceedings laying claim to the Baker Street business the shocking truth was revealed, causing considerable distress to Annie, and embarrassment to her children. Herbert's illegitimacy, of which he was deeply ashamed and which he felt sullied the memory of his parents, was a fact he thereafter made every effort to conceal. Anna Maria was unsuccessful in pressing her claim, but the revelation cost the Druce estate additional legacy duty and Annie was no longer able to support her daughter-in-law. Anna Maria was obliged to go to the Marylebone Workhouse, where she relied on such funds as Annie could afford to feed the children. She did not institute any further litigation until after Annie's death in 1893.

In 1894 Anna Maria was living in modest lodging houses, making ends meet by passing worthless cheques and creating scenes at the office of her husband's executor until he gave her money to go away. She had researched the family papers, looking for details of a piece of copyhold land once owned by her father-in-law, which was no longer in the Druce family, and eventually discovered that the land had once been the property of the Duke of Portland, who had disposed of it by transfer. Copyhold was an ancient form of land tenure granted by a feudal lord, under which it could revert back to him, but to Anna Maria the Duke's ownership meant only one thing, that Thomas Druce and the Duke of Portland were one and the same; and it followed that the burial in 1864 had been a sham, the Druce will invalid and her son was Duke of Portland and heir to the massive Portland estates, which also included properties passed to the de Walden family on the death of the 5th Duke. To prove her point she needed to open the family vault, but ownership had passed to Herbert, who adamantly refused to grant permission to open it on the grounds that it was an act of desecration – although it is tempting to suppose that Herbert was prepared to do anything he could to obstruct the woman who had caused such grief to his family.

In 1897 Anna Maria wrote to the cemetery authorities, who agreed to transfer ownership of the vault to her son. She engaged a broker, Edward Phillips, who raised loans for her, and sold some Druce bonds on the strength of the millions she claimed were Sidney's. Her application to open the grave was heard by the Consistory Court of London on 9 March 1898. Anna Maria's solicitor, Mr Wright, had assembled a plausible case, carefully omitting any mention of the supposed double identity with the Duke of Portland, which he may have felt would not help his client. He was correct, as this was probably the only court hearing at which Anna Maria was heard with any sympathy. Thomas Druce, it was claimed, had become insane, and other people had faked his death and obtained probate in order to get hold of his property, and cheat Walter, who in 1864 had been just 12, out of his rights. It was asserted that, when the vault was opened in 1893 for Annie's burial, Walter's coffin, which was on top of that of Thomas Druce, had dropped, revealing that the lower one was just a shell weighted with lead. (The coffins of Thomas and Walter Druce actually lay in the vault side by side.) Anna Maria claimed to have seen and recognised her father-in-law, whom she had never met, in 1874. She had been passing the Berkshire County Lunatic Asylum in Maidenhead, and had seen Druce there as an inmate under the name of Dr Harmer. She had later been told that he had lived on as late as 1884. Dr Forbes Winslow, the head of the asylum, testified that he had once had a patient called Dr Harmer, a former homeopathic doctor who used to stand in the hospital grounds and dance like a bear. Shown a photograph of Mr Druce – and Wright took care not to reveal when it was taken – he identified it as a picture of Dr Harmer. Wright added fuel to the case by pointing out that Thomas Druce's death certificate, which gave the cause of death as abscesses, exhaustion and gangrene, had not been signed by a medical man. The court granted leave to open the grave, and there the whole matter might have ended except for the determined opposition of Herbert Druce, who proceeded to throw every possible legal obstacle in the way. At this difficult time, Anna Maria gained a new ally, the journalist John Sheridan Sheridan, who, recognising that others too could make money from the case, interviewed her at length and made their discussion headline news in *Lloyd's Weekly Newspaper*. Before long, Highgate Cemetery was besieged with thousands of sightseers, all of whom wanted to see the Druce tomb.

In March 1898, however, *The Times* published some highly damaging revelations. Dr Harmer's widow had been disturbed by the suggestion that her husband had been other than himself, and it was pointed out that Harmer had died aged 63 in 1893, when Thomas Druce would, if alive, have been 99. Dr Forbes Winslow soon backtracked on his identification, saying only that the photograph resembled Dr Harmer. *The Times* also recalled Anna Maria's original suggestion that Druce was the Duke of Portland, which was implausible if she claimed he was alive in 1884. The article also mentioned, but did not explore, the implications of a codicil in Druce's will, the bequest of £1,000 to a son George, of a former marriage.

Anna Maria's reasons for the Duke's imposture as reported in *Lloyd's Weekly Newspaper* were both romantic and tragic. Although there was no evidence that the future 5th Duke of Portland and his younger brother, 46-year-old George Bentinck MP, had ever known Annie May, it was claimed that in 1848 they had both been in love with her, which had led to a quarrel. Their father, said Anna Maria, had not only encouraged the suit of the younger brother, but had behaved insultingly towards his eldest son, who suffered from an unpleasant skin disease. The only true part of her story was that on 21 September 1848 George, who had been walking to a dinner engagement, failed to arrive and was found dead outside the gates of Welbeck Park. The cause of death was given as heart disease.

Anna Maria also claimed that, following his brother's death, John had suffered 'the keenest remorse and the most abject fear',[2] though whether this was guilt at having precipitated a fatal heart attack or something more sinister she would not say, but added that it was for protection that he adopted a new persona, that of Thomas Charles Druce. In 1864, said Anna Maria, anxious that the complexities of his double life could increase his risk of exposure, he determined to rid himself of his fictitious alter ego. She further claimed that George Vassar, an employee of Thomas Druce, had told her that shortly before the burial he had been asked to bring lead down from the roof of Druce's house to put in the coffin. (Vassar, now 70 years old, denied this story with tears of indignation in his eyes.) Even after the sham burial, she said, the Duke remained in fear and decided to feign madness, under the name of Harmer, so that he might be able to plead insanity if accused of any crime. This contradicted what was said at the Consistory Court, but Anna Maria was adept at changing her story when it suited her. She also claimed that the marriage of Thomas Druce and Annie May had been delayed because of uncertainties about the lady's birth – she was purportedly the illegitimate daughter of the 5th Earl of Berkeley. This was demonstrable nonsense, as Annie May had been born many years after the Earl's death.

As the year progressed, and Herbert Druce successfully delayed all endeavours to have the vault opened, Anna Maria became obsessed with the idea that he would try to steal her father-in-law's coffin. She consequently went to Highgate Cemetery almost every day, accompanied by a mining engineer, to check that all was well. In June she saw some workmen digging new graves and ordered them to stop what they were doing, convinced that they were tunnelling to the Druce vault. It took more than two hours for cemetery officials and the mining engineer to persuade her that from the point where the men were working such a feat would have been impossible.

In the same month she issued a writ against Mr Alexander Young, the only surviving executor of Thomas Druce's will, with the object of obtaining revocation of probate on the grounds that Druce had not died in 1864. She also gained a new witness. An appeal for information in *Lloyd's Weekly Newspaper* had been answered by 68-year-old Mrs Margaret Hamilton, who said she had known Thomas Druce since girlhood and had seen him after 1864. The Duke, she added dramatically, had been directly responsible for the death of his brother after striking him in the chest during a quarrel. Protests by the Bentinck family that the future 5th Duke had been in London on the date of his brother's death were ignored.

It is not surprising that both press and public took the view that Herbert Druce's opposition showed he had something to hide. 'The remark heard on every hand is: "If Mrs Druce be a deluded lady, why not have this straight-away proved by opening the grave and the coffin therein?" An impartial public naturally infers that Mrs Druce's contention gives her opponents an uneasy feeling of uncertainty as to the contents of that coffin . . .'.[3] Herbert's solicitors were convinced that, even if the coffin was opened, after thirty-four years the contents were unlikely to be more than an unidentifiable skeleton. In December 1898 Herbert succeeded in regaining ownership of the vault.

In February 1899 Anna Maria's entire case collapsed. The newspapers had been digging into Thomas Druce's past and had uncovered the story of his first marriage. On 19 October 1816, Thomas Druce, declaring his age to be 21, had married Elizabeth Crickmer in Bury St Edmunds, both bride and groom showing their father's occupation as 'farmer'. (The future 5th Duke of Portland was then only a month past his sixteenth birthday.) Their children, Henry Druce, Charles Crickmer Druce, George Druce and Frances Elizabeth Druce, were born in 1817, 1818, 1819 and 1821 respectively. Perhaps this rapid family expansion was too much for Druce, since he deserted his wife before the birth of their daughter, leaving her to bring up the children in poverty. Elizabeth later traced him to London, where he had established himself as a successful draper, and persuaded him to provide an allowance. Henry joined the Navy and died at sea, while the two younger sons went to Australia. Frances married a butcher named John Izard and settled in London. Elizabeth Druce died in the summer of 1851, and soon afterwards Thomas Druce and Annie May were married.

Anna Maria was able to cope with this development only by denying it was true, but her day was almost done. She was about to be challenged by a new pretender to the Portland millions, George Hollamby Druce. A widower with several children, he was the son of George Druce snr, the third son of Thomas's Druce marriage to Elizabeth Crickmer. George snr had gone to Australia in 1851 and become first a miner and then a farmer. He had married a widow, Mrs Cadle, the former Mary Hollamby. George jnr (referred to from now on as George) was born at Campbell's Creek, Victoria, in 1855. A carpenter by trade, he maintained a keen interest in mechanical engineering, through which he hoped he would make his fortune. He had a workshop where in about 1893 he began to work on the invention of a perpetual motion machine. Patiently he built model after model, and despite repeated disappointment never gave up. In 1898 he read about the Druce case in the newspapers, without at first realising that he was a descendant of Thomas Charles, but in 1901 he made an application to intervene in Anna Maria's case against Alexander Young. Anna Maria was adamant that George was no relation at all of Thomas Charles Druce, but 'an impudent, audacious, and absolute [*sic*] ignorant impostor'.[4]

The hearing of the application to revoke probate in December 1901 was effectively the end of Anna Maria's case. Dr Edmund Shaw gave evidence that he had attended Thomas Druce in his final illness, as did Dr William Blasson and an elderly servant, Cathcrine Bayly. All vividly recalled Druce's unpleasant death. He had died of gangrene of the bowel, and the body had smelt so offensive it had been necessary to wrap it in a sheet sprinkled with chloride of lime. Herbert testified that he had seen his father's body and had signed the death certificate as informant. The apparent inconsistency about the lack of a doctor's signature was clarified when it was established that until 1874 doctors were not required to sign death certificates. Anna Maria was by now in a state of hysterical agitation, accusing all the witnesses of lying and declaring that Thomas Druce's coffin contained a wax effigy made by Tussauds. She claimed that Mrs Hamilton was really the late Duchess of Abercorn and had sworn on her deathbed that Druce was the 5th Duke. She would not believe that Mrs Hamilton was still alive, and referred to a Henry Walker, who had once stoked the fires at Welbeck, refusing to believe that he had been dead for many years: 'I have seen him alive . . . I said "You're Henry Walker." He said "I'm not," I said "You're a liar, you are living in the same house as he lived,"' she exclaimed unconvincingly.[5]

The jury did not need to deliberate. They found that the will had been properly executed and that Thomas Druce had indeed died in 1864. Thereafter Anna Maria's appearances in court were less frequent, and increasingly desperate and pathetic. Edward Phillips was unable to do any more for her, and retired from the case.

George Hollamby Druce arrived in England in May 1903, together with 38-year-old Thomas Kennedy Vernon Coburn, a barrister and solicitor who had abandoned his practice in Australia to devote all his energies to securing his client's rights. Perhaps he had not a great deal to lose: Coburn had achieved some notoriety in Australia during his involvement in the land-boom period, had almost been struck off the rolls and was twice declared insolvent – 'his career has been rather a checkered one,' observed J. Howden, a Melbourne finance agent. 'He is very clever and smooth-spoken, but is regarded with suspicion here, and is considered unreliable.'[6] George had little money or education, but with Coburn's assistance had raised funds for travel and research by selling mortgage debentures at £50 apiece. George was 'a quaint little fellow, as eccentric as his grandfather',[7] said the writer Bernard O'Donnell, who shared lodgings with him. He appeared quite serious and earnest about his claim, but any spare moments were devoted to his perpetual motion machine. Assisted by Coburn, he gathered information about the Bentinck and Druce families, interviewing people who had known Thomas Druce and the 5th Duke. The one thing he was never able to find was a baptismal record of Thomas Druce, whose exact age must remain a mystery.

George tried to raise further funds by selling Druce bonds to investors in England, who were told that George's father was the eldest son of Thomas Charles Druce. A meeting of supporters was held, but the plans abruptly fell apart. Someone had been researching the Australian Druce family and discovered a fact that both George and Coburn had tried hard to conceal: there was a grandson of Charles Crickmer Druce, named Charles Edgar, born in 1870, who clearly had priority over George. In 1899 Charles Edgar and a family syndicate assisted by Arthur Trewinnard, a relative by marriage, had attempted to promote his claim, but after a dispute the syndicate broke up. Trewinnard later described Charles Edgar as 'a dull and stupid man, [who] could not be induced to take any active part in the matter, and the result was that the arrangements for prosecuting his claim fell through'.[8] It was only after this that George saw his chance. Trewinnard was of the opinion that George did not have the intellectual capability to commit a complex fraud, but he knew who did – Thomas Coburn.

As soon as Charles Edgar's name was mentioned, George flew into a temper. He said his cousin was illegitimate, and he would have nothing to do with him. Efforts were made to persuade George that someone should be sent to Australia to get a signed agreement from Charles Edgar renouncing his claim, but George would not be reasoned with and the potential investors withdrew. George's cousin, John Ebenezer Crickmer, a stockbroker of Messers Crickmer Hilder and Towse, then suggested that his firm should incorporate a company and sell shares to the public. This plan was agreed, but John failed to mention the existence of Charles Edgar to his partners. When they found out, they withdrew, refusing to pay any costs, saying they had been misled. As a result, John Crickmer left the firm and registered the company himself. Coburn went to Australia, and on 17 April obtained a signed statement from Charles Edgar Druce in which he agreed to share the Portland estates equally with George if the claim was successful.

Despite these difficulties, George had some valuable allies, Mrs Hamilton, whose stories about her youthful friendship with the Duke were full of intricate detail, and the *Daily Express*, which by July had interviewed both George and Coburn and was publishing daily articles about the case. John Sheridan Sheridan, once Anna Maria's champion, abandoned her and threw in his lot with George, who eventually rewarded him with commission notes entitling him to 10 per cent of the proceeds of his claim. Sheridan was well aware of the necessity of shoring up George's case, since he had been introduced to Trewinnard and had learnt all about Charles Edgar Druce. Obtaining an introduction to Mrs Hamilton, he carefully nursed her as a potential witness, distancing her from possible rivals and providing for her financially. Sheridan tried to draw Phillips into the case again, but, suspicious of Mrs Hamilton's story, Phillips asked Sheridan if he had been coaching her, to which he replied: 'Of course I have, what do you think?'[9] Among the many letters Phillips had received about the case was one from a Robert Caldwell in America, who had claimed to have important information. Phillips had treated the letter as 'one from a maniac',[10] and left it in his file, but shortly after Sheridan had looked at the file Phillips found that the letter was missing. Phillips declined to have anything further to do with Sheridan.

Anna Maria was soon back in court waving a copy of the *Daily Express*, which she said was printing lies, and she demanded costs, which had never been awarded to her. This appearance was her last despairing act in the Druce case. She seems to have been utterly alone, abandoned even by her children. Her funds all gone, she was later admitted to Hampstead Workhouse.

On 22 July 1905 G.H. Druce Ltd was incorporated with capital of £11,000 in shares (about £750,000 today). There was no lack of takers, and blocks of shares were soon changing hands at a substantial premium. The directors were George Hollamby Druce and two Crickmer cousins, Charles James, a retired wine merchant, and John Ebenezer. George had transferred the rights under his claim to the company, and if successful, shareholders were promised £100 for each £1 share they held. This breached the agreement with the Australian debenture holders, who contacted George to establish their rights, but he failed to respond.

Coburn saw no reason to inform the shareholders in G.H. Druce Ltd about the existence of Charles Edgar, but when, as was inevitable, they found out, he reassured them that George's nephew was illegitimate. He failed to mention that counsel's opinion had been sought on the matter and it had been confirmed in July 1906 that there was no proof to support this allegation.

A critical development in George's claim was the emergence of two new witnesses, both of whom had read about the case in the newspapers. English-born Miss Robinson, a stout middle-aged lady who was resident in New Zealand, had written to say that she had once acted as secretary to the Duke of Portland, having been introduced to him by Charles Dickens. Not only had the Duke told her about the imposture, but she had recorded his words in a diary that was still in her possession. Irish-born Robert Caldwell, living in New York, whose letter to Phillips had mysteriously disappeared, had met with a better reception from George Druce and his advisers. He claimed he had known the Duke both as the Duke and as Druce, and had actually assisted with the mock burial, obtaining the lead with which to weight the coffin. Edmund Kimber, George's London solicitor, went to America to interview Caldwell and returned to report to the committee of shareholders that he was satisfied that his story was true. Both of these individuals were brought to England, Miss Robinson arriving with a younger lady companion, Miss Maude O'Neill. Immediately there was a new sensation, as Miss Robinson complained to the police that valuable documents, including letters from Charles Dickens and the Duke of Portland, had been stolen from her trunk during the voyage. Extensive investigations were made, but no evidence could be found to justify her claim.

The attack of George and his solicitor on the evidence of Thomas Druce's death was now simplified by the fact that William Blasson had died in 1904 and Young, Shaw and Catherine Bayly were old and infirm. The claimant's resources would never be sufficient to take on the financial might of the Portland dukedom, but there was an easier target. Herbert Druce had both sworn an affidavit and testified in court that his father had died on 28 December 1864 and that he had seen him in his coffin. If George's claim was true, then Herbert Druce had committed perjury. George therefore instituted proceedings against Herbert Druce. The case would probably cost several thousand pounds, but he had no doubts as to where he could get the money.

In June 1907 an informal meeting of the shareholders of G.H. Druce Ltd was advised that the case was now so strong that the onus of proof was no longer on George but on his opponents. George's descent from Thomas

Druce and Elizabeth Crickmer was beyond doubt, they had a witness to the fake burial, and it only remained to prove that Druce and the Duke were the same man. It was now implied that the young future Duke had commenced his imposture by the time he was 16 and had lied about both his name and his age on his marriage to Elizabeth Crickmer. Dazzled by the promise of millions, George and his associates did not think this improbable. Coburn told the excited throng that he had spent five years gathering evidence, and that he honestly believed not only that G.H. Druce was the grandson of the 5th Duke of Portland but also that he would be able to establish the point in court. He was greeted with loud cheering. Only one more thing was required, George told them: more money for the forthcoming trial. He was willing to offer 3,000 £1 shares to existing shareholders at £2 a share. Any not so taken up would go on the market, where he believed they would sell at £4. The meeting closed with the shareholders expressing their unabated confidence in his claim. A series of articles later published as pamphlets in which Mrs Hamilton confirmed the Duke's imposture was a key part of the campaign to persuade the public to part with their money. One article was by Coburn, but the rest, published under the name of George Hollamby Druce, were written by Kenneth George Henderson, manager of the *Idler* magazine and grandson of Frances Izard. The question of establishing identity was then an uncertain science. *Was Druce the Duke?* presented a host of clues to convince the public. There was one admitted photo of the Duke and also one of Druce, and the pamphlet declared that persons who had known the Duke had picked out Druce's picture as a lifelike picture of the Duke, while business associates of Druce identified a photo of the Duke as Thomas Druce. The photographic evidence would have been more convincing but for the fact that the Duke was cleanshaven, apart from side whiskers, while Druce had a substantial bushy beard and moustache. It was, however, no great leap of imagination to suggest that the eccentric Duke had specially made false whiskers that he wore when masquerading as Druce. Other 'evidence' stated that the two men were similar in height, build and manners, and both suffered from a hereditary skin disease. The most dubious section was the one headed 'Habits of life generally', which listed, among other things, 'secrecy and reserve, subterranean wanderings, passion for building and making alterations to buildings, mysterious journeyings, and peculiar style of closed carriage', all of which may well have been true of the Duke, but there was no evidence at all that these traits were also those of Thomas Druce.[11] Some research had been done to identify where the Duke and Thomas Druce were at different periods, in an effort to show that blanks in the history of one could be explained by activity of the other. The Duke's Army career, which coincided with Druce bringing up a family in Bury St Edmunds, was an inconvenience explained away by suggesting that it was an appointment on paper only.

By the autumn of 1907 most of the shares in G.H. Druce Ltd had been sold, but by then two more companies had been launched by John Sheridan Sheridan, the Druce-Portland Company in October, with the object of promoting George's claims, and The New Druce-Portland Company in November, which acquired Sheridan's commission notes. If George was successful, the holder of each 5s share would receive £16.

On 25 October 1907 Herbert Druce was summoned before magistrate Mr Plowden of the Marylebone Police Court, and some of the best legal minds in the country appeared in a case where 'laughter in court' was virtually the rule of the day. The prosecution was led by the brilliant Llewellyn Atherley-Jones KC MP. His formidable opponents were Horace Avory KC and Sir Charles Matthews KC. The audience in the crowded court included the 6th Duke of Portland. Anna Maria Druce took no part in the case. She was by now an inmate of the London County Asylum.

Atherley-Jones, emphasising Herbert Druce's continued refusal to permit the coffin to be opened, made the powerful point that, if it was shown that the funeral had been spurious, there would be an intestacy so far as Thomas Druce was concerned, Herbert Druce would have to surrender all the property he had received under his father's will and George Druce would then succeed to the whole of Thomas Druce's property. He made no mention of Charles Edgar Druce, and it may well have been that at that point he had not been advised either of that person's existence or of his true relationship to George.

Mr Avory asked for an adjournment of two weeks to prepare his defence, and one of the first things he wanted to examine was Miss Robinson's diary, which she had given to Edmund Kimber. On 29 October Herbert's solicitors, Messrs Freshfields, wrote to Kimber to make an appointment to view the diary. Kimber replied that the diary had been returned to Miss Robinson, who had been subpoenaed to produce it in court, and he could not produce the original until she went into the witness box, but would be happy to provide a copy. Freshfields pointed out that the magistrate had said that the defence should be able to inspect the diary, and on 1 November Kimber replied with some disturbing news: the diary had been stolen. Miss Robinson had gone shopping with it in her handbag. While she was looking in a shop window, a man had come up and told her that there was a spider on her shoulder. She was distracted and the man disappeared with her bag. Kimber added that this was the sixth theft of important documents, and alleged that they had been carried out by agents employed by Freshfields's clients.

When the hearing resumed on 8 November, Avory boldly read the correspondence in court. Atherley-Jones dissociated himself from the unwise allegation, and Kimber was obliged to apologise. Avory must have known he had already won. He was too experienced not to realise that important documents going mysteriously missing at a critical moment, and wild allegations of theft, showed a very serious weakness in the prosecution's case. 'You at the proper time will know what is the proper inference to be drawn from this proceeding,' he said.[12]

Next, 71-year-old Robert Caldwell took the stand, amid considerable excitement. He was a brazen and careless liar, happy to tell any story that suited him (as long as the people he mentioned were dead), unconcerned that some of his claims contradicted those of Anna Maria and utterly oblivious to the fact that many of his statements could be disproved by official records. He told the court that as a young man he had suffered from a disease that had made his nose bulbous and unsightly. Arriving in England in 1855, he consulted Dr Morell Mackenzie, the renowned specialist, and was told that his condition was incurable. Having heard of a gentleman in India who could help him, he travelled there and met British Army Captain Arthur Wellesley Joyce, who not only cured him but gave him the secret of the cure. (A later interview with Joyce's daughter revealed that Wellesley Joyce was a Limerick man, who had never been to India.) Returning to England, he again called on Morell Mackenzie, who invited him to apply the cure to a poor man, which he did. It was through the specialist that he was introduced to the Duke of Portland at Welbeck Abbey, early in 1864.

The Duke, claimed Caldwell, had suffered from a similar malady, and so he was invited to commence treatment, which was carried out sometimes at Welbeck Abbey and sometimes at Druce's bazaar in London, where he was introduced to Druce's wife and children and stayed as a guest. In 1864, at the Duke's direction, he had employed a carpenter to construct a coffin. On 27 December he bought about 200lb of sheet lead, which was placed in the coffin, and a funeral took place on the following day, a magnificent affair with fifty mourning coaches filled with old retainers of the Duke from Welbeck. Caldwell had no difficulty in recognising the photographs of the Duke and Druce that were produced in court as being of the same man, adding, to the amusement of the spectators, that he had seen the Duke put on a false beard.

When Avory began his cross-examination, he revealed that the Druce-Portland affair was not the first scandalous mystery in which Caldwell had been involved. In November 1878 the body of Alexander Turney Stewart, a multimillionaire who had died two years earlier, was stolen from his family crypt in St Mark's Churchyard, New York. The newspaper-reading public was kept amused for several months as detectives spread their investigations over most of the eastern United States. In 1880 Judge Henry Hilton, the administrator of Stewart's estate, announced that he had paid a ransom and recovered the remains, which he had had interred at Garden City Cathedral.

After Hilton's death in 1899 Caldwell had approached the *New York Herald*, offering to sell it a story for $10,000 in which he accused Judge Hilton of forging Stewart's will and stealing the remains himself. He claimed to be a trustee of twenty-seven compromising letters that had passed between Judge Hilton and Cornelia, Stewart's widow, who had died in 1886.

Avory suggested that, once the *New York Herald* had refused to purchase the original story, Caldwell, popularly known as 'the great American affidavit maker',[13] had taken it away and 'cooked it and served it up again'[14] with embellishments (that is, forged letters), which Caldwell hotly denied.

Caldwell was obliged to backtrack on his claim to have seen Morell Mackenzie in 1855 (Mackenzie, born in 1837, had opened his clinic in 1862), saying he had been given a recommendation to him in 1857 and carried it about for several years. 'Waiting for him to grow up, I suppose?' asked Avory.[15]

Avory next tried to discover more about the supposed cure of the poor man.

'What did you do to his nose?'

'Ah, you would like to get at that.' (A roar of laughter) 'You would go into the business yourself if you could.' (More roars of laughter)[16]

Caldwell claimed he had cured two rajahs, who had paid him £5,000 each, while the Duke had paid him £10,000, of which half was for putting the lead in the coffin.

Asked why he had abandoned this remunerative business, Caldwell said that the whole medical faculty were after him for dispensing medicines without being a doctor. 'You find me a man with a bulbous nose and I'll cure him in a month. That is a fair offer, but I should want £5,000.' (Laughter)[17]

Caldwell had a poor memory for his own lies. When questioned at the adjourned hearing a week later, the two rajahs had become a German and an Italian, and he denied dispensing medicines at all, saying he had removed hair from the Duke's nose and applied an ointment. Avory now led Caldwell into even deeper waters, as he asked him about the living arrangements at the Baker Street Bazaar, since Caldwell had claimed that Druce, his wife and five children all slept and dined there, and they were waited on by eight servants.

'If there was no bedroom, kitchen nor dining room at Baker Street Bazaar your story must be untrue?' asked Avory, who was clearly aware that the bazaar did not incorporate living accommodation. 'I throw in the servants too. Supposing there were not any, your story about them must also be untrue?'[18] He also challenged Caldwell about the date of the funeral, which had actually taken place on 31 December, and his supposed recollections of Welbeck Abbey, the underground rooms, magnificent 100ft ballroom and picture gallery.

'Now just listen to me,' said Avory, dangerously. 'Suppose these underground rooms, picture gallery and ballroom were never constructed until 1872, your whole story must be untrue?'[19] Under this barrage of questioning Caldwell could do little more than stubbornly insist that he was telling the truth.

Avory later established that Caldwell had been in service with a Mr Christy of Londonderry between 1863 and 1871, the period when he was supposed to have been such a favourite of the Duke, and Caldwell was reduced to the ridiculous excuse that the Londonderry man had been his brother, with whom he had exchanged names.

The next star witness was the writer of the missing diary, a lady who stated her name as Miss Robinson, her age as 56 and that she was originally from America, where her father had owned a tobacco plantation. Not one of these statements was true. She said that as a schoolgirl she had been introduced to Druce and had once attended a party at Gadshill, the home of Charles Dickens, where Druce sang songs to entertain the children. In May 1868 she had met Dickens again in Boston, and he had suggested that she should become a secretary for Druce at Welbeck Abbey. Dickens later took her to Welbeck, where she recognised Druce as the man she had met when she was a child. Her duties were to receive packets for the Duke at her lodgings, which were sent to her under the name of 'Madame

Tussaud' and contained letters for him in the name of Druce, and she also posted letters for him. She ceased to be on friendly terms with the Duke in 1876, and went to New Zealand.

Avory naturally pressed her as to how much she had received in expenses to come to England, and led to a slip of the tongue that the court found hilarious:

'Have you had anything on account from anybody?'

'I have.'

'How much?'

'Not overmuch. I cannot tell you how much. I have not kept a diary.' (Laughter)[20]

It was easy for Avory to cast doubts on the veracity of her claims with questions such as 'Supposing Mr Dickens left America in April and was in Liverpool on 1 May 1868, how can you reconcile that to your story?', and 'Are you aware that it has been publicly proclaimed by the Dickens family that Mr Dickens had nothing to do with the Duke?'[21] Shown samples of handwriting, the supposed secretary was unable to identity that of the Duke and was obliged to admit that samples of the Duke's and Druce's writing had been written by different hands. She was also unable, despite several attempts, to spell 'Tussaud'. Further questioned about her meetings with Dickens, Miss Robinson was reduced to pleading that her memory was fading, and after being allowed a break of ten minutes returned to the witness box and sat still, her eyes closed, saying she felt unwell. She later denied all knowledge of the mock funeral.

Mrs Hamilton, another prolific liar, stated that she had been born in Rome, the daughter of Robert Lennox Stuart, a great friend of the 5th Duke of Portland. From the age of about 14 she had known the Duke as Mr Druce and visited him at the Baker Street Bazaar; he used to refer to her affectionately as 'Madge'. On being shown a photograph of Druce, she at once identified the sitter as the Duke, or 'Dear old Scott'. The Duke, she said, had always gone around with a false beard in his pocket, confiding 'Well, of course, you know I am Mr Druce when I put that on.'[22] She also claimed that the Duke had wanted to marry her, but her father had refused permission. The Duke had told her about the supposed death of Druce, and she had seen him after the mock funeral. In her earlier affidavits she had said nothing about the Duke having a affliction of the nose, but she now said there had been some ugly lumps on his nose and that she had heard a gentleman she thought was named Cardwell was going to help cure him.

The remaining witnesses called by the prosecution were a parade of past employees or associates of Druce and the Duke. They did their best to recall events more than forty years in the past, peered at old photographs and gave their impressions of whether either man wore wigs, false whiskers or eyebrows. So many claimed to be privy to the 'secret' that the onlookers must have wondered just how it had remained a secret for so long. Henry Marks, the son of Druce's fishmonger, said he had seen a coffin being made and some rolls of lead, but contradicted Caldwell's story by saying there had been only two funeral carriages and not fifty. (This was confirmed by the records of the funeral directors.) He recalled that the coffin had been made at the time of his marriage, but his evidence foundered when Avory produced a certificate showing that Marks had been married in 1865. An engineer named James Rudd who had worked at Welbeck from 1872 said that the Duke did not entertain visitors and that he had never heard of Miss Robinson or 'Madge' and was not aware of the alleged friendship with Mr Stuart.

Many of the shareholders of G.H. Druce Ltd were, like the public, convinced that Caldwell was lying, but Coburn said he still thought the man was truthful. The committee met to discuss the matter and decided to send one of their number, a Mr Hill, to Londonderry to make enquiries. When Hill returned he described Caldwell as 'a damned old fraud'.[23] The committee decided to have no more to do with him. Caldwell called on George and Coburn, asking them for money to go to America to get documentary proof of his statements. They told him he was no longer wanted. Borrowing £10 from the company secretary, he went away.

On Friday 13 December Atherley-Jones, having closed his case, made an extraordinary announcement: he disowned one of his own witnesses. After the suspicion cast upon Caldwell's evidence, he said he felt that it would not be proper to rely upon his testimony. The following day the Bow Street Magistrates granted a warrant to arrest Caldwell for perjury, and the police went at once to the home of Charles Crickmer, where Caldwell had been lodging. They were too late. The previous Thursday Caldwell had taken a cab to Waterloo, where he caught the train to Southampton. That afternoon he departed by liner for New York.

On 16 December Avory opened the case for the defence. He wasted little breath on Caldwell, except to describe him as 'the most noxious perjurer that ever polluted the fountain of justice'.[24] He had few witnesses to call. Alexander Young had died the preceding August, and Dr Shaw was too infirm to travel to court. Perhaps the prosecution had hoped that

Miss Bayly would also be unable to testify, but, aged almost 77, she appeared and was able to confirm everything she had said previously. Additionally, she insisted that from 1848 to the date of his death Thomas Druce had never spent a night away from his home except in the company of his family – a statement which, if true, would have rendered his appearance as the Duke impossible.

Herbert Druce, under enormous public pressure to stop the undignified proceedings, finally relented, and on 21 December *The Times* announced that consent had been given to open the grave of Thomas Druce. On the same day, Robert Caldwell arrived at Hoboken, New Jersey, well aware of what lay in store for him. The news of the warrant had been transmitted by wireless telegram, and he and the other passengers were able to read about it in a daily paper that was published on board ship. Taken into custody by a US Marshal, he was arraigned before a US Commissioner, who appointed doctors to examine him. On being told that Caldwell was 'desperately ill',[25] the Commissioner fixed bail at $5,000 and Caldwell went home to Staten Island to stay with his daughter.

As the hoardings started to go up around the Druce grave, the seasonal pantomimes made topical allusions to the case that was the sensation of the day. The meeting of the Consistory Court on 27 December to hear the application to exhume was a formality. Three days later the lid of the coffin was lifted to reveal, not as many had supposed, a skeleton, nor a wax effigy or even lead weights, but 'a shrouded human figure which proved to be that of an aged, bearded man'.[26] The body was stiff, desiccated and partially mummified. The features were easily recognisable, and the reddish brown hair, eyebrows and beard were entirely natural and still attached to the skin. George William Thackrah, who had worked for Druce from 1860 until just before his death, was present, and at once identified the body as that of his former employer. Two journalists, who had been instructed not to publish prematurely and were guarded by a policeman, nevertheless managed to signal the result. On emerging from the shed, one blew his nose on a red handkerchief, and colleagues with field glasses and a telescope understood from this that a body had been found and alerted the press.

A few days later, after George had held two long conferences with his legal advisers, Coburn told the press that Atherley-Jones was satisfied that the body was not that of Druce; however, Dr Pepper's subsequent report left little doubt that the body was indeed that of the shopkeeper. On 6 January Atherley-Jones withdrew the prosecution and Herbert Druce was discharged, 'his character for truthfulness absolutely and conclusively vindicated'.[27]

Soon afterwards, Mary Robinson was arrested and charged with perjury. In court she adopted a vacant stare and pretended not to understand what was happening, while Kimber said he thought she was of unsound mind. She was committed for trial. The police had been suspicious of her ever since she claimed to have been robbed on the voyage, and had been gathering information from the New Zealand authorities. Born Mary Anne Webb in May 1841, she was the daughter of a police sergeant of Mortlake, Surrey. In 1863 she had married a butcher, William Robinson, who in 1869 was employed as a shepherd on the Duke of Portland's estate, but was dismissed after three months for neglecting the sheep, while Mrs Robinson was known to be 'a loose character in Worksop'.[28] The couple then emigrated to New Zealand, where William worked as a butcher. After his death there in 1884, Mrs Robinson went to live in Christchurch with her four children. Maude 'O'Neill' was in fact one of her daughters. In Christchurch Mrs Robinson was suspected of some minor thefts, but there was insufficient evidence for a prosecution. In 1906 she and Maude were living in Thomas Street when the house burned to the ground. An insurance claim stated that, apart from a cash-box, all her possessions, including plate and jewellery, had been destroyed. The police suspected that the valuables had been removed before the fire broke out, but in the absence of proof the money was paid. The Robinsons next moved to Falsgrave Street, Christchurch, but in February 1907 were ordered to leave following complaints made to the landlord by neighbours. They had observed that Mrs Robinson had been in the habit of leaving her daughter alone in the house, which had then been frequented by men.

Waiting in Holloway prison for her trial, Mrs Robinson had ample opportunity to consider her position, and on 27 January she indicated that she wished to make a statement. Admitting her true origins and confessing to many of her lies, she nevertheless omitted the fact that she had forged letters that purported to show that she had been the Duke's mistress. Given her history, the story she now told, which shifted much of the blame to others, may not be entirely believable. She said that in 1906 she had read an account of the Druce case in a newspaper, which claimed that the Duke had been a wizard. The newspaper gave the address of a Mr Druce, to whom she wrote saying that the article was mistaken and that she had known the Duke. About a month later, she said, a man called at her house with an offer. He gave his name as Druce and said the case needed funds and if she would write what he asked she would receive £4,000. He wanted her to write a book with all that she could say or invent, and as there was another witness coming from America she was to claim she came from there too. She never saw the man again, but when she met George Hollamby Druce in London she felt sure that the two were related. As she compiled her history, George Druce and Mr Coburn kept in touch with her by letter, sending her pamphlets about the case, and cabled her £250 to enable her to come to England. When she arrived in Plymouth early in 1907, Coburn and Kimber immediately demanded the diary. She gave it to them, but later asked for it back on two occasions, since she wanted to refresh her memory before she gave evidence. Kimber refused, saying it was at his bank. When George called on her, however, he said that investors were being brought round to Kimber's office to look at the diary and that it was raising a lot of money for them. Mrs Robinson and her daughter lodged at Sisters Avenue, Clapham, where they waited in vain for Kimber to bring them some funds. Instead, they received a letter from him claiming that Scotland Yard was after her and that she was a bad character who had been chased out of New Zealand by the police there. As a final resort they called on Mr Watt, chairman of the committee of shareholders of G.H. Druce Ltd, and after that a Mr Crickmer called a few times to bring them money. Kimber later wrote to her with a list of things he wanted her to swear to in court, many of which she was unhappy about, and Coburn called and said he wanted her to swear she had seen lead put in the coffin, which she refused to do.

After several efforts to get the diary back, Mrs Robinson paid a solicitor to retrieve it for her. She then read it though and made a copy. 'I wanted my tale in the witness box to appear a little feasible, even though it was all lies.'[29] She insisted that the story she had told about the diary's theft was true. Several people had been eager to get hold of it: Freshfields, the defence solicitors, Kimber, who undoubtedly wanted it back, Coburn, who said he wanted to make copies of it, Allen, Caldwell's solicitor, who said he could make money out of it from the newspapers, and Watt, who was anxious on behalf of the shareholders. On 10 April 1908 Mrs Robinson was sentenced to four years in prison.

Mrs Hamilton was also arrested and tried for perjury. Born Margaret Jane Atkinson in Holme, Westmoreland, in March 1830, she claimed to have married William Hamilton, a master mariner, in the 1850s. There is no record of such a marriage, but in 1861 the couple were living as man and wife in Great Crosby, Lancashire, with a son and daughter.[30] She later parted from Hamilton and claimed to have worked as a housekeeper before coming to London. Mrs Hamilton's case was considered to be far more serious than that of Mrs Robinson. She had told, retold and embellished her lies for ten years and continued to persist in them. Her stories had been the foundation of the prospectus of G.H. Druce Ltd, on the basis of which many people had bought worthless shares. Mr Justice Grantham believed she ought to have been imprisoned for seven years, but in view of her advanced age she was sentenced to eighteen months' hard labour.

Robert Caldwell never stood trial. An application for his extradition was adjourned when medical reports showed he was suffering from paranoia. His daughter revealed that she had long suspected him to be insane. For many years he had been claiming friendships with distinguished men and special knowledge of sensational cases. When he began to talk about the Druce affair she had been about to take steps for his committal, but had not done so because London solicitors arrived and said that his stories could be corroborated. In February 1908 Caldwell was sent to the Manhattan State Hospital for the insane on Ward's Island. He died on 12 January 1911, aged 76.

Thomas Coburn, afraid of prosecution, had burned all his papers. Reduced to penury, he wrote begging letters to his friends, asking for 'a few shillings, for I am actually without money for stamps and fares' and for work: 'If only a pound a week to keep me from actual physical want.'[31] What became of him later is unknown. The Director of Public Prosecutions gave serious thought to taking action against George Druce, Kimber, Henderson, Coburn and Sheridan, but eventually decided not to proceed in view of the difficulty in proving fraudulent intent.

In March 1908 George presided at a meeting of the shareholders of G.H. Druce Ltd. The company had ceased to trade, all its capital was exhausted and there were liabilities of £300. He wanted it clearly understood that the proposed liquidation would not affect the continuation of proceedings to establish his claim, adding that he was unable to answer any questions that might affect litigation involving the directors. Whether any of his listeners still believed in him was not recorded. Charles Crickmer seconded the resolution to wind up the company, which was carried without discussion. The investors received nothing. The shareholders in the two companies formed by Sheridan were more fortunate. On 6 December 1907 a restraining order had prevented the directors from parting with any of the money subscribed. The holders of the 5s shares eventually received 4s a share.

George Druce settled in Oakland California, where in 1913 he told the correspondent of the *Oakland Tribune* that there was a tunnel between the

Duke of Portland's London mansion and the Baker Street Bazaar and that the coffin had contained only a dummy. He claimed to have been offered 'ample funds . . . by several wealthy women', the consideration in return being marriage. The lawsuit he had lost he described as 'a skirmish',[32] and announced his intention of returning to England to continue the fight. Gradually his funds were exhausted and his dreams became wistful thoughts of what might have been. He remained in Oakland, working as a carpenter and janitor. By 1937 he was living in a rooming house at 723 Sixth Street, blind and existing on a pension. He died in 1942.

Herbert Druce died on 11 April 1913. In a deliberately low-key funeral, he was buried in the family vault. Anna Maria Druce died in the London County Asylum on 17 March 1918.

It is to Mr Plowden, the magistrate for the Druce case, that the final words can be left. 'No-one can now doubt that Thomas Charles Druce existed in fact . . . Sufficient to say that this case is an illustration of that love of the marvellous which is so deeply ingrained in human nature, and is likely to be remembered in legal annals as affording one more striking proof of the unfathomable depths of human credulity.'[33]

Notes

Chapter 1: The Price of Omnium

1. Anon., *The Trial of Charles Random de Berenger, Sir Thomas Cochrane, Commonly Called Lord Cochrane, the Hon. Andrew Cochrane Johnstone, Richard Gathorne Butt, Ralph Sandom, Alexander McRae, John Peter Holloway, and Henry Lyte for a Conspiracy in the Court of King's Bench Guildhall, on Wednesday 8th and Thursday 9th June 1814, with the Subsequent Proceedings in the Court of the King's Bench* (London, Butterworth and Son, 1814), p. 5.

2. S. Johnson, *A Dictionary of the English Language* (London, Thomas Tegg, 1813), p. 762.

3. S. Pope, *Considerations, Political Financial and Commercial Relative to the Important Subject of the Public Funds, Addressed to Stock-Holders in General, and More Particularly to the Holders of Omnium* (London, Oriental Press, 1802), p. 2.

4. *London Chronicle*, 21 February 1817, p. 176.

5. Anon., *The Case of Thomas Lord Cochrane K.B., Containing the History of the Hoax, the Trial, the Proceedings the House of Commons, and the Meeting of the Electors of Westminster* (Edinburgh, J. Dick, 1814), p. 8.

6. Sir Leslie Stephen and Sir Sydney Lee (eds), *Dictionary of National Biography* (repr. London, Oxford University Press, 1973), vol. 10, p. 959.

7. This is the only extant account of the conversations between de Berenger and Cochrane Johnstone, but it is consistent with what is known of both men.

8. Baron C.R. de Berenger, *The Noble Stock-jobber, or Facts Unveiled, Irrefutably to Disprove Lord Cochrane's Affidavits* (London, R.S. Kirby, 1816), p. 49.

9. De Berenger, *Noble Stock-jobber*, pp. 64–5.

10. *Ibid.*, p. 257.

11. *Ibid.*, p. 293.

12. Anon., *Trial of de Berenger*, p. 25.

13. *Ibid.*, p. 144.

14. John Brown (ed.), *An Antidote to Detraction and Prejudice, Respecting the Family, Character, and Loyalty, of Charles Random Baron de Berenger; with a Biographical Memoir; an Account of his Arrest at Leith; his Singular Progress to, and Treatment in, London, Correspondence &c.* (London, printed for the editor, 1814), p. 56.

15. Anon., *Trial of de Berenger*, p. 487.

16. De Berenger, *Noble Stock-jobber*, appendix, p. 68.

17. *Ibid.*, p. 67.

18. 'Court of Kings Bench, Saturday June 18', *Observer*, 19 June 1817, p. 3.

19. Anon., *Parliamentary Debates* (London, T.C. Hansard, 1816), vol. 32, p. 1146.

20. *The Times*, 8 March 1817, p. 3.
21. The National Archives (TNA): PRO TS 11/44/165, 'The King ag^t Richard Gaythorne Butt', p. 2.
22. 'Caraboo', *Notes and Queries*, 3rd series, vol. 8, 29 July 1865, p. 94.
23. 'Inquest', *Bristol Daily Post*, 29 December 1864, p. 2.

Chapter 2: The Princess of Javasu

1. J.M. Gutch, *Caraboo. A Narrative of a Singular Imposition Practised upon the Benevolence of a Lady Residing in the Vicinity of the City of Bristol, by a Young Woman of the Name of Mary Willcocks, alias Baker, alias Bakerstendht, alias Caraboo, Princess of Javasu* (London, Baldwin Cradock and Joy, 1817), p. 50.
2. Gutch, *Caraboo*, p. 51–2.
3. *Ibid.*, p. 37.
4. *Ibid.*, p. 68.
5. *Ibid.*, p. 1.
6. *Ibid.*, p 1.
7. *Ibid.*, p. 3.
8. *Ibid.*, p. 68.
9. *Ibid.*, p. 7.
10. 'Caraboo', *Notes and Queries*, 3rd series, vol. 7, 1 April 1865, p. 269.
11. Gutch, *Caraboo*, p. 14.
12. *Ibid.*, p. 15.
13. *Ibid.*, n. 10 p.12.
14. Archbishop R. Whateley, 'Notice of the Pretended Princess Caraboo', *The Rose the Shamrock and the Thistle*, April 1863, p. 517.
15. Gutch, *Caraboo*, p. 20.
16. *Ibid.*, p. 19.
17. 'Curious and Authentic Particulars of the Life and Adventures of Carraboo, Alias, Mary Baker, Alias - - !', *Bristol Mirror*, 21 June 1817, p. 3.
18. Gutch, *Caraboo*, p. 27.
19. *Ibid.*, p. 47.
20. *Ibid.*
21. 'Curious and Authentic Particulars', p. 3.

Chapter 3: The Viscount of Canada

1. Archibald Swinton, *Report of the Trial of Alexander Humphreys [sic] or Alexander, Claiming the Title of Earl of Stirling, before the High Court of Judiciary at Edinburgh for the Crime of Forgery* (Edinburgh, Thomas Clark, 1839), p. 189.
2. Abel Stevens (ed.), 'Mademoiselle Le Normand', *National Magazine*, vol. 2 (New York, Carlton and Phillips, 1853), p. 439.
3. International Genealogical Index.
4. William Turnbull (ed.), *The Stirling Peerage. Trial of Alexander Humphrys or Alexander Styling himself Earl of Stirling* (Edinburgh, William Blackwood and Sons, 1839), footnote p. 8.
5. Anon., *Remarks on the Trial of the Earl of Stirling by an English Lawyer* (London, Lewis and Co., 1839), p. 30.
6. Swinton, *Report of the Trial of Alexander Humphreys*, p. ix.
7. *Ibid.*
8. Thomas C. Banks (as Sir Thomas C. Banks Bart. N. S.), *An Analytical Statement of the Case of Alexander, Earl of Stirling and Dovan &c. &c. &c.* (London, James Cochrane and Co., 1832), p. 99, appendix 6: Copy of the Minutes of Election of the Sixteen Peers of Scotland 2 September, 1830.
9. Banks, *An Analytical Statement*, Appendix 13, p. 118.
10. *Ibid.*, Appendix 7, p. 104.
11. Revd Charles Rogers, 'History of Alexander Humphrys or Alexander, Claimant of the Earldom of Stirling', in

Memorials of the Earl of Stirling and of the House of Alexander (Edinburgh, William Patterson, 1877), vol. 2, appendix 4, p. 218.

12. Turnbull (ed.), *The Stirling Peerage*, p. 13.
13. *Ibid.*, pp. 14–15.
14. Banks, *An Analytical Statement*, appendix 9, p. 112.
15. A.H. Alexander (as Earl of Stirling), *Narrative of the Oppressive Law Proceedings, and Other Measures, Resorted to by the British Government, and Numerous Private Individuals, to Overpower the Earl of Stirling, and Subvert his Lawful Rights* (Edinburgh, James Walker, 1836), p. 20.
16. Rogers, 'History of Alexander Humphrys', p. 219.
17. Alexander, *Narrative of the Oppressive Law Proceedings*, p. 13.
18. *Ibid.*, p. 14.
19. Turnbull (ed.), *The Stirling Peerage*, pp. 24–5.
20. 'Sales by Auction', *The Times*, 22 October 1832, p. 8.
21. 'Advertisement', *The Times*, 6 November 1832, p. 4.
22. Turnbull (ed.), *The Stirling Peerage*, p. 30.
23. Rogers, 'History of Alexander Humphrys', p. 222.
24. *Ibid.*, p. 222.
25. Turnbull (ed.), *The Stirling Peerage*, footnote p. 10.
26. Alexander, *Narrative of the Oppressive Law Proceedings*, p. 1.
27. *Ibid.*, p. 4.
28. *Ibid.*
29. *Ibid.*, p. 2.
30. *Ibid.*, p. 19.
31. *Ibid.*, p. 22.
32. *Ibid.*, p. 29.
33. Swinton, *Report of the Trial of Alexander Humphreys*, appendix 8, p. xxxix.
34. 'Private Correspondence', *The Times*, 28 April 1838, p. 5.
35. Swinton, *Report of the Trial of Alexander Humphreys*, p. 258.
36. Turnbull (ed.), *The Stirling Peerage*, pp. 39–40.
37. Swinton, *Report of the Trial of Alexander Humphreys*, p. 144.
38. *Ibid.*, p. 274.
39. *Ibid.*, p. 292.
40. *Ibid.*, p. 192.
41. *Ibid.*, p. 299.
42. *Ibid.*
43. *Ibid.*, p. 300.
44. *Ibid.*
45. *Ibid.*, p. 347.
46. Joseph Babington Macaulay, *The Life of the Last Earl of Stirling* (Paignton, W.A. Axworthy, 1906), p. 62.
47. Stevens (ed.), 'Mademoiselle Le Normand', pp. 439–40.
48. A.H. Alexander (as Earl of Stirling), *Two Letters Addressed to the Right Honourable Thomas Lord Denman* (Paris, J. Smith, 1845), p. 1.
49. *Ibid.*, p. 2.

Chapter 4: The Sting

1. Anon., *The Times Testimonial. Report of the Trial of the Action Bogle versus Lawson* (London, John Hatchard and Son, 1842), p. 8.
2. International Genealogical Index.
3. 'The Times Testimonial', *The Times*, 18 August 1841, p. 2.
4. Anon., *The Times Testimonial*, p. 9.
5. *Ibid.*, p. 10.
6. *Ibid.*, p. 11.
7. 'Extraordinary and Extensive Forgery and Swindling Conspiracy on the Continent', *The Times*, 26 May 1840, p. 6.
8. *Ibid.*

9. *Ibid.*
10. *Ibid.*
11. Anon., *The Times Testimonial*, p. 20.
12. 'Bogle v. Lawson', *The Times*, 18 August 1841, p. 2.
13. *Ibid.*, p. 3.
14. *Ibid.*
15. *Ibid.*
16. 'Bogle v. Lawson', *The Times*, 17 August 1841, p. 7.
17. Anon., *The Times* Archives, Bogle Case, Litigation 2.
18. Anon., *The Times Testimonial*, p. 30.
19. 'Bogle v. Lawson', *The Times*, 17 August 1841, p. 5.
20. 'Bogle v. Lawson', *The Times*, 18 August 1841, p. 4.
21. *Ibid.*
22. International Genealogical Index.
23. *Ibid.*
24. Anon., *The Times Testimonial*, p. 33.
25. *Ibid.*

Chapter 5: The Bank with No Scruples

1. Anon., *The Annual Register, or a View of the History and Politics of the Year 1856* (London, F. & J. Rivington, 1857), Chronicle, p. 33.
2. 'The Late John Sadleir esq.', *Cork Daily Reporter*, as quoted in *Clonmel Chronicle*, 20 February 1856, p. 2.
3. 'Death of Mr Sadleir M.P.', *Freeman's Journal*, 19 February 1856, p. 2.
4. 'Suicide of Mr John Sadleir M.P.', *Morning Advertiser*, 18 February 1856, p. 2.
5. 'Death of Mr Sadleir M.P.', *Morning Chronicle*, 19 February 1856, p. 7.
6. 'Suicide of Mr John Sadleir M.P.'
7. 'The Tipperary Joint Stock Bank', *Kilkenny Monitor*, 26 February 1856, p. 3.
8. 'The Inquest on Mr Sadleir, M.P.', *The Times*, 20 February 1856, p. 10.
9. *The Times*, 10 March 1856, p. 8.
10. Anon., *The Annual Register*.
11. 'London and County Joint Stock Bank', *Tipperary Free Press*, 19 February 1856, p. 4.
12. 'The Late Mr Sadleir M.P.', *Waterford Chronicle*, 1 March 1856, p. 1.
13. Anon., *The Annual Register*.
14. 'The Late Mr Sadleir M.P.', *Clonmel Chronicle*, 27 February 1856, p. 4.
15. 'The Tipperary Joint Stock Bank', *Freeman's Journal*, 29 April 1856, p. 4.
16. British Library, Aberdeen papers, Add. MS. 43248, f. 194.
17. *Ibid.*, f. 193.
18. 'Breaking the Pledge', *The Nation*, 1 January 1853, p. 291.
19. A.M. Sullivan, *New Ireland* (London, Sampson Low, Marston, Searle & Rivington, 1877), vol. 1, p. 377.
20. 'The Late Mr Sadleir M.P.', *Carlow Sentinel*, 23 February 1856, p. 3.
21. 'The Tipperary Joint Stock Bank', *Freeman's Journal*, 29 April 1856, p. 4.
22. *Ibid.*
23. *Ibid.*
24. *Ibid.*
25. 'The Tipperary Joint Stock Bank', *Clonmel Chronicle*, 30 April 1856, p. 2.
26. 'The Late John Sadleir', *Tipperary Free Press*, 9 November 1858, p. 3.
27. *Ibid.*
28. *Irish Chancery Reports* (Dublin, Hodges Smith and Co, 1861), vol. 11, p. 8.
29. *Irish Chancery Reports* (Dublin, Hodges Smith and Co., 1857), vol. 5, p. 199.
30. 'Winding up of the Tipperary Bank', *Freeman's Journal*, 5 March 1856, p. 2.
31. 'The Adjourned Inquest on Mr Sadleir M.P.', *The Times*, 26 February 1856, p. 12.
32. *Ibid.*

33. 'The Late Mr Sadleir', *Clonmel Chronicle*, 27 February 1856, p. 2.
34. *Ibid*.
35. *Ibid*.
36. 'The Tipperary Bank', *Carlow Sentinel*, 1 March 1856, p. 3.
37. 'The Tipperary Joint Stock Bank', *The Times*, 3 March 1856, p. 7.
38. 'Felo de Se', *The Nation*, 23 February 1856, p. 409.
39. Sullivan, *New Ireland*, pp. 378–9.
40. 'London and County Bank', *Tipperary Free Press*, 4 April 1856, p. 1.
41. Anon., *The Annual Register*.

Chapter 6: A Racing Certainty

1. 'The Convict William Kurr', *Police Guardian*, 24 August 1877, p. 4.
2. George Dilnot (ed.), *The Trial of the Detectives* (London, Geoffrey Bles, 1928), p. 16.
3. Detective Inspector Andrew Lansdowne, *A Life's Reminiscences of Scotland Yard* (London, The Leadenhall Press Ltd, 1893), p.11.
4. Belton Cobb, *Critical Years at the Yard – The Career of Frederick Williamson of the Detective Department and the CID* (London, Faber and Faber, 1956), p. 120.
5. Dilnot, *Trial of the Detectives*, p. 231.
6. *Ibid*., p. 23.
7. *Ibid*., p. 26.
8. *Ibid*., p. 28.
9. 'Police', *The Times*, 8 December 1876, p. 11.
10. *Ibid*.
11. Dilnot, *Trial of the Detectives*, p. 29.
12. George Dilnot, *The Story of Scotland Yard* (London, Geoffrey Bles, 1926), p. 237.
13. Dilnot, *Trial of the Detectives*, p. 95.
14. *Ibid*., p. 96.
15. 'Charge against Detectives', *The Times*, 3 August 1877, p. 11.
16. Dilnot, *Trial of the Detectives*, p. 31.
17. 'The Detectives and Mr Froggatt', *The Times*, 26 October 1877, p. 11.
18. *Ibid*.
19. Dilnot, *Trial of the Detectives*, p. 32.
20. *Ibid*.
21. 'Frauds and Aggravated Misdemeanour', *Police Gazette*, 13 October 1876, p. 2.
22. Dilnot, *Trial of the Detectives*, p. 103.
23. *Ibid*., p. 37.
24. 'The Detectives and Mr Froggatt', *The Times*, 14 November 1877, p. 11.
25. Dilnot, *Trial of the Detectives*, p. 38.
26. 'The Charge of Conspiracy against Detective Officers', *The Times*, 20 July 1877, p. 12.
27. TNA: PRO HO, 144/21/60045, piece 6.
28. J.G. Littlechild, *The Reminiscences of Chief Inspector Littlechild* (London, The Leadenhall Press, 1894), p. 53.
29. Dilnot, *Trial of the Detectives*, p. 47.
30. A.W. Basset, *The Scotland Yard Scandal and Other Stories of Crime* (London, Austin Rogers and Co., 1928), p. 14.
31. *Ibid*., p. 18.
32. Ex-Chief Inspector John Meiklejohn, *Real Life Detective Stories* (London, John Dicks Press, 1912), p. 130.
33. 'Forger Benson Must Go', *New York Herald*, 15 May 1888, p. 10.

Chapter 7: The Grappler

1. Ernest Terah Hooley, *Confessions* (London, Simpkin Marshall Hamilton Kent and Co., 1924), p. 8.
2. *Ibid*., p. 22.
3. These and other estimates of Hooley's personal finances come from his memoirs, *Confessions*.

4. 'Hooley Companies', *Money*, 3 September 1898, p. 565.

5. Hooley, *Confessions*, p. 149.

6. *Ibid.*, p. 73.

7. *Ibid.*, p. 12.

8. *Ibid.*, p. 8.

9. Anon., *The Hooley Book* (London, John Dicks, 1904), p. 28.

10. 'The Cycle Boom', *The Economist*, 16 May 1896, p. 618.

11. 'The Hooley Failure', *The Economist*, 30 July 1898, p. 1113.

12. 'Cyclomania', *Financial Times*, 27 April 1896, p. 4.

13. 'Beeston Pneumatic Tyre Co Ltd', *Money*, 2 May 1896, p. 625.

14. 'Beeston Pneumatic Tyre', *Financial Times*, 1 May 1896, p. 3.

15. 'City Notes', *Irish Field and Gentleman's Gazette*, 21 March 1896, p. 388.

16. 'The Grappler Tyre Company', *Financial Times*, 18 May 1896, p. 7.

17. 'City Notes', *Irish Field and Gentleman's Gazette*, 2 May 1896, p. 541.

18. 'City Notes', *Irish Field and Gentleman's Gazette*, 9 May 1896, p. 565.

19. 'The Grappler Pneumatic Tyre and Cycle Company Ltd', *Evening Irish Times*, 27 May 1896, p. 5.

20. *Ibid.*

21. *Ibid.*

22. 'City Notes', *Irish Field and Gentleman's Gazette*, 30 May 1896, p. 658.

23. 'Mr Hooley as a Company Promoter', *Pall Mall Gazette*, 27 May 1898, p. 5.

24. Hooley, *Confessions*, p. 50.

25. Anon., *Hooley Book*, p. 25.

26. 'Results of the Hooley System of Finance', *The Economist*, 20 August 1898, p. 1213.

27. 'The Money Market', *The Times*, 23 November 1896, p. 4.

28. Hooley, *Confessions*, p. 55.

29. *Ibid.*, p. 25.

30. *Ibid.*, p. 160.

31. *Ibid.*, p. 95.

32. *Ibid.*, p. 146.

33. 'Hooley', *The Cycle*, 19 December 1896, no 158.

34. Anon., *Hooley Book*, p. 106.

35. Hooley, *Confessions*, pp. 153–4.

36. 'Mr Hooley's Latest Scheme', *The Economist*, 10 July 1897, p. 987.

37. *Ibid.*

38. 'More Hooley Finance', *The Economist*, 28 August 1897, p. 1232.

39. 'Men of Millions', *Financial Times*, 21 February 1898, p. 8.

40. 'Drucker v. Hooley', *The Times*, 11 May 1898, p. 3.

41. *Ibid.*

42. 'The Grappler Tyre Company', *Financial Times*, 18 May 1898, p. 7.

43. *Ibid.*

44. *Ibid.*

45. 'Mr Hooley and the Grappler Company', *Financial Times*, 20 May 1898, p. 6.

46. *Ibid.*

47. 'Mr Hooley and the Grappler Tyre Company', *The Economist*, 21 May 1898, p. 767.

48. 'Mr Hooley as a Company Promoter', *Pall Mall Gazette*, 27 May 1898, p. 5.

49. *Ibid.*

50. 'The Hooley Failure', *The Economist*, 30 July 1898, p. 1113.

51. Anon., *Hooley Book*, p. 52.

52. *Commonwealth*, quoted in Anon., *Hooley Book*, pp. 61–2.

53. Anon., *Hooley Book*, p. 130.

54. 'Mr Hooley on his Financial Position', *Telegraph*, 10 June 1898, p. 7.

55. 'The Affairs of Mr E. T. Hooley', *The Times*, 25 July 1898, p. 3.
56. *Ibid.*
57. Hooley, *Confessions*, p. 274.
58. 'In re Hooley', *The Times*, 28 July 1898, p. 14.
59. 'In re Hooley', *The Times*, 11 August 1898, p. 4.
60. 'In re E. T. Hooley', *The Times*, 1 November 1898, p. 13.
61. 'In re E. T. Hooley', *The Times*, 18 August 1898, p. 10.
62. 'The Charges against Mr Hooley', *The Times*, 7 March 1899, p. 12.
63. Hooley, *Confessions*, p. 177.
64. *Ibid.*, p. 288.
65. *Ibid.*, p. 291.
66. *Ibid.*, p. 1.
67. *Ibid.*, p. 5.
68. *Ibid.*, p. 13.
69. *Ibid.*, p. 299.
70. 'Hooley Companies', *Money*, 8 October 1898, pp. 645–6.
71. 'Financier's Affairs', *The Times*, 22 February 1939, p. 16.
72. 'Hooley Companies', *Money*, 8 October 1898, p. 645.

Chapter 8: The Greatest Liar on Earth

1. *Wide World Magazine* (London, George Newnes Ltd, 1898), 1/1, p. 3.
2. *Ibid.*, 1/5, p. 451.
3. *Ibid.*
4. *Ibid.*, p. 454.
5. *Ibid.*
6. *Ibid.*, p. 462.
7. *Ibid.*, p. 471.
8. *Ibid.*, p. 475.
9. 'The Adventures of Louis de Rougemont', *Wide World Magazine*, 1/6, p. 617.
10. ' "?" by an Australian', *Daily Chronicle*, 9 September 1898, p. 5.
11. *Ibid.*
12. 'A New Crusoe', *Daily Chronicle*, 10 September 1898, p. 6.
13. *Ibid.*
14. 'British Association', *The Times*, 13 September 1898, p. 8.
15. *Ibid.*
16. *Daily Chronicle*, 13 September 1898, p. 4.
17. 'The British Association, a Retrospect', *The Times*, 19 September 1898, p. 12.
18. *Home News*, 16 September 1898, p. 4.
19. 'The Annual Meeting of the British Association', *The Times*, 15 September 1898, p. 7.
20. *Daily Chronicle, Grien on Rougemont, or the Story of a Modern Robinson Crusoe* (London, Edward Lloyd Ltd, 1898), p. 13.
21. *Evening News*, 13 September 1898, p. 4.
22. *Ibid.*
23. 'A Yachtsman's View', *Daily Chronicle*, 12 September 1898, p. 5.
24. 'M de Rougemont and His Artist', *Daily Chronicle*, 13 September 1898, p. 5.
25. 'De Rougemont and Jensen', *Daily Chronicle*, 14 September 1898, p. 5.
26. 'Is Mr de Rougemont's Story True?', *Daily Chronicle*, 12 September 1898, p. 5.
27. *Grien on Rougemont*, p. 12.
28. *Ibid.*
29. *Ibid.*
30. *Ibid.*, p. 13
31. 'De Rougemont at the "Chronicle" Office', *Daily Chronicle*, 15 September 1898, p. 5.
32. 'De Rougemont', *Daily Chronicle*, 17 September 1898, p. 5.
33. 'Professor Forbes and M de Rougemont', *Daily Chronicle*, 20 September 1898, p. 5.

34. 'The Octopus Story', *Daily Chronicle*, 20 September 1898, p. 5.
35. 'De Rougemont', *Daily Chronicle*, 22 September 1898, p. 5.
36. *Wide World Magazine*, 1/7, p. 3.
37. *Wide World Magazine*, 2/7, p. 4.
38. *Ibid.*, p. 8.
39. *Ibid.*, p. 18.
40. 'De Rougemont', *Daily Chronicle*, 23 September 1898, p. 5.
41. 'The Narrative of M de Rougemont', *Daily Chronicle*, 26 September 1898, p. 6.
42. *Wide World Magazine*, 2/8, p. 115.
43. 'De Rougemont', *Daily Chronicle*, 14 October 1898, p. 5.
44. *Evening News*, 3 October 1898, p. 4.
45. 'M. de Rougemont's Lecture', *Daily Graphic*, 4 October 1898, p. 4.
46. *The Times*, 7 October 1898, p. 1.
47. 'De Rougemont', *Daily Chronicle*, 7 October 1898, p. 5.
48. *Ibid.*
49. *Ibid.*
50. 'The Rougemont Fraud', *Daily Chronicle*, 10 October 1898, p. 5.
51. *Ibid.*
52. 'Another London Adventure', *Daily Chronicle*, 8 October 1898, p. 5.
53. 'An Earlier Experiment', *Daily Chronicle*, 8 October 1898, p. 5.
54. 'De Rougemont's "Confidences"', *Daily Chronicle*, 15 October 1898, p. 6.
55. *Ibid.*
56. *Ibid.*
57. 'Rougemont', *Daily Chronicle*, 11 October 1898, p. 5.
58. 'Rougemont', *Daily Chronicle* 12 October 1898, p. 8.
59. 'Rougemont', *Daily Chronicle*, 15 October 1898, p. 5.
60. 'Rougemont', *Daily Chronicle*, 13 October 1898, p. 8.
61. 'De Rougemont', *Daily Chronicle*, 14 October 1898, p. 5.
62. 'Rougemont', *Daily Chronicle*, 17 October 1898, p. 5.
63. 'The Topic of the Hour', *London Morning*, 12 October 1898, p. 1.
64. 'Rougemont', *Daily Chronicle*, 13 October 1898, p. 7.
65. *Wide World Magazine*, 2/9, p. 227, quoting 'An Amended Motto', *The World*, 12 October 1898, p. 25.
66. 'George Newnes (Limited)', *The Times*, 1 August 1899, p. 3.
67. Hulda Friederichs, *The Life of Sir George Newnes, Bart* (London, Hodder & Stoughton 1911), p. 129.
68. H.L. Grin (as Louis de Rougemont), *The Adventures of Louis de Rougemont, as Told by Himself* (London, George Newnes Ltd, 1899), p. 113.
69. *Ibid.*, p. 122.
70. H.M. Mill, *An Autobiography* (London, Longmans Green and Co., 1951), p. 99.
71. 'My Friend Mr Green', *The Sketch*, 12 October 1898, p. 516.
72. 'De Rougemont. Fiasco at the Bijou', *Argus*, 18 March 1901, p. 5.
73. *Ibid.*
74. 'De Rougemont in Melbourne. An Unsympathetic Audience', *The Age*, 18 March 1901, p. 6.
75. Frank Clune, *The Greatest Liar on Earth* (Melbourne, Hawthorn Press, 1945), p. 21.
76. 'The Tivoli – De Rougemont', *Sydney Morning Herald*, 25 March 1901, p. 5.
77. 'Entertainment', *The Times*, 30 July 1906, p. 1.
78. The Hon. Sir John Kirwan, *An Empty Land: Pioneers and Pioneering in Australia* (London: Eyre and Spottiswoode, 1934), p. 141.
79. *Ibid.*, pp. 141–2.
80. *Ibid.*, p. 142.

Chapter 9: The Juggler with Millions

1. 'The Westralian Mining Market', *The Economist*, 24 June 1899, p. 903.
2. 'London and Globe Finance Corporation', *The Times*, 18 December 1900, p. 12.
3. Charles E. Drummond Black, *The Marquess of Dufferin and Ava* (London, Hutchinson and Co., 1903), p. 363.
4. 'London and Globe Finance Corporation', *The Times*, 18 December 1900, p. 12.
5. *Ibid.*
6. Birth certificate of James Whittaker Wright.
7. Raymond Radclyffe, *Wealth and Wild Cats: Travels and Researches in the Gold-fields of Western Australia and New Zealand* (London, Downey and Co., 1898) p. 203.
8. *Ibid.*, pp. 200–1.
9. Black, *The Marquess of Dufferin and Ava*, p. 379.
10. *Ibid.*
11. 'London and Globe Finance Corporation (Limited)', *The Times*, 17 December 1901, p. 7.
12. 'Company Meetings. London and Globe Finance', *Financial Times*, 25 October 1899, p. 3.
13. *Ibid.*
14. *Ibid.*
15. 'The Whitaker Wright Companies', *The Times*, 28 January 1902, p. 13.
16. 'Why Westralians are Weak', *Financial Times*, 1 November 1900, p. 7.
17. Sir Alfred Lyall, *The Life of the Marquess of Dufferin and Ava* (London, John Murray, 1905), vol. 2, p. 304.
18. 'London and Globe Finance Corporation (Limited), *The Times*, 10 January 1901, p. 13.
19. *Ibid.*
20. *Ibid.*
21. 'London and Globe Finance', *Financial Times*, 10 January 1901, p. 3.
22. *Ibid.*
23. 'Globe Meeting', *Pall Mall Gazette*, 10 January 1901, p. 4.
24. 'Chat on Change', *Daily Mail*, 5 January 1901, p. 2.
25. 'The Money Market', *The Times*, 23 May 1901, p. 4.
26. 'British America Corporation (Limited)', *The Times*, 4 June 1901, p. 3.
27. *Ibid.*
28. *Ibid.*
29. *Ibid.*
30. *Ibid.*
31. 'The Whitaker Wright companies. Further Revelations', *The Times*, 31 July 1901, p. 13.
32. *Ibid.*
33. *Ibid.*
34. *Ibid.*
35. Lyall, *The Life of the Marquess of Dufferin and Ava*, vol. 2, p. 305.
36. The Whitaker Wright Companies', *The Times*, 28 January 1902, p. 13.
37. 'The Whitaker Wright Companies', *The Times*, 22 January 1902, p. 4.
38. The Whitaker Wright Companies', *The Times*, 28 January 1902, p. 13.
39. *Ibid.*
40. 'The London and Globe Finance Corporation (Limited)', *The Times*, 24 December 1902, p. 10.
41. 'Rex v. Whitaker Wright', *The Times*, 12 January 1904, p. 14.
42. TNA: PRO FO 5/2570, letter from Abrahams and Co., 18 September 1903.
43. 'The Charge against Mr. Whitaker Wright', *The Times*, 6 August 1903, p. 10.
44. The Marquess of Reading, *Rufus Isaacs First Marquess of Reading by his Son* (London, Hutchinson, 1943), p. 114.

45. 'Rex v. Whitaker Wright', *The Times*, 12 January 1904, p. 14.
46. 'Rex v. Whitaker Wright', *The Times*, 14 January 1904, p. 12.
47. 'Rex v. Whitaker Wright', *The Times*, 19 January 1904, p. 13.
48. 'Rex v. Whitaker Wright', *The Times*, 20 January 1904, p. 3.
49. *Ibid.*
50. *Ibid.*
51. *Ibid.*
52. 'Rex v. Whitaker Wright', *The Times*, 21 January 1904, p. 14.
53. *Ibid.*
54. 'Facing the Ordeal', *Daily Mail*, 21 January 1904, p. 3.
55. 'Rex v. Whitaker Wright', *The Times*, 22 January 1904, p. 13.
56. *Ibid.*

Chapter 10: The Double Duke

1. 'The Druce Case', *Daily Mail*, 17 August 1898, p. 4.
2. 'Alleged Sham Burial', *Lloyd's Weekly Newspaper*, 13 March 1898, p. 13.
3. 'Druce Mystery', *Lloyd's Weekly Newspaper*, 27 March 1898, p. 1.
4. 'Druce v. Young', *The Times*, 28 November 1901, p. 15.
5. 'Druce v. Young', *The Times*, 5 December 1901, p. 14.
6. TNA: PRO DPP 1/11, Rex v. Robinson, item 3, p. 5.
7. Bernard O'Donnell, *The Trials of Mr Justice Avory* (London, Rich & Cowan Ltd, 1935), p. 93.
8. TNA: PRO DPP 1/11, Druce v. Lord Howard de Walden. Note of Messrs Baileys Shaw and Gillett's attendance on Mr Trewinard (*sic*) on 6th May 1908.
9. TNA: PRO MEPO 3/175, Statement to AC CID, Edward Phillips, 23 June 1908, p. 13.

10. *Ibid.* p. 6.
11. Thomas K.V. Coburn, *The Portland Millions. Was Druce the Duke?* (privately printed, *c.* 1905), pp. 9–10.
12. 'The Police Courts', *The Times*, 9 November 1907, p. 15.
13. *Ibid.*
14. *Ibid.*
15. *Ibid.*
16. *Ibid.*
17. *Ibid.*
18. 'The Police Courts', *The Times*, 16 November 1907, p. 15.
19. *Ibid.*
20. 'The Police Courts', *The Times*, 20 November 1907, p. 18.
21. 'The Police Courts', *The Times*, 22 November 1907, p. 3.
22. 'The Police Courts', *The Times*, 28 November 1907, p. 13.
23. TNA: PRO MEPO 3/175, Statement of Frederick Hargrave, 15 July 1908.
24. 'The Police Courts', *The Times*, 17 December 1907, p. 3.
25. 'The Druce Case', *The Times*, 23 December 1907, p. 9.
26. 'The Druce Case', *The Times*, 14 January 1911, p. 10.
27. 'The Police Courts', *The Times*, 7 January 1908, p. 12.
28. TNA: PRO MEPO 3/175, Statement of Mrs Wilkinson, Rex v. Mary Anne Robinson, Perjury, 11 January 1908.
29. 'The Police Courts', *The Times*, 25 February 1908, p. 14.
30. 1861 census.
31. TNA: PRO MEPO 3/175, Further statement of Francis George Coles, 30 June 1908.
32. 'Title Claimant Now in Oakland', *Oakland Tribune*, 20 January 1913, p. 12.
33. 'The Police Courts', *The Times*, 7 January 1908, p. 12.

Bibliography

Chapter 1: The Price of Omnium

Anon., *The Case of Thomas Lord Cochrane K.B., Containing the History of the Hoax, the Trial, the Proceedings in the House of Commons, and the Meeting of the Electors of Westminster* (Edinburgh, J. Dick, 1814)

Anon., *The Trial of Charles Random de Berenger, Sir Thomas Cochrane, Commonly Called Lord Cochrane, the Hon. Andrew Cochrane Johnstone, Richard Gathorne Butt, Ralph Sandom, Alexander McRae, John Peter Holloway, and Henry Lyte for a Conspiracy in the Court of King's Bench Guildhall, on Wednesday 8th and Thursday 9th June 1814, with the Subsequent Proceedings in the Court of the King's Bench* (London, Butterworth and Son, 1814)

Anon., *De Berenger Detected, The Letter of C.R. De Berenger to his Solicitor, Dated 17 February 1814, Printed in Refutation of his Fabricated History of the Stock-Exchange Fraud, Recently Published* (London, May 1816)

Anon., *The Calumnious Aspersions Contained in the Report of the Sub-Committee of the Stock Exchange, Exposed and Refuted in so far as Regards Lord Cochrane, K.B. and M.P., the Hon Cochrane Johnstone, M.P. and R.G. Butt, Esq.* (2nd edn, London, W. Lewis, 1814)

Anon., *Parliamentary Debates* (London, T.C. Hansard, 1816)

Brown, John (ed.), *An Antidote to Detraction and Prejudice, Respecting the Family, Character, and Loyalty, of Charles Random Baron de Berenger; with a Biographical Memoir; an Account of his Arrest at Leith; his Singular Progress to, and Treatment in, London, Correspondence &c.* (London, printed for the editor, 1814)

Burke, Sir John Bernard, *Burke's Genealogical and Heraldic History of the Landed Gentry* (London, Burke's Peerage, 1965–72)

Cochrane, Thomas, 10th Earl of Dundonald, *The Autobiography of a Seaman*, 2 vols (London, Richard Bentley, 1859, 1860)

De Berenger, Baron C.R., *The Noble Stock-jobber, or Facts Unveiled, Irrefutably to Disprove Lord Cochrane's Affidavits* (London, R.S. Kirby, 1816)

Hennessey, Elizabeth, *Coffee House to Cybermarket: 200 Years of the London Stock Exchange* (London, Ebury Press, 2001)

Johnson, Samuel, *A Dictionary of the English Language* (London, Thomas Tegg, 1813)

Mackenrot, A., *Secret Memoirs of the Honourable Andrew Cochrane Johnstone of the Honourable Vice Admiral Sir Alex. Forrester Cochrane, K.B. and of Sir Thomas John Cochrane, a Captain in the Royal Navy* (London, printed for the author, 1814)

McRae, Alexander, *A Disclosure of the Hoax Practised upon the Stock Exchange 21st February, 1814; with Some Remarks on the Extraordinary Letter of Lord Cochrane to Lord Ellenborough* (London, published for the author, 1815)

Pope, Simeon, *Considerations, Political Financial and Commercial Relative to the Important Subject of the Public Funds, Addressed to Stock-Holders in General, and More Particularly to the Holders of Omnium* (London, Oriental Press, 1802)

Smith-Hughes, Jack, *Six Ventures in Villainy* (London, Cassell, 1955)

Stephen, Sir Leslie, and Lee, Sir Sydney (eds), *Dictionary of National Biography* (repr. London, Oxford University Press, 1973)

Thomas, Donald, *Cochrane, Britannia's Sea Wolf* (St Helens, Cassell Military Paperbacks, 2001)

ARCHIVES

TNA: PRO TS 11/44/165
TNA: PRO TS 11/42
TNA: PRO T 1/3890

Chapter 2: The Princess of Javasu

Atkyns, Robert, *The Ancient and Present State of Glostershire* (London, W. Herbert, 1768)

Cave, Charles Henry, *A History of Banking in Bristol* (Bristol, W. Crofton Hemmons, 1899)

Fry, Edmund, *Pantographia* (London, John and Arthur Arch, 1799)

Gutch, J.M., *Caraboo. A Narrative of a Singular Imposition Practised upon the Benevolence of a Lady Residing in the Vicinity of the City of Bristol, by a Young Woman of the Name of Mary Willcocks, alias Baker, alias Bakerstendht, alias Caraboo, Princess of Javasu* (London, Baldwin Cradock and Joy, 1817)

Hager, Joseph, D.D., *Explanation of the Elementary Characters of the Chinese; with an Analysis of their Ancient Symbols and Hieroglyphs* (London, Richard Phillips, 1801)

Raffles, Thomas Stamford, *The History of Java*, 2 vols (Kuala Lumpur, Oxford University Press, Asia Historical Reprints, 1978)

Walker, Roy S., *The Book of Almondsbury* (Buckingham, Barracuda Books Ltd, 1987)

Wells, John, *Princess Caraboo: Her True Story* (London, Pan, 1994)

PERIODICALS

Notes and Queries
The Rose the Shamrock and the Thistle

Bibliography

WEBSITES

http://freepages.genealogy.rootsweb.com/~walkersj/Phipps8.htm: for Phipps family genealogy pages; accessed March 2005

http://freepages.genealogy.rootsweb.com/~walkersj/lechmere.htm: for details of Elizabeth Worrall and Richard Lechmere, accessed March 2005

Chapter 3: The Viscount of Canada

Alexander, A.H. (as Earl of Stirling and Doven &c. &c. &c.), *Address to the Right Honourable the Peers of Scotland. To which is added a particular statement of his case by T.C. Banks Esq.* (Edinburgh, William Tait, 1831)

Alexander, A.H. (as Earl of Stirling) *Narrative of the Oppressive Law Proceedings, and other Measures, Resorted to by the British Government, and Numerous Private Individuals, to Overpower the Earl Of Stirling, and Subvert his Lawful Rights* (Edinburgh, James Walker, 1836)

Alexander, A.H. (as Earl of Stirling), *Two Letters Addressed to the Right Honourable Thomas Lord Denman* (Paris, J. Smith, 1845)

Anon., *Remarks on the Trial of the Earl of Stirling by an English Lawyer* (London, Lewis and Co., 1839)

Banks, Thomas C. (as Sir Thomas C. Banks Bart. N.S.), *An Analytical Statement of the Case of Alexander, Earl of Stirling and Dovan &c. &c. &c.* (London, James Cochrane and Co., 1832)

Dicta, Dimitriadis, *Mademoiselle le Normand* (Paris, Perrin, 1990)

Erickson, Carolly, *Josephine* (London, Robson Books, 1999)

Hayes, John L., *Vindication of the Rights and Titles, Political and Territorial, of Alexander, Earl of Stirling and Doven, and Lord Proprietor of Canada and Nova Scotia* (Washington, Gideon and Co., 1853)

Macaulay, Joseph Babington, *The Life of the Last Earl of Stirling* (Paignton, W.A. Axworthy, 1906)

Marquiset, Alfred, *La Célèbre Mlle Lenormand* (Paris, unknown publisher, 1911)

Mauguin, Georges, *L'Imperatrice Josephine: Anecdotes et curiosités* (Paris, J. Peyronnet, 1954)

Rogers, Revd Charles, 'History of Alexander Humphrys or Alexander, Claimant of the Earldom of Stirling', in *Memorials of the Earl of Stirling and of the House of Alexander*, 2 vols (Edinburgh, William Patterson, 1877), vol. 2, appendix 4, p. 210

Stevens, Abel (ed.), 'Mademoiselle Le Normand', *National Magazine* (New York, Carlton and Phillips, 1853), vol. 2, pp. 435–40.

Swinton, Archibald, *Report of the Trial of Alexander Humphreys [sic] or Alexander, Claiming the Title of Earl of Stirling, before the High Court of Judiciary at Edinburgh for the Crime of Forgery* (Edinburgh, Thomas Clark, 1839)

Turnbull, William Esq. (ed.), *The Stirling Peerage. Trial of Alexander Humphrys or Alexander Styling himself Earl of Stirling* (Edinburgh, William Blackwood and Sons, 1839)

Urban, Sylvanus (ed.), *The Gentleman's Magazine* (London, John Nichols and Son, 1819), vol. 89 (NS 12), pp. 98, 290

WEBSITE

www.familysearch.org: International Genealogical Index

Chapter 4: The Sting

Anon., *The History of The Times*, vol. 1, *The Thunderer in the Making, 1785–1841* (London, *The Times*, 1935; Kraus reprint, 1971), vol. 2, *The Tradition Established, 1841–1884* (London, *The Times*, 1939; Kraus reprint, 1971)

Anon., *The Times Testimonial. Report of the Trial of the Action Bogle versus Lawson* (London, John Hatchard and Son, 1842)

Cunninghame-Graham, R.B, *Doughty Deeds: An Account of the Life of Robert Graham of Gartmore, Poet and Politician, 1735–1797* (London, William Heinemann Ltd, 1925)

Sala, George Augustus, *Twice round the Clock; or the Hours of Day and Night in London* (London, W. Kent and Co., 1861)

'*The Times* Testimonial', *Sharps London Magazine* (1846), pp. 59–63

ARCHIVES

The Times Archives, Bogle Case, Litigation 2

WEBSITE

http://www.florin.ms/cemetery.html, accessed January 2006: Alphabetical Register of the Protestant Cemetery of Florence

Chapter 5: The Bank with No Scruples

Anon., *The Annual Register, or a View of the History and Politics of the Year 1856* (London, F. & J. Rivington, 1857)

Hynes, M., 'Sadleir, M.P., Banker', in James White (ed.), *My Clonmel Scrapbook* (3rd edn, Clonmel, Tentmaker Publications, 1995)

Irish Chancery Reports, vols 5, 11 (Dublin, Hodges Smith and Co., 1857, 1861)

McDermot, B.C., 'Letters of John Scully to James Duff Coghlan', *Irish Genealogist*, vol. 6, no. 1, pp. 54–76; no. 2, pp. 227–46; no. 3, pp. 353–69

O'Shea, James, *Prince of Swindlers* (Ireland, Geography Publications, 1999)

Sullivan, A.M., *New Ireland*, 2 vols (London, Sampson Low, Marston, Searle & Rivington, 1877), vol. 1, ch. XV, 'The Suicide Banker', pp. 354–81

Thomas, Revd H., BA, *John Sadleir, or The Ruined Speculator* (Melbourne, Wilson, Mackinson & Fairfax, 1856)

Bibliography

ARCHIVE

British Library, Add. MS 43248, Aberdeen papers

Chapter 6: A Racing Certainty

Basset, Arthur Ward, *The Scotland Yard Scandal and Other Stories of Crime* (London, Austin Rogers and Co., 1928)

Browne, Douglas G., *The Rise of Scotland Yard* (London, George G. Harrap and Co. Ltd, 1956)

Clarke, Sir Edward, *The Story of my Life* (London, John Murray, 1918)

Cobb, Belton, *Critical Years at the Yard – The Career of Frederick Williamson of the Detective Department and the CID* (London, Faber and Faber, 1956)

Dilnot, George, *The Story of Scotland Yard* (London, Geoffrey Bles, 1926)

Dilnot, George (ed.), *The Trial of the Detectives* (London, Geoffrey Bles, 1928)

Howe, Sir Ronald, *The Story of Scotland Yard* (London, Arthur Barker Ltd, 1965)

Lansdowne, Detective-Inspector Andrew, *A Life's Reminiscences of Scotland Yard* (London, The Leadenhall Press Ltd, 1893)

Littlechild, J.G., *The Reminiscences of Chief Inspector Littlechild* (London, The Leadenhall Press, 1894)

Meiklejohn, ex-Chief Inspector John, *Real Life Detective Stories* (London, John Dicks Press, 1912)

ARCHIVES

TNA: PRO HO 144/21/60045
TNA: PRO HO 144/21/60045B
TNA: PRO CRIM 4/914

Chapter 7: The Grappler

Anon., *The Hooley Book* (London, John Dicks, 1904)

Hooley, Ernest Terah, *Confessions* (London, Simpkin Marshall Hamilton Kent and Co., 1924)

PERIODICALS

The Economist
Irish Field and Gentleman's Gazette
Money

Chapter 8: *The Greatest Liar on Earth*

Barrett, Charles, *White Blackfellows* (Melbourne, Hallcraft Publishing Co. Pty Ltd, 1948)

Clune, Frank, *The Greatest Liar on Earth* (Melbourne, Hawthorn Press, 1945)

Daily Chronicle, Grien on Rougemont, or the Story of a Modern Robinson Crusoe (London, Edward Lloyd Ltd, 1898)

Friederichs, Hulda, *The Life of Sir George Newnes, Bart.* (London, Hodder & Stoughton, 1911)

Grin, H.L. (as Louis de Rougemont), *The Adventures of Louis de Rougemont, as Told by Himself* (London, George Newnes Ltd, 1899)

Kirwan, The Hon. Sir John, *An Empty Land: Pioneers and Pioneering in Australia* (London, Eyre and Spottiswoode, 1934)

Mill, H.M., *An Autobiography* (London, Longmans Green and Co., 1951)

Wide World Magazine (London, George Newnes Ltd, from 1898)

Chapter 9: *The Juggler with Millions*

Ashley, F.W., *My Sixty Years in the Law* (London, John Lane The Bodley Head, 1936)

Black, Charles E. Drummond, *The Marquess of Dufferin and Ava* (London, Hutchinson and Co., 1903)

Felstead, Sidney Theodore, *Sir Richard Muir*, ed. Lady Muir (London, John Lane The Bodley Head, 1927)

Horne, M.A.C., *The Bakerloo Line: A Short History* (London, Douglas Rose, 1990)

Jackson, Stanley, *Mr Justice Avory* (London, Victor Gollancz Ltd, 1935)

Lougheed, Alan, 'The London Stock Exchange Boom in Kalgoorlie Shares, 1895–1901', *Australian Economic History Review*, 35, 1 March 1995, pp. 83–102

Lyall, Sir Alfred, *The Life of the Marquess of Dufferin and Ava*, 2 vols (London, John Murray, 1905)

Radclyffe, Raymond, *Wealth and Wild Cats: Travels and Researches in the Gold-Fields of Western Australia and New Zealand* (London, Downey and Co., 1898)

Reading, The Marquess of, *Rufus Isaacs First Marquess of Reading by his Son* (London, Hutchinson, 1943)

ARCHIVES

TNA: PRO FO 5/2570
TNA: PRO HO 45/10281/105947
TNA: PRO J 17/651

Chapter 10: The Double Duke

Archard, Charles J., *The Portland Peerage Romance* (London, Greening and Co., 1907)

Besterman, Theodore, *The Druce–Portland Case* (Duckworth, London, 1935)

Bradbury, D.J., *Welbeck and the 5th Duke of Portland* (Mansfield, Wheel Publications, 1989)

Coburn, Thomas K.V., *The Portland Millions. Was Druce the Duke?* (Privately printed, c. 1905)

Coburn, Thomas K.V., 'The Druce Claim to the Portland Millions', in Robert Barr (ed.), *The Idler* (London, Chatto and Windus, 1905–6), vol. 29, pp. 791–3

Druce, G.H., 'Which is the Duke?', in Robert Barr (ed.), *The Idler* (London, Chatto and Windus, 1905–6), vol. 28, pp. 356–64

Druce, G.H., 'The Druce Case', in Robert Barr (ed.), *The Idler* (London, Chatto and Windus, 1905–6), vol. 28, pp. 518–29, 630–45; vol. 29, pp. 114–28

Henderson, Kenneth, 'Fresh Evidence on the Druce Case', in Robert Barr (ed.), *The Idler* (London, Chatto and Windus, 1905–6), vol. 29, pp. 396–402

O'Donnell, Bernard, *The Trials of Mr Justice Avory* (London, Rich & Cowan Ltd, 1935)

Turberville, A.S., *A History of Welbeck Abbey and its Owners*, 2 vols (London, Faber and Faber, 1938)

ARCHIVES

TNA: PRO BT 31/11183/85345
TNA: PRO BT 31/12175/95549
TNA: PRO DPP 1/11
TNA: PRO HO 45/10541/157177
TNA: PRO HO 144/1020/160196
TNA: PRO MEPO 3/174
TNA: PRO MEPO 3/175
TNA: PRO MEPO 3/176
TNA: PRO TS 18/272

WEBSITE

http://www.nottingham.ac.uk/mss/online/online-mss-catalogues/cats/port_londonpll.html#druce6, accessed December 2005: Nottingham University Portland Collection P1 L1/1–13, abstracts

Index